10 ⁰⁰/₁

The Ruler's Imperative

Strategies for Political Survival in Asia and Africa

SOUTHERN ASIAN INSTITUTE SERIES

The Southern Asian Institute of Columbia University seeks a deeper understanding of that vast and tumultuous area stretching from West Pakistan in the west to Indonesia and the Philippines in the east. To understand the problems facing its leaders and its diverse peoples requires sustained training and research. Our publications are intended to share with others whatever concepts and propositions might be useful in forwarding economic and political development, in accommodating tradition and change, and in the search of each people for international security.

The Ruler's Imperative focuses on one problem crucial for all political leaders—how they use whatever political resources they may command or mobilize in their efforts to remain in power and to effect their polity.

The Ruler's Imperative

Strategies for
Political
Survival
in Asia and
Africa

by W. Howard Wriggins

Columbia University Press

New York and London

1969

Copyright © 1969, Columbia University Press
Library of Congress Catalog Card Number: 73-90431
Printed in the United States of America

To My Father and Mother
Charles C. Wriggins
and Evelyn W. Wriggins

Preface

This is a study of political leadership in independent Africa and Asia. It assumes that the ruler's first imperative, and his most urgent desire, is to retain his position at the apex of government, for only from there can he affect the future of the polity he seeks to rule. Leaders of most emerging countries, however, are unsure of their position. The chances are no better than even that they will successfully hold office for their full term. Their political structures are new; grounds for legitimacy are uncertain; contention is often rife. Resources are scant, demands are on the rise, and bureaucracies sluggish and unresponsive to the ruler's will. In the face of these handicaps, what do leaders do to retain their office and to improve their ability to get things done?

Based on the extensive monographic literature devoted to politics and development in African and Asian countries since their independence, and on the author's personal knowledge of a number of Asian countries, this study examines the political strategies leaders have used in their efforts to stay in power. It outlines characteristic political problems of the new states, discusses the goals leaders typically set beyond assuring their own personal position, and discusses the principal political groups they must fashion into supporting coalitions. The bulk of the study examines eight different strategies—their characteristics, their advantages, and their liabilities—which leaders have been using. In most instances, the discussion of each strategy is preceded by a brief vignette of a leader who used to advantage that particular strategy.

Although the discussion is based on generally familiar materials, the approach—focusing on political strategies leaders use in the "aggregation of power" and in building their supporting coalition—is not common in the literature. In order to illustrate the widespread applicability of this approach to understanding politics, examples have been drawn from countries as far apart as Indonesia and Tanzania. Because this perspective is not typical of recent literature in comparative politics, it was decided to shape these materials single-handedly, rather than to depend upon a collection of individual essays by specialists of different countries or to concentrate solely on those several countries the author knew well at first-hand. The advantages of attempting a single synthesis illuminated by one perspective seemed to outweigh the risks of possible errors of emphasis or fact.

There has been a conscious effort to avoid specialized jargon and to write straightforward prose in order to bring these observations within reach of a broad spectrum of interested laymen, as well as to more committed scholars concerned with comparative politics and political development.

A year's leave of absence from the U.S. Department of State's Policy Planning Council gave me time for most of the research and preliminary drafting. I am particularly indebted to Professors Arnold Wolfers and Robert Osgood and Dean Francis Wilcox for inviting me to the Washington Center of Foreign Policy Research at the School of Advanced International Studies in Washington. W. W. Rostow, then Chairman of the Policy Planning Council, generously supported my request for leave.

My intellectual debts are too many to acknowledge in detail here. Some of my most helpful consultants, those who have been willing over the years to discuss with me the politics of their own countries, I know, would prefer to remain unnamed. It is a pleasure to acknowledge my particular debt to Gabriel Almond for inspiration and guidance in my first research endeavor, and to Myron Weiner and Dankwart Rustow, whose encouragement on this project materially helped to overcome original hesitation and whose criticism was helpful throughout. Lucian Pye, John Plank, Robert H. Johnson, Samuel P. Huntington, C. B. Marshall, Lewis Edinger, David Bayley, and Sally Wriggins also read the manuscript through and gave me the benefit of their criticism. Tony Barrett criticized early formulations of the African examples. Douglas Ashford, Guy Pauker, John Badeau, Gray Cowan, Wayne Wilcox, James Guyot, S. M. Ikram and Barbara Ward Jackson commented on specific parts. To my students at the School of Advanced International Studies in Washington and at the Southern Asian Institute of Columbia University, and particularly to research assistants Joungwon A. Kim, Robert Clark, and Krishnan Nanda go warm thanks.

These critics have given me much good advice which I have not always taken; the views expressed are entirely my own responsibility.

The Rockefeller Foundation made possible my stay at the Washington Center of Foreign Policy Research, and the Ford Foundation's initial grant for the Southern Asian Institute of Columbia University supported the final drafting and preparation of the manuscript. Without the first institution, this study could not have been considered or begun; without the second its completion would have been long delayed.

I am grateful, too, to Suzanne Joiner for typing at the research stage, and to Elaine Clark, Denise Jefferies, Patricia Leuba, Susan Schubert and Patty Francy for typing and editorial assistance as the manuscript took shape. Mrs. Kalyani Raghavan helped in checking references.

W. Howard Wriggins

Contents

I

The
Approach

1 The Approach

The search for personal influence is at the center of the job of being President. To analyze the problem of obtaining power, one must try to view the Presidency from above the President's shoulder, looking out and down with the perspective of *his* place. . . . My treatment of events and men has no other purpose than to clarify the nature of the search for personal power.

Richard Neustadt

What must a ruler do to remain in power and to affect his country's affairs? Once positioned at the apex, where can he find political resources to muster on behalf of his position and his purposes? How does he deal with those who seek to displace him? How can he best use his person, his trusted associates, and whatever political or governmental assets he has to strengthen his own influence and achieve his ends beyond mere survival in the president's or prime minister's office?

This essay examines the experience of rulers in emergent Africa and Asia during the past twenty years with such questions as these in mind. The materials drawn upon are generally familiar to students of comparative politics. It is the angle of vision which has some claim to originality. Not that this way of looking at politics is new. On the contrary, it has an ancient lineage reaching at least as far back as Kautilya and Aristotle.

3

To look at politics this way in Africa and Asia has seemed useful for a number of reasons. Contemporary comparative politics literature has tended to set aside the sweaty, contentious matter of political competition as our models have become more abstract and our "political systems" more sophisticated. In seeking an inclusive analytical scheme encompassing all possible relevant aspects of a political society, we have too often forgotten the core of the matter.[1] Starting with the ruler of a non-communist country in Asia and Africa, this study explores his problem of staying in power, precariously poised as he so often is (or feels himself to be) on an uncertain political base. It discusses his political circumstances, the goals he typically sets, and the sources of power he seeks to win and aggregate into supports for his regime. He is usually competing against others who want to bring him down. At the center of this study are the strategies he uses to acquire the backing he must have if he is to retain and improve his position at the apex of government. For only from there can he and his associates use governmental power to effect change, cope with misery, and deal with foreign threats or whatever other purposes he may seek beyond mere political survival. One reason for this approach, therefore, is the desire to bring back into focus the ruler's imperative—the need to stay in power—and how he seeks to retain and improve his position in emerging Africa and Asia.

As the leaders of most new countries perceive their situation, political supports are uncertain. Offices they hold lack the legitimacy of having been long established. Or, as newcomers to these offices, who like as not seized power by coup d'état, their claim to occupy them may be dubious. Political institutions often appear to be insufficiently established to contain the political forces that the independence struggle, popular politics, and new communications have generated. Dissidence is widely expected; political disruption is all too easy. Searching for the means to stay in power is a more urgent matter for these real political actors than it is for rulers in more established polities.

Rulers cannot count on many of the governmental capabilities which go with top responsibility in the more developed states. They

---

[1] Notable exceptions are Aristide Zolberg, *Creating Political Order—The Party-States of West Africa* (Chicago, Rand-McNally, 1966, 168 pp.); Dankwart A. Rustow, *A World of Nations: Problems of Political Modernization* (Washington, D.C., Brookings Institution, 1967, 306 pp.); Samuel P. Huntington, *Political Order in Changing Societies* (New Haven, Yale University Press, 488 pp.).

often cannot insure even limited peace and order throughout their realm. Many other functions of government taken for granted in more developed countries are not performed the way the politically active believe they should be. Taxes are hard to extract; exploitative economic activities are difficult to regulate; and urgently voiced demands of relatively well-organized groups may challenge the ruler's position of control. The bureaucracy itself may be unable to function effectively, either from inner weaknesses or as a result of the resistance of the society to the government's enterprises. Only if the leader's power position is improved in relation to those elements in the society capable of obstructing government activity can he bring reality nearer to his vision.

How leaders tackle their problem of aggregating power in order to ensure their own political survival has an effect upon the way the polity develops. To turn Marx's famous phrase about the class struggle on its head, one might say that "struggles between political leaders are the engines of history." The manner of their contention affects the political institutions and practices they leave behind. The more clearly leaders perceive the costs and advantages of the way they carry on their political competition, the more aware they may be of the possible side effects and the heritage they are preparing for their successors.

This approach to politics in underdeveloped countries is not considered to be grand theory, nor is it an inclusive scheme into which all relevant phenomena fit. It is, rather, an attempt to look out of the president's or prime minister's window, to see his problems as he sees them. It centers attention on the ruler's search for allies and his effort to rally support for himself so that he can stay in power long enough and with sufficient capability to get certain things done. It assumes that every leader has some choice in the way he tackles his job, for no two leaders would deal with their problem of aggregating and using political power in exactly the same way. It is, in sum, a study of alternative strategies leaders have used in their efforts to gain or to sustain control, and to use that control to effect their will or whim upon the polities they "rule."[2]

---

[2] For a parallel approach, although concerned more specifically with executive power in the United States, see Richard E. Neustadt, *Presidential Power* (New York, John Wiley, 1960, 224 pp.), p. vii.

PROBLEMS FACING NEW STATES

Never before have so many entities calling themselves states laid claim to the perquisites and responsibilities of national sovereignty. Never before has the configuration of world politics and the existence of international institutions been so favorable to amplifying new voices and giving young states a visible role in world affairs.

Over seventy states and a handful of remaining colonies divide the great arc stretching from Indonesia and the Philippines in the South Pacific, through the Indian subcontinent into the Middle East and curving south to sub-Saharan Africa. A number, such as Morocco, Jordan, Syria, Lebanon, and Egypt, were never technically colonies, though they experienced protracted tutelage under European civilian or military administration. Turkey once ruled extensive domains in Europe and the Middle East. Ethiopia was a colony for only a few years. Nepal, Thailand, Afghanistan, and Liberia have been politically independent for generations. Over fifty of these states have come to independence since the middle of World War II.

Presiding over each is a small band of men and women on whose purposes and skills so much depends. They and their political abilities stand between their countries and the twin evils of chaos and tyranny. Their search for power sufficient to their purposes is conditioned by the circumstances of their gaining office and the peculiar social, political, and economic conditions of their country. These underlying problems are discussed in Chapter 2.

LEADERSHIP GOALS

Rulers are beset with the anguishing challenge of compressing into decades the changes which took centuries to accomplish elsewhere. They are attempting to build the institutions of state authority. They seek to develop a national sense of mutual identity and national loyalty to replace the parochial loyalties characteristic of their present societies. They must achieve a productive and flexible economy, one capable of meeting the challenge of rapidly growing demands and changing opportunities for comparative advantage. An increasingly large proportion of the people can no longer be excluded from some form of political participation. Democratic representative practices may be impractical in many countries today and may even be abrogated where they once existed. But tyrannous or authoritarian rule is usually made out to be only an unavoidable and temporary expedient.[3]

In the more established states, these challenges presented themselves over many generations, giving time for each to be absorbed in turn. In new countries, by contrast, they have all descended at once upon hard-pressed political leaders. And the task is made harder because the yardstick by which they are judged—and tend to judge themselves—is usually of foreign make, derived from different historical experiences and cultural traditions.[4] These tasks require substantial governmental capability if men of government are to help achieve them.

Moreover, regardless of whether a government is democratic or authoritarian, it normally performs a number of complex functions that require continued governmental capability. Leaders endeavor to develop a capacity to defend the territorial entity and generally to reduce external friction affecting themselves. They seek to sustain internal order; they usually attempt to establish a degree of domestic justice, in some measure commensurate with local standards, and to provide a modicum of economic prosperity. They usually try to reduce domestic tensions and conflicts, and provide means for defining collective goals and allocating values among the major groups in the society.[5] All these functions demand political capability or power in the hands of those who rule. Perhaps the most difficult of all is the challenge of succession: the preparation of orderly and peaceful means for replacing rulers in ways that bestow legitimacy on successors.[6]

[3] On "system development problems," see Gabriel A. Almond and G. Bingham Powell, Jr., Comparative Politics: A Developmental Approach (Boston, Little Brown, 1966, 348 pp.), pp. 314-27.

[4] Robert E. Ward and Dankwart A. Rustow (eds.), Political Modernization in Japan and Turkey (Princeton, Princeton University Press, 1964, 502 pp.), pp. 465-66.

[5] Carl J. Friedrich, Man and His Government (New York, McGraw-Hill, 1963, 737 pp.), p. 390; Shmuel N. Eisenstadt, The Political Systems of Empire (New York, Free Press of Glencoe, 1963, 524 pp.), p. 7; Harold Laswell, Politics: Who Gets What, When, How? (New York, Whittlesey, 1936, 264 pp.), p. 3; Howard Wriggins, "Foreign Assistance and Political Development," in Brookings Institution, Development of the Emerging Countries (Washington, Brookings Institution, 1962, 239 pp.), pp. 181-214.

[6] David Easton, A Systems Analysis of Political Life (New York, John Wiley, 1965, 507 pp.), Ch. 2.

The goals leaders set themselves derive largely from these imperatives of governance or from the standards they learned in their
schools, adopted in the struggle for independence, defined since
coming to responsibility, or have had set by growing popular
demands. These goals are discussed in Chapter 3.

AGGREGATING POWER—GROUPS IN POLITICS

Some of the pioneers in comparative politics studies have
chosen to avoid the concept "power" altogether.[7] However, for purposes of this study, there is no single notion which so conveniently
suggests the real and daily preoccupation of successful leaders. For
their main concern must be how to elicit or induce actions by others
which they, as leaders, desire but which the others would not otherwise perform. To be sure, there is often a reciprocal relationship,
as the "more powerful" person must adjust his aims and his actions
if he is to elicit the desired behavior from the "less powerful."[8]
Power is ambiguous, too, because it implies the capacity to use or
threaten the use of force at the time that its success derives from
consent. All this is neither neat nor clear-cut. But its very ambiguity
well reflects the nature of the political behavior to be examined.
To acquire sufficient power calls for a wide range of activities about
which it is difficult to be precise; power's components are combined
in many different ways by each practitioner.

In order to aggregate sufficient power, the successful political
leader in a new country—as well as in the more established states—
identifies individuals and groups who have power over still others
and whose support is worth winning because they add to his strength
or weaken his opponent's. He attempts to combine these distinguishable, often disparate components of power, drawing them around
himself and his government. He seeks to influence their activities,
so that they assist him in pursuing his own purposes. He may thus
organize components of power already existing. He may find new
groups, hitherto quiescent, and awaken them to a sense of common
grievance or concerted destiny in order to add their political strength
to his cause.

---

[7] Notably Gabriel Almond and James S. Coleman, *The Politics of the Developing Nations* (Princeton, Princeton University Press, 1960, 591 pp.).

[8] Robert A. Dahl, "The Concept of Power," *Behavioral Science*, Vol. II, No. 3
(July, 1957), 201-15.

In the real world of politics, particularly in emerging countries, it is a hard political fact that the political groups to be combined generally retain a good deal of autonomy and are capable of sharing or withholding their support. Armies may turn against their ruler; bureaucracies may distort or even sabotage his program; traditional religious groups may delay modernizing changes he seeks to promote and they oppose; ethnic minorities may yearn to secede; and the few well-organized unions may delay production until their demands are met. Political competitors may build a following on such groups and block progress toward the ruler's purposes or even bring about his downfall. These and other similar possibilities are what makes the political task of staying on top such an uncertain and contingent matter.

The components of power, that is, the groups of people who in their combination have the potentiality for exerting power to uphold or to challenge a regime, must be organized, inspired, negotiated with, bribed, or in other ways persuaded to throw their weight behind the ruler, or at least to acquiesce in his position or his program. The process of winning them to the ruler's cause can be likened to the search for political coalitions of support. Chapter 4 discusses the process of coalition building and the main characteristics of the more important political groups to be found in most emerging countries.[9]

ALTERNATIVE STRATEGIES FOR AGGREGATING POWER

The leader finds that different groups want mutually contradictory things. The support of some can be won only by strategies which alienate others. Often, demands of political supporters or opponents rise more rapidly than the ability of the political system to satisfy; loads outpace capabilities. Bureaucracies are sluggish or lack the necessary skills to carry out his wishes; private groups capable of helping to meet some of the new demands may have been destroyed in the political struggle or are only now beginning to function. The very components of power he attempts to develop and enlist may come to threaten his leadership. A leader's ability to enlist support rests in part upon his reputation for power, a highly sub-

[9] For coalition building, see particularly William Riker, *The Theory of Political Coalitions* (New Haven, Yale University Press, 1962, 300 pp.).

jective matter, dependent largely upon intangible whisperings or half-conscious private calculations of probable individual or group advantage. Ethnic loyalties, cultural affinities, familial relationships, the leader's reputation, and his personality may all contribute to his ability to win—or antagonize—potential supporters.

Leaders might use many alternative strategies to build their own coalitions of support around themselves and their government and to undermine the coalitions of their opponents. Which they choose depends upon their circumstances, the political resources they command or can generate, their political skills, the priority they attach to different goals, and how their opponents are able to set limits to their choices and impose imperatives they cannot avoid. The balance of this study identifies eight of the most important strategies leaders use to aggregate power. It discusses the characteristics of each strategy, its advantages and liabilities, and the dynamic it generates which must then be dealt with.[10]

Leaders lay great stress upon projecting their personalities—attempting to deal with the manifold problems of governance in developing countries through personalized, charismatic leadership. This is the strategy most often turned to. Others devote attention to organization, building the right kind of loyal personal organization within the army, police, or bureaucracy; or constructing a political party to give shape and consistency to the activities of large numbers of followers. Others emphasize the importance of ideology as it affects the perceptions and values of the politically active. Some devote substantial resources to rewarding the faithful and those susceptible to the ruler's influence; others prefer—or see no better alternative than—intimidating their opponents into acquiescence or their wavering followers back into line. A number of leaders have stressed developing the economy to improve their chances of political survival. A few have consciously expanded political participation of hitherto passive elements of the population, thus adding recruits to their banner; others have sought to reduce active participation. Finally, some have used foreign policy in ways which have strengthened their political positions at home. These alternative strategies are discussed in Chapters 5 through 12.

But no ruler depends on only one of these strategies. Each com-

[10] Other strategies could be added, but after an extensive review of the monographic literature on developing countries, these appeared to be the most prominent.

bines them in his own unique mix. Chapter 13 cites a number of sample strategic mixes and assesses their advantages and liabilities, both for aggregating power and for pursuing the additional goals most rulers seek.

Such an approach should not be construed as suggesting that leaders in new countries are invariably more "power hungry" than leaders of older states. The intensity of concern for power or political capability varies greatly between individuals and regimes.[11] Yet it remains generally true that for a leader to effect his policies, he must at the very least succeed in staying in power for some time and have additional power to spare to achieve his goals beyond mere survival. If it were possible to measure the attention a ruler gives to different problems, it could probably be shown that he devotes more time and effort to aggregating around himself and his government sufficient political power to permit him to stay on top than to any other single purpose. If he looks carefully at his peers in Asia and Africa, he would note that the chances are less than even that they will be able to run out their constitutional term.[12] "Uneasy lies the head that wears the crown" was true in Shakespeare's kingdoms. It is also true of the bulk of emerging countries. The extended tenure of men like Prime Minister Nehru and Presidents Bourguiba, Houphouët-Boigny, Nasser, and Sukarno are exceptions; yet even they faced moments of uncertainty as to their own political survival.

THE VICISSITUDES OF POLITICS

Perhaps of all human activities involving relationships with others, politics imposes more problematic situations on its practitioners than any.[13] It is essentially an uncertain affair, full of ambiguities and imponderables. Politics is not a matter of structure and process, neatly defined, but rather a drama of human beings,

[11] Arnold Wolfers, "The Pole of Power and the Pole of Indifference," World Politics, Vol. IV, No. 1 (October, 1951), 39-63; Myron Weiner, "The Struggle Against Power: Notes on Indian Political Behavior," World Politics, Vol. XIII, No. 3 (April, 1956), 392-403.

[12] Fred Von der Mehden calculated that between the end of World War II and 1964, when his assessment was made, in 84 "developing countries," 49 had experienced coups or attempted coups. Politics in the Developing Nations (Englewood Cliffs, N. J., Prentice Hall, 140 pp.), p. 19.

[13] Friedrich, Man and His Government, p. 17.

responding to and attempting to affect the behavior of one another. It is highly contingent and chancy activity. As Dahl reminds us, even with all our analytical sophistication, politics remains an art. The unknowns are so numerous that a ruler's choice of one course as against another depends in substantial part upon his own inner dispositions and his own conceptions of the reality with which he deals.[14]

Many of the leaders of emerging countries are seriously seeking to shape a sound political future for their countries in the midst of great difficulties. Others, however, seek no such end, but are out to make the most of their present opportunity for themselves and their families, feathering their private nests as they bilk the public. To generalize without close appraisal of the personal characteristics of specific leaders invites easy error.

Moreover, each political situation is in many respects unique not merely because of the diverse qualities and ambitions of individual leaders. Each polity's history, institutional framework, social organization, and communications system is different, and their combination is unique. Any generalizations about politics in countries ranging from Malaysia through India, Egypt, and Ethiopia, down to Ghana, Nigeria, and Tanzania at this stage are bound to be more suggestive than firm. Nevertheless, we must seek out consistencies beyond uniqueness to improve our understanding. This essay, therefore, consciously seeks that unsatisfying middle ground between the peculiar and contingent individual case and the grand but esoteric world of the general theorist, by focusing on one of those problems which besets nearly all men of politics.

As should be obvious, there is no guarantee that all new states will be able to stay the course. Some are likely to experience acute internal difficulties. The bad luck of misfit leadership or insoluble problems may bring decline from within. Systematic infiltration and externally provoked internal takeover may bring from without an end to independence. Some may even become subservient to ambitious neighbors who themselves have only recently gained independence. Not all societies will succeed in creating for themselves a satisfactory polity.

It is difficult enough to assess those who bear the ultimate responsibility in one's own country, when public affairs are refracted through the prism of intimates or the press. It is far more tempting

[14] Robert A. Dahl, *Who Governs? Democracy and Power in an American City* (New Haven, Yale University Press, 1961, 355 pp.), pp. 307-08.

to weigh up the strengths and weaknesses of another country's leadership and political process, far away. However, the matters under discussion are too serious to allow easy offhand grading of performance, as if any of us knew what were in fact correct answers for other people's political predicaments. Coping with intractable problems, leaders of emerging countries, like our own, face uncertain and contingent judgments every political day. One hopes that they may be foresighted and forebearing in the use of their offices and their influence. There is no assurance that this will be so. Nevertheless, this study seeks to avoid the pleasures of praising and blaming, on the assumption that a better understanding of how statesmen attempt to retain and use their opportunity to affect their country's policies is reward enough.

Chapters 2, 3, and 4 discuss the characteristic problems facing leaders of new countries, the goals they set, and the groups out of which they seek to form their coalitions of support. For the serious reader, these are essential background chapters. Those less patient, who wish to hurry on to the discussion of political strategies, may turn to Chapters 5 and beyond.

II

Problems, Goals, and Groups in Politics

2 Some Problems of New States

Among the new nations of the world . . . bits of Western practices have been fed into formerly dependent areas through colonial and imperial relationships. With independence, all the problems that have habitually plagued the West, whether political, social or economic, have descended all at once on the new nations.

David Apter

$\mathbf{T}$o stay in power and effect governmental policies, the new leader must cope with a host of complicated problems, for which his experience gives little precedent. From his position, he sees these difficulties more clearly than when he was attempting to win independence or was in opposition. These underlying social and economic problems shape the environment of his political activities. The uncertainty of his position makes it prudent for him to tackle these problems in ways which will be least likely to weaken his support.[1]

How a regime comes to power affects the political problems it

[1] One of the early efforts to characterize the political process as it relates to underlying problems, and one still highly recommended, is that of Lucian Pye, "The Non-Western Political Process," *The Journal of Politics*, Vol. XX, No. 3 (August, 1958), 468-86. Greater detail is encompassed in Edward A. Shils, *Political Development in the New States* (The Hague, Gravenhage, Mouton and Co., 1962, 91 pp.). The final chapter in Howard Wriggins, *Ceylon, Dilemmas of a New Nation* (Princeton, Princeton University Press, 1960, 505 pp.) draws some generalizations from that detailed case study of one country.

must deal with if it is to stay in power. Among the first-generation leaders of independent Africa and Asia, most received their power directly from the hands of the outgoing French and British colonial administrators. To be sure, the recipients gained their position as inheritors by demonstrating superior organizational or agitational skill, and they forced the pace at which authority was extended to elected representatives by the colonial governments. But the latter were the ones who generally defined the rules of the game and worked out the constitutional framework within which political competition took place.[2]

Within the municipal and state governments, where power was earliest delegated to elected representatives, considerable numbers of individuals gained experience at publicly articulating demands, compromising and adjusting them in order to gain a broader coalition of support, and overseeing the civilian bureaucracy. The system of courts and legal processes defined political liberties and procedures which came to be the standard for open, competitive political processes; these were established more deeply in former British than in French or Dutch colonies.[3]

Within such an arena, it was to the leader's advantage to activate large numbers on behalf of independence, for thus he demonstrated to the colonial authorities the extent of his own popularity, and how difficult the task of rule would be in the future if they did not transfer power soon. In the process, expectations became inflated beyond the possibility of satisfaction; groups became activated which could not easily return to quiescence after independence. Promoting demands as a means of embarrassing the colonial regime and as a by-product of party competition in open political contention would pose a major problem to the new men who replaced the colonial administrators. The orderly and peaceful transition to independence in these instances permitted the bureaucracy to be handed over virtually intact. The new governments inherited an institution capable of assisting them to maintain law and order and a substantial degree of economic control. But as a rule the bureaucracies were not dynamic instruments for promoting economic development; despite the ideological preference many leaders had to expand the economy primarily through governmental initiatives.[4] Since the

---

[2] For the typical process in British areas, see Wriggins, Ch. IV.

[3] Zolberg, *Creating Political Order*, pp. 77-79.

[4] Michael Brecher, *Nehru, A Political Biography* (Boston, Beacon Press, 1962, 267 pp.), Ch. XII.

transfer of power involved little change in the social and economic structure, in the main, those who had been prominent before independence continued to be so afterwards. However, princes, tribal chieftains, aristocratic families, and small but traditionally influential caste groups such as the Brahmins in India were soon seriously challenged by representative politics which gave influence to numbers at the expense of those with inherited position.

In sum, for those who received power in a peaceful transfer, the problems they faced were encompassed by four questions: How can we cope with the political participation and inflated demands resulting from the independence fight? How can we deal with our opponents? How can we insure the loyalty and broaden the energy of the bureaucracy we inherited? How can we demonstrate we are really independent?

A second mode of gaining power can be seen in such countries as Indonesia and Algeria. They gained independence only after a protracted military campaign which required a virtual *levée en masse* of the populace and the development of a large army to overcome the metropolitan forces sent against them. Many real assets were destroyed; normal civilian bureaucracies were disrupted; and economic relationships which had been interwoven between metropole and the dependency were disrupted. The protracted conflict blocked orderly, open political processes; it imposed instead closed politics more characteristic of wartime crisis. Hatreds generated by the military action, the demanding tasks it imposed, and the opportunities for radical changes in station it brought with it generated intense enthusiasm and a high level of mass mobilization. The élan of the conflict induced a strong sense of national unity in the face of the enemy. When independence was finally achieved, there appeared to be a solidarity lacking in those countries where independence had not been fought for.

On the other hand, acute problems quickly imposed themselves. The army was by far the largest single organized entity in the society. Large numbers resisted demobilization; the burden of military expenditures ran far beyond what was required to meet expected external threats or domestic disorders. Even though there were severe differences within the army, military leaders threatened to wield the single most important political weight; civilian power was beholden to its complaisance. In Indonesia, Sukarno saw the Communist Party of Indonesia (the PKI) as the balancer of the army; in Algeria, civilians never regained control but remained in fact politically junior to the generals. The disrupted bureaucracy could not perform even minimum functions. Many of the economic enterprises on which pre-independence prosperity had depended were disrupted or destroyed during the fighting or the bitterness of the aftermath. Civilian processes for aggregating demands and developing a tolerable working consensus on what should be done could not be readily reestablished.

The first type of regimes have experienced a number of orderly changes of political leadership; the latter regimes have found no orderly means of succession. Instead, they had had to suffer coups d'état engineered from within the army.

And this brings forward a third means of gaining power, the coup d'état. A coup d'état usually occurs where previous regimes have signally failed to fulfill even the minimal functions of governance; it is often the result of a long period of military involvement in politics.[5] The pattern is familiar. A faction within the army secretly prepares, penetrating the critical battalions near the capital, defining objectives, identifying the key individuals who must be apprehended and the installations which must be seized. The numbers must be few to assure against police informers. The stakes are high, since failure means an end to a promising career if not to life itself. After the key leaders have been arrested and strategic installations possessed, there comes the inevitable manifesto, promising that the work of government shall go on, that corruption and profiteering will end, that the society will be renovated, and that all good things are now possible.[6]

If the leader of the coup is well placed in the army, he will automatically command the authority of the army, at least. If the previous regime has been repugnant to important elements of the populace for its arbitrariness, ruthlessness, corruption, or sloth, the new group may be temporarily accepted. But unless the leaders are unusually skilled at winning and sustaining popular backing by virtue of their personalities, they will quickly have to prove themselves able to govern better than their predecessors. They have torn the fabric of legitimacy. Is their right to rule better than anyone else's?[7]

---

[5] Dankwart A. Rustow, *A World of Nations: Problems of Political Modernization*, pp. 179-81.

[6] Feliks Gross, *The Seizure of Political Power in a Century of Revolution* (New York, the Philosophical Library, 1958, 398 pp.), pp. 40-42; unpublished case studies by Joungwon A. Kim.

[7] Rustow, *A World of Nations*, pp. 69-70.

The new leaders risk becoming obsessed with the fear that what they did to others will be done to them. Surveillance must be increased. The police penetrates secretly to nip in the bud any possible counterorganization. The regime prefers secrecy in order to complicate the task of those who would bring it down by the very steps which brought it to power.

Something has to be done with the civilian leaders who have been replaced. Should they be politically retired for a number of years as in Pakistan or exiled or executed as in some other countries? As open politics is replaced, how does the leader know what the popular traffic will bear in the way of discipline, taxes, or postponed consumption? Following a coup d'état, how can popular participation be safely opened up again? How can coup leaders be replaced by means other than another coup, which may lead, as in Syria, to a numberless series of increasingly destructive and disorderly successions?

A fourth road to power, open only to the few, is that of inheritance. There are a number of persisting or refurbished monarchies still, and their problems of aggregating power are different from those of the leaders who have come to power by another route. Haile Selassie of Ethiopia, King Mahendra of Nepal, King Zahir of Afghanistan, and King Faisal of Saudi Arabia are examples. These are the relatively backward and isolated among the underdeveloped countries, except for Ethiopia, since they have never experienced the disruption (and the stimulus) of direct foreign rule. In these societies, to inherit the right to rule is the most effective form of legitimacy.

The problems of the monarchs generally derive less from the simple fact of having inherited the throne than from the very backwardness of the countries they rule over compared to the needs for change and the increasingly confident voices of those who seek a renovation of their archaic societies. Organizations for articulating demands are few; ethnic, regional or tribal differences are serious; and groups live in isolation from each other. Their governments have not yet penetrated deeply into the traditional society. Generally, the rulers lack institutions favoring gradual change and thus fear that changes will undermine their own positions. Like the ruling house of Afghanistan, however, they may come to recognize that if they block all change they will be swept aside, as was King Faisal of Iraq. The serious among them accept the need for modern skills to improve their government's performance and to tackle the debased standard of living. They are also aware that with new skills come new ideas, as the young Turks demonstrated in Turkey prior to World War I, or the educated Indians, Ceylonese, or Ghanaians in the British colonial experience made clear even before World War II. Old organizational forms must be made more effective, but the most loyal followers are often the most unwilling to change. The modernizers all too often challenge the old mode of rule entirely.[8]

Many additional problems exist, however, which most leaders in Africa and Asia must deal with, regardless of how they came to power. The seriousness of each and their relative importance will depend upon the specific conditions in that country. The characteristic problems derive from the fragmented society; the weak, unintegrated polity; the intemperance of political contention; and the economy's sluggishness; as well as the difficulties of economizing, of investing productively, and of productive innovation.

Most *societies* in new states are *fraught with divisions.* They have aptly been called mosaic societies, made up of countless pieces, each distinguished and separated from the others.[9] If the leader is to address a substantial proportion of his people, the chances are good he will need at least one interpreter and maybe more. Countries as small as Ghana, with 7.5 million people have over five major languages, while India's millions speak eight major languages and some eight hundred dialects. In the Philippines, no one language can be understood by as much as one third of the people. Religious and regional differences often confirm and reinforce these language differences. Each group is likely to find its special meaning within its own distinctive way of life. Relationships which cut across and so diminish these long-standing differences are rare. Diversity is exaggerated in a number of countries by the existence of large foreign minorities. Numerous foreign immigrants in many countries—such as the Chinese in Southeast Asia, and Indians in Ceylon and East Africa—make up as much as one quarter of the total population of a country (as in the Ivory Coast, for example). This impedes national cohesion. While the leader himself is likely to be city bred and to prefer urban ways, the bulk of his people are rural folk whose loy-

[8] Donald N. Levine, *Wax and Gold, Tradition and Innovation in Ethiopian Culture* (Chicago, University of Chicago Press; 1965, 315 pp.), Ch. 7.

[9] Carleton Coon, *Caravan, The Story of the Middle East* (London, Jonathan Cape, 1952, 376 pp.), Ch. 1.

alties are bounded by family, clan, or ethnic unit.[10] Men and women within these units are closely knit, but see people outside their small circles as suspect.[11] Such elements in the society are the most fundamental fragments of all. It is on their base that a satisfactory polity must be erected.

There are other substantial differences. Compared to the metropolitan country where the leader is likely to have studied, the social distance between him and the mass is large. Traditionally, in areas of high organization, such as the ancient civilization of Asia, distances have been great; the august leadership could generally count on an apathetic mass. In tribal Africa, the differences were usually not so marked. The traditional gap between elite and mass in most underdeveloped countries was accentuated by the colonial experience, when the leader and those like him were educated in foreign schools and trained in foreign enterprise or administration, becoming differentiated from the rest in totally new ways. Those who went to the metropole were separated from those who remained at home. To be sure, the fissures created by the intrusion of Western activities often resulted in men of different ethnic and religious backgrounds coming together in common educational, recreational and work experiences. These common experiences transcended some of the indigenous ethnic and tribal divisions and helped create the first generation national elite. But the gap between the Western-educated and the populace continues as a substantial impediment to national integration.[12] Educational differentiation is related to the sharp dif-

[10] Riggs has coined the word "clect" combining clique and sect, for still another intermediate entity. Fred W. Riggs, *Administration in Developing Countries, The Theory of Prismatic Society* (Boston, Houghton Mifflin, 1964, 477 pp.), pp. 164-73.

[11] Edward Banfield, *The Moral Basis of a Backward Society* (Illinois, Glencoe Free Press, 1958, 204 pp.), has defined the concept of "amoral famialism" for this approach toward the world, as he found it in a village in southern Italy. Tribalism, casteism, and ethnic group loyalties are of the same order in other countries. See, for example, Fred Frey, unpublished manuscript, "Political Attitudes in Development"; G. Morris Carstairs, *The Twice Born* (Bloomington, Indiana University, 1961, 343 pp.), pp. 42-43; Surindar Suri, *1962 Elections, A Political Analysis* (New Delhi, Sudha Publications, 1962, 201 pp.), *passim.* The difference between "brother" and "stranger" is sharply noted by J. Donald Kingsley, "Bureaucracy and Political Development, with Particular Reference to Nigeria," pp. 301-18 in Joseph La Palombara (ed.), *Bureaucracy and Political Development* (Princeton, Princeton University Press, 1963, 481 pp.), p. 306.

[12] This phenomenon is familiar in the literature on South Asia. See Wriggins, *Ceylon*, pp. 29-33. For its reflection in West Africa, see Ruth Schachter Morgen-

ference which separates his generation from his father's and from that of the younger men now coming forward. This can be seen nearly everywhere, but it is accentuated in emerging countries because the dramatic changes of the past forty years have affected different generations in radically disparate ways. It is compounded by the fact that in nearly all these societies, the elders have traditionally been endowed with prerogative decision on virtually all aspects of the life of their family, tribe, or caste groups. Recent younger generations have experienced the sense of being cribbed and constrained by the judgments of their elders. But the educated youth now coming forward have found their elders' judgments and conventional wisdom particularly irrelevant to the tasks they now must face. The distance between the present generation and its elders is probably greater today than most of these societies have ever known.

The new leader has great difficulty in uncovering—or promoting—consensus on major issues of public affairs. Large numbers are attached to the traditional, often virtually sacred ways and see in a rejuvenated indigenous past the guide to present and future. Some look back to the exciting period of the independence struggle for organizational and ideological models. Others see the colonial bureaucracy as the guide to organizational effectiveness. Still others look abroad and take their guidance from the former metropole or some imagined replica of the United States, the Soviet Union, or Communist China. No agreement on political practices exists; nor is there much attachment to political institutions. Nearly all articulate leaders concur that economic matters should not be left to the forces of the market but should be shaped by public policy. However, few agree on just what direction the economy should take. There is lack of consensus on the procedures quite as much as on the ends of government.[13]

---

thau, *Political Parties in French-speaking West Africa* (London, Oxford, Clarendon Press, 1964, 445 pp.), p. 335; and David Hapgood, *Africa: From Independence to Tomorrow* (New York, Atheneum, 1965, 221 pp.), Ch. 4. On the other hand, the "gap" can easily be exaggerated, as pointed out, for example, by Richard L. Sklar, *Nigerian Political Parties: Power in an Emergent African Nation* (Princeton, Princeton University Press, 1963, 578 pp.), p. 503.

[13] For significant discussion see Clifford Geertz (ed.), "The Integrative Revolution," *Old Societies and New States: The Quest for Modernity in Asia and Africa* (New York, Glencoe Free Press, 1963, 310 pp.), pp. 105-58. See also

All these diversities impede the growth of mutual identification, the subjective prerequisite for a modern nation state. The ruler himself finds it hard to understand the interests, fears, or demands of some tribes or ethnic interest groups. He sees how few of his associates or potential allies can imagine the needs, the fears, and the aspirations of those in other groups.[14] These diversities enormously complicate the transaction of government business. They pose the problem of national integration as one of his major concerns and contribute to the intemperance of politics.

His polity faces some characteristic problems. Political integration is difficult. In no case has it proved a simple matter to develop a truly integrated political society out of these diversities. During the exciting independence struggle there seemed to be a sense of common endeavor and shared destiny. But in most instances, this perception of mutual identity was short-lived. Afterwards, men of different communities have eyed each other more as rivals than as men facing a common task. Only rarely has there developed a substantial consensus on major cultural and ideological issues which sustained itself for any length of time. A great deal of the leader's energy in post-colonial countries is applied to settling disputes and quieting jealousies.[15] Ethnic loyalties, communal identifications, and parochial differences remain the chief source of political differences. Indeed, the ruler is likely to perceive what might be called a new parochialism. Ancient differences, long hidden by forgetfulness or

---

Wriggins, "Problems of Unity in New Nations," *American Political Science Review*, Vol. LV, No. 2 (June, 1961), 313-20; David Apter, *The Political Kingdom in Uganda: A Study in Bureaucratic Nationalism* (Princeton, Princeton University Press, 1961, 498 pp.), p. 47; Aristide Zolberg, *One-Party Government in the Ivory Coast* (Princeton, Princeton University Press, 1964, 374 pp.), pp. 40-41; George E. Taylor, *The Philippines and the United States: Problems of Partnership* (New York, Praeger, 1964, 325 pp.), p. 168; Herbert Feith, *The Decline of Constitutional Democracy in Indonesia* (New York, Cornell University Press, 1962, 618 pp.), pp. 27-28; Lucian Pye (ed.), *Communications and Political Development* (Princeton, Princeton University Press, 1963, 381 pp.), p. 60; Gordon H. Torrey, *Syrian Politics and the Military, 1945-1958* (Columbus, Ohio State University Press, 1964, 438 pp.), pp. 22-23; Dennis Austin, *Politics in Ghana, 1946-1960* (London, Oxford University Press, 1964, 459 pp.), p. 420; Morgenthau, *Political Parties*, pp. 335-36 and *passim*.

[14] On the problem of empathy, see Daniel Lerner, *The Passing of Traditional Society* (Glencoe, Ill., Free Press, 1958, 466 pp.), pp. 47-52.

[15] See Leonard Binder, "National Integration and Political Development," *American Political Science Review*, Vol. LVIII, No. 3 (September, 1964), 622-31.

damped down by common antagonism to the outsider, come to the fore when groups begin to search the past to strengthen their sense of identity or contend against each other for the fruits of influence and the perquisites of office.[16] As Clifford Geertz put it, "Alongside of, and interacting with, the usual politics of party and parliament, cabinet and bureaucracy, or monarch and army, there exists, nearly everywhere, a sort of para-politics of clashing public identities and quickening ethnocentric aspirations."[17] An observer of these matters in India goes so far as to contend that the main unifying theme in political behavior is the determination of all to combine against that ethnic or caste group which appears to be bettering its position by comparison with others in the society.[18] Integrating a nation out of the multiple diversities encompassed within a colonial society has not been accomplished anywhere and is a discouraging task.[19]

Even more basic, few are the rulers who can count on their sovereign capability, even within their own territories. If one could obtain a candid view, the typical new leader of an emerging country experiences most of the time a sense of the very narrow limits of his power. Often substantial geographical areas within the realm lie outside the range of his authority. These may be the "lands of insolence," where peoples like the Kurds, the Nagas, or the Kachins actively resist encroachment from the central government. The ruler is likely to be all too aware of the regionally preponderant power of local chieftains, potentates or warlords, as in the Northwest Frontier area where Afghanistan and Pakistan meet. If a local notable cannot be induced to cooperate by political and economic means, very little can be done about it short of a test of arms which the

[16] Wriggins, Ceylon, Ch. VI.

[17] Geertz, Old Societies, p. 124. See also Karl Von Vorys, "Toward a Concept of Political Development," The Annals, Vol. 358 (March, 1965), 14-19, 16.

[18] Suri, 1962 Elections, p. 50.

[19] On the difficulties of handling various kinds of conflict in emerging countries, see Shmuel N. Eisenstadt, "Breakdowns of Modernization," Economic Development and Cultural Change, Vol. XII, No. 4 (July, 1964), 345-67, 347. Geertz has a thoughtful discussion of the process of appropriate adjustment between the modern civil identifications and the primordial ties, so that "government can proceed freely without threatening the cultural framework of personal identity." Old Societies and New States, pp. 154-55; see also Von Vorys, "Toward a Concept of Political Development," The Annals, Vol. 358 (March, 1965), 16.

ruler may not want to risk.[20] There may be, on the other hand, remote areas where until recently governments have not attempted seriously to assert regular influence, such as the Northeast Frontier Agency area in Assam State, India, and Thailand's northeast.

The difficulties of the new leader may be more administrative in character, in that the executive arm of his government simply lacks the capability to effect his will through bureaucratic, logistical or other inadequacies. Several Western observers have noted the low overall level of institutional power in many underdeveloped societies. Large sections of the society may be outside the range of governmental influence.[21] Government may be so lacking in capability that rulers cannot carry out their commitments, let alone have assurance that they can perform even minimum functions.[22] Indeed, new leaders have often found their major problem to be the survival of national authority itself, the example of Nigeria being only the extreme case.

These matters may not be important in countries which are geographically remote from other powers and therefore are relatively safe from external encroachment, such as Ethiopia before the Italian invasion of the 1930s, Saudi Arabia, or Mali; or where little government capability is needed since governments set only modest goals and the people have been generally satisfied with what little the government does, as in Nepal or in Northern Nigeria.

But the new states are rarely of this sort. Most leaders have outlined vaulting goals, inducing spacious expectations in their followers. High ambitions require efficient performance. Accordingly the goals leaders have set call for notable sovereign capability, while the social and institutional impediments to capability are deeply discouraging.

This predicament is intensified by the tendency of parochial groups to resist rule by any but their own. It is debasing in an intensely personal fashion to be ruled by anyone outside one's tribal, ethnic, or traditional group. In leading the anti-colonial struggle, the leader

[20] The notion of the "land of insolence" is from the Arabic and applies to the Middle East. See Coon, Caravan, Ch. 16. Indonesia is said to face a similar problem. See Herbert Feith, Decline of Constitutional Democracy in Indonesia, pp. 520-38.

[21] Fred Frey in an unpublished manuscript on "Some Stages of Political Development," p. 9.

[22] Hapgood, Africa, Chs. 4 and 7. Charles B. Marshall, "Reflections on a Revolution in Pakistan," Foreign Affairs, Vol. XXXVII, No. 2 (January, 1959), 247-56.

often gained local support when he could show that independence would bring an end to the centralizing tendencies of the colonial regime. The continuing resistance of parochial groups to centralizing political control impedes new leaders at the center of new nations.[23]

The lack of sovereign capability in the executive is not the only reason governance is difficult. The leader also finds the demands of politics ambiguous. He is often unsure of what substantial groups within his polity are hoping for. Because they lack interest group organizations or leadership skilled in brokering their aspirations with the central authority, parochial and traditional groups do not have the means for sustained expression of their demands or of aggregating contradictory demands into alternative policies.[24] Often there is a perplexing mercurial quality to political life as groups abruptly form and assert their demands without the benefit of experience in compromise. Buddhists suddenly entered the political arena in Ceylon and South Vietnam; linguistic groups burst into political life in India. Tribal antagonisms break out in Nigeria; people run amok in Indonesia and massacre many thousands of communists, sympathizers, and others.[25] Leaders may face apathy and exploding activation alternately, without the sustained plurality of interests which in more developed societies balance each other and often leave governments considerable room for independent maneuver. Ideally, leaders seek that rare compromise which will maximize the greatest return to the greatest number. More likely, they may have to settle for the most tolerable distribution of half-loaves to the major contending groups in the society and to their often shifting and temporary small allies.[26]

Where most men believe that the personalities and processes of

[23] Geertz, Old Societies and New States, p. 127.

[24] Almond and Coleman, The Politics of the Developing Nations, pp. 38-45; Eisenstadt, "Breakdowns of Modernization," Economic Development and Cultural Change, Vol. XII, No. 4 (July, 1964), 345-67, 351.

[25] Movement politics are particularly prone to such manifestations. Religious group activation has been notably dramatic in this respect, as for example Buddhist politics in Ceylon. See Wriggins, Ceylon, Ch. 6; Jerold Schecter, The New Face of Buddha (New York, Coward McCann, 1967, 300 pp.); Chs. 8, 9, and 10; John Mecklin, Mission in Torment (Garden City, Doubleday, 1965, 318 pp.).

[26] See Myron Weiner on this process in Indian politics, The Politics of Scarcity, Public Pressures and Political Response in India (Chicago, University of Chicago Press, 1962, 251 pp.), Ch. 9; and Dahl, Who Governs? passim, on the way it works in New Haven. Eisenstadt, "Breakdowns of Modernization," pp. 24-26; Pye, Communications and Political Development, p. 150.

governance are appropriate, government is endowed with legitimacy. Even when a particular act of government may be to one's personal disadvantage, it will still be felt as acceptable. By contrast, in most emerging countries much is of dubious authority. After the first flush of enthusiasm fades, the leader's authority after independence is rarely taken for granted. The channels for political contention, the operational code which defines the rules of the game, the assumptions of the principal protagonists, and the reliability of the sanctions against those who break the rules remain in doubt. In most countries, the practices and institutions introduced during the colonial period often, by that fact, were brought into question after independence.

Typically, the new leader will find political contention in his country intemperate, a characteristic which will give him great difficulty. A number of elements contribute to political intemperance.

Where the society is fragmented and group antagonism widespread strong contention should be expected. The art of compromise is difficult to practice when mutually suspicious groups compete against each other in an open political arena. Often covert contention has been practiced for generations, as different families, castes, communities, and tribes have been competing against each other for status, economic opportunity, access to jobs in the public service, or even for land and grazing rights. "The vision of a single nation submerged under colonial control fades before the reality of competitive sub-societies, each of which tends to view independence as a mandate to reassert its traditional heritage and strengthen its claims against those of other groups."[27] It would be surprising if, when the foreigners leave, these profound issues would be dealt with in a moderate and restrained fashion.

Moreover, within the tightly knit traditional society there were

[27] Ann Ruth and Dorothy Willner, "The Rise and Role of Charismatic Leaders," *The Annals*, Vol. 358 (March, 1965), pp. 77-88, 85. "As long as kinship is an important link between the educated and their rural constituents, division among the elite on such constitutional matters as federalism, independence, or the position of "chiefs" . . . is often taken by their kinsmen as a signal for settling entirely unrelated traditional issues over land, women or water. This was one of the dynamics behind the Ivory Coast incidents of 1949-1952." Morgenthau, *Political Parties*, pp. 353-54. Geertz, *Old Societies and New States*, p. 124; Donald Kingsley in J. La Palombara (ed.), *Bureaucracy and Political Development*, p. 306. Selig Harrison in *India, The Most Dangerous Decades* (Princeton, Princeton University Press, 1960, 350 pp.), reports analogous modern differences being utilized to settle old scores.

usually firm restraints which disciplined ambition and set limits to who could properly bid for the higher stakes. And in an evolved polity, constitutional, legal, or other limits set more modern bounds to unbridled competition. But in transitional societies, some individuals or groups are freed of the old restraints without yet being constrained by newer rules of the game.[28]

An intensity is added to contention by the stakes of political success or failure. Political life in developing countries is often seen as if one man's gain is another man's equivalent loss. Though not a zero sum game, it often approaches just that. This is particularly so where competition for effective power, for relative status, or for the appurtenances of power are at issue. If, as in many Western countries, after one loses office, one can return to one's law firm at a higher income, rise in social status, and have more time for leisure, not much is lost if one is retired by a political defeat. But in many underdeveloped countries, the stakes of losing office are very great, indeed. Political life may be the open road to advancement if one has that talent; such a life may also be the most expeditious way to improve one's status and income. Politics may represent a full-time profession for many who, in their youth, undertook to battle for independence. Losing office under such circumstances may project one not only into poverty, which is bad enough, but into obscurity and demeaning dependence on former subordinates, which in highly status-conscious societies may be worse. Intense contention, therefore, may derive from the desperate personal need for political success.

Politics may also represent emotional release, a channeling of frustrations and anxieties into political energies which may have great force for a time. When this occurs, intense contention may have little to do with the objective interests or rational calculations of active participants, but represent the release of pent-up passions.

The small size of many political elites contributes to intense competition. It is not merely that many emerging countries are in themselves small, with populations under 10 million people. Even in larger countries the full-time political participants are relatively few. There is an acutely personal dimension. Promising young men, whose families, clans, or communities have been jockeying against each other for generations, square off at school or university, competing

[28] See, for example, W. H. Morris-Jones, *The Government and Politics of India* (Doubleday, Anchor, 1967, 227 pp.), pp. 50-51.

for debating honors, scholarships, or academic openings. In the course of their early competition at school, rivalry is built in. The contention continues at university. When they embark on political careers, they can work together only intermittently. They know each other all too well and expose each other's weaknesses. This phenomenon is observable in South Asia. To understand Indian state politics and Ceylon national politics usually requires familiarity with the early personal relationships of leading contenders and associates. On the basis of African observations, David Apter notes that it is by no means rare for the successful contender to taunt the defeated, flaunt his power, and provoke the defeated "opposition" to acts which permit the ruler to take stern measures against his erstwhile competitor.[29]

There is little confidence that the institutional framework is adequate to resolve deeply felt differences. Particularly during periods of rapid change, the new groups fear that they will be ignored— and therefore must assert their views and interests with great vigor; those who are already established fear that the institutions will be unduly responsive to new demands, and they will lose completely their status, opportunity, or income. Means for moderating claims to change or to defend the status quo are lacking. Seen from either perspective, it is critically important to push one's position hard enough to win the political game.

As Myron Weiner put it:

A modern political system has no single mechanism, no single procedure, no single institution for the resolution of conflict; indeed, it is precisely the multiplicity of individuals, institutions and procedures for dispute settlement that characterizes the modern political system—both democratic and totalitarian. In contrast, developing societies with an increasing range of internal conflict, typically lack such individuals, institutions and procedures. It is as if mankind's capacity to generate conflict is greater than his capacity to find methods for resolving conflict; the lag is clearly greatest in societies in which fundamental economic and social relationships are rapidly changing.[30]

[29] David E. Apter, "Some Reflections on the Role of Political Opposition in New Nations," Comparative Studies in Society and History, IV (The Hague, Mouton and Co. 1961-1962), 154-168; 164. Until the Zaim coup in Syria in 1949, Syrian politics were a horrible example of what such rivalries could do to a "representative" system; Torrey, Syrian Politics, p. 22.

[30] Myron Weiner, "Political Integration and Political Development," The Annals, Vol. 358 (March, 1965), 52-64, 60; see also Carl Friedrich, Man and His Government, p. 339.

Moderation in politics is made even less likely by the fact that the future balance of political forces appears to be in the process of being critically shaped during the early years of independence.[31] Victory for one's own group may give one's family, clan, tribe, or region long-run advantages which cannot be ensured unless the game is vigorously played from the outset. This is more clearly seen in British and French West Africa than in South Asia. In most instances in West Africa, and in Tanganyika, too, the early winners in the game were still the principal figures in 1968: Sékou-Touré, Houphouët-Boigny, and Nyerere. In South Asia, Nehru remained at the apex for nearly twenty years, but his successors were severely challenged in the 1967 elections. In Ceylon, a Senanayake was the first prime minister, and his son was elected prime minister in 1952 and again in 1965. Yet from 1956 to 1965 other leaders and parties had had a chance at responsibility.

Since the states are new and constitutionalism is not yet well-established, the rules of the political game are in flux. The man on the losing side all too often correctly fears that the winner will so change the rules that he must resign himself to perpetual defeat, as Nkrumah so dramatically demonstrated to the discomfiture of his opponents—until a coup d'état abruptly removed him from office.

Intense political competition is favored by a sense of economic cramp and narrowing opportunity. In some new countries, particularly if they gained their independence in the late forties or early fifties, economic prosperity was bolstered by the remaining wartime balances or the boom in commodity prices during the Korean War. Those countries which have come to independence more recently have not had such advantages. Indeed, in most of the liberated African states, leaders gained responsibility at a time of intensifying economic difficulty.

The ruler's economy poses characteristic difficulties. Most of the emerging countries are deep in poverty. Per capita annual incomes average roughly $100 in most countries in Asia and Africa.[32]

[31] Clark Kerr, John T. Dunlop, Frederick H. Harbison, and Charles A. Myers, *Industrialism and Industrial Man; The Problems of Labor and Management in Economic Growth* (Cambridge, Harvard University Press, 1960, 321 pp.), p. 68.

[32] This figure excludes Israel, Cyprus, Kuwait, Saudi Arabia, and Japan as exceptional, and Liberia, Laos, Burundi, Rwanda, and Malawi for which figures were not available. Figures are for the year 1958. *Yearbook of National Accounts Statistics, 1964* (New York, United Nations Statistical Office, Department of Economic and Social Affairs, 1965), pp. 389-92.

Contrasts of income within specific countries make the real economic significance of such figures uncertain. Their political implications are equally difficult to assess. Only after a person begins to improve his situation does he begin truly to aspire to more. At some point in the shifting equation of income and aspiration, however, poverty provokes demands for change which can be politically organized and exploited by rulers or by their political opponents.

Although the bulk of the population works on the land, the production of food crops for local consumption has remained archaic and inefficient. Insufficient economic infrastructures are believed still to inhibit development. Communications are lacking; sources of energy, and essential financial, productive, and distributive institutions are simply not there or are grossly insufficient. The external economies taken for granted by industry in developed countries are only rarely found in association with one another in emerging Africa and Asia. Social overheads like safe drinking water and even minimal housing in rapidly growing urban centers are all too rare. Perhaps felt most directly in the political arena is the demand for schooling, which in most countries far outstrips the government's ability to satisfy. In India, for example, between 1950 and 1959 the school population grew by 20 million students, going up 100 per cent in a mere decade; in Nigeria, the numbers trebled in the same period. In Egypt, they went up roughly 140 per cent. Egypt's annual rate of population growth went from 1.8 per cent in 1937-1946 to 2.5 per cent in 1958-1961. India's reportedly climbed from 1.7 per cent on the average between 1937 and 1951 to 2.2 per cent during the 1958-1961 period, and it is now thought to be nearly 2.6 per cent. Pakistan's is reported to be even higher. These seem like small increments, but they cumulate rapidly, a rate of 1.5 per cent doubles the population in 47 years, 2 per cent in 35 years, and 2.5 per cent in only 28 years.[33]

The increases in the numbers of the youthful call for heavy educational outlays. The economies have not yet expanded sufficiently to find places for those who are entering the labor market in ever larger numbers and with a new level of expectation as a result of their training. More unproductive elderly people must now be cared for. Urban unemployment is already widespread, producing a numerous—and growing—group of disgruntled men in the cities, with time on their hands, susceptible to easy organization. Rural under-

[33] Computed from the UN *Statistical Yearbook*, 1948, 1949, 1952, 1962.

employment, though endemic and economically unproductive, is politically less serious, but does provide a political potential for the future if artfully organized.

The scarcity of resources in almost all instances is real enough. It is made more serious by the fact that those controlling the resources a country does possess are often reluctant to move into activities most likely to lead to productive development. Investment in land, apartment houses, or office buildings in the capital makes individual economic sense as a hedge against inflation. It is also congenial to local status values, tends to be more secure, and requires less unfamiliar managerial skills than embarking on an industrial enterprise. The import business and local trading, involving high markups and small inventories, tend to produce higher profit margins with less risk than is the case with more productive investment. There is a high preference for liquidity, in part because of chronic political instability. The desire to have a nest egg abroad, if possible, is strong. There is a widespread expectation that future investment opportunities, foreseeable but indefinite, will prove more rewarding than those available today.[34]

The decision to embark on a major investment commits not only funds, when one prefers to remain liquid, but also a major portion of one's personal responsibility.[35] Cooperation with others is as difficult in economic as in political affairs. Where there is much distrust, only personal supervision or management held within the family can be counted upon to make proper returns to the investors. Local lending institutions, if they exist, are often high-cost and conservative in the enterprises they will back. The hard, patient personal application required for management of complex enterprises all too often is found largely among religious or ethnic minorities, or foreign communities, who are seen as interlopers and exploiters by nationalists claiming to speak on behalf of the majority indigenous communities.[36] Trained young men are reluctant to go to the rural areas for productive work but prefer high-status jobs in the cities. The

---

[34] On this see Albert O. Hirschman, *The Strategy of Economic Development* (New Haven, Yale University Press, 1958, 217 pp.), pp. 20-21.

[35] *Ibid.*, p. 19.

[36] David McClelland, *The Achieving Society* (Princeton, N.J., Van Nostrand, 1961, 512 pp.), Ch. 7, especially p. 281. Everett E. Hagen, *On the Theory of Social Change: How Economic Growth Begins* (Homewood, Illinois, The Dorsey Press, 1962, 557 pp.), pp. 240-50; 446-70.

traditional values or standards unwittingly inculcated by the example of colonial administrators devalue the man who dirties his hands.

The technology readily available abroad is usually capital-intensive and labor saving, while at home capital is scarce and labor cheap. Adaptations which economize on capital and increase the labor component require a readiness to innovate, a quality possessed by only the very few. And labor itself requires a heavy investment in training. Where private entrepreneurs lack either the means or the will to invest and innovate, government enterprise often attempts to take its place. But it is the rare bureaucracy in emerging countries which possesses the rigorous applied energy, the cost-consciousness, and the innovative flexibility necessary to promote rapid and economical investment.

These essentially internal problems are compounded by external difficulties. Foreign investments have usually concentrated on extractive industries, and while these have brought new technologies, management practices, and capital into the country, the side-effects of development have often been limited. Moreover, most emerging countries remain dependent upon the export of raw materials to earn the foreign exchange needed to meet current import requirements and to finance investment programs. Yet the world market price of individual raw materials fluctuates substantially from year to year.[37] If each country had a diversified range of products to export, gains in one might well offset losses in another, and some sustained foreign exchange earnings could be counted upon. However, most emerging countries are dependent upon only one or two exports which account for the bulk of their earnings.[38] Technological advances in the developed countries are providing substitute materials which dampen the world market prospects for many of the raw material exports of emerging countries, and thus far the underdeveloped countries have been unable to do anything about these adverse developments, despite collective efforts through the United Nations Conference on Trade and Development (UNCTAD) and other channels.

The uncertainty in foreign exchange earnings means that the

[37] William Butler, "Trade and the Less Developed Areas," *Foreign Affairs,* Vol. XLI, No. 2 (January, 1963), 372-83, 375.

[38] For example Pakistan depends on jute for approximately 70 per cent of its earnings. Ghana between 50 and 75 per cent on cocoa. Ceylon depends upon tea alone for some 70 per cent of its earnings, and the other 30 per cent is divided between coconut products and rubber.

developing country must adjust vital imports each year to its export earnings or run the risk of accumulating serious balance of payments deficits. Such fluctuations in import programs contradict the need for maximum economy in capital development programs so that, if they are to be carried forward efficiently, they must be phased to the requirements of the investment sequence and not be subject to stops and starts determined by fluctuating foreign exchange availabilities. These and other difficulties have encouraged most emerging countries to seek ways of insulating their economies from external economic forces by such means as high tariffs, multiple exchange rates, and industrial self-sufficiency directed toward such a small market as to be highly inefficient.

Leaders of developing countries face problems which, in their combination, would discourage the most optimistic leader in developed countries. These difficulties have much to do with the goals leaders set as they seek to overcome these difficulties, or to circumvent them while sustaining themselves in power. The next chapter discusses these goals.

3 On Goals and Disappointments

For men to plunge headlong into an undertaking of vast change, they must be intensely discontented yet not destitute, and they must have the feeling that by the possession of some potent doctrine, infallible leader or some new technique they have access to a source of irresistible power. They must also have an extravagant concept of the prospects and potentialities of the future. Finally, they must be wholly ignorant of the difficulties involved in their vast undertaking. Experience is a handicap.

Eric Hoffer

The political goals leaders set themselves affect the way they use the power they have available. Their goals will also affect their ability to extend and retain that power. Goals justify their political aspirations and activities to themselves, to their entourage, and to the wider public.

The goals they voice come from many sources. A substantial proportion derive directly from the problems facing emerging polities discussed in Chapter 2. But there are other points of origin, and not all problems apparent to the outside observer will necessarily be dealt with. Leaders inherit many of the goals they talk of; these may be part of the symbolic coin of political discourse developed during the independence struggle. Leaders may commit themselves to goals they believe will win them popular support or the backing of key groups in their societies. Some may seek their positions of leadership to bring into being a better society. If large numbers of men are to be moved to action, great purposes beyond all probability of realization must be held up before them. Leaders also may set different private goals, concealing from the population their own sense of political vulnerability while attempting to use their period in office to improve their own power or their wealth.

To talk of goals in any rigorous sense is admittedly difficult. Today's end becomes tomorrow's means for yet another end, and so on in infinite sequence. Goals are often defined in relation to what a person or political group believes to be available capability. As capability or power improves, goals often rapidly expand, while available means affect the nature and scope of the end to be achieved. Moreover, the means adopted to pursue political ends will affect the end itself.

Public goals are usually stated in a generalized form, encompassing many possible alternative specific activities. This ambiguity improves the chances that large numbers of individuals and groups will support the proponents of such goals. An unduly narrow or precise definition of objectives risks alienating possible associates or allies. In some instances—particularly where leaders are unsure of themselves— grand goals may be articulated as a substitute for action, not as a serious guide to action, for there is less risk of being discredited when trying the impossible than when trying the possible.[1] Taking statements of political goals at face value can be misleading. Nevertheless, political goals defined by leaders for a polity generally do have something to do with what leaders are striving to achieve, the way resources are allocated, and the level and direction of public aspiration. Often they are the yardsticks by which most leaders, ultimately, come to be judged.

It will be sufficient here to discuss the major goals which most statesmen in emerging countries have set themselves, for there is a notable similarity among their stated purposes. Characteristics of each goal will be identified and its political utility considered.

LEGITIMACY, THE UNACKNOWLEDGED SEARCH

The new leader seeks to draw about himself and his government the cloak of legitimacy; he seeks to have it understood, without question, that he is properly entitled to rule. Having legitimacy, he

[1] Eric Hoffer, *The True Believer: Thoughts on the Nature of Mass Movements* (New York, Mentor, 1958, 160 pp.), p. 72.

and his government are assured of their authority. With legitimacy much is simple; without it, everything is difficult. To be able to take for granted the near magic acquiescence in one's right to rule over others is the ideal situation for a political leader. Such acceptance requires little performance to sustain it; political responses are prompt and usually unquestioning; and the person being influenced is seldom aware of his acquiescence. In well-established states much of the time procedures for selecting the ruler and his entourage are generally accepted and automatically confer legitimacy.[2]

Legitimacy has many forms and faces. Inheritance is the simplest and surest for the man thus blessed. In traditional societies still relatively untouched by more modern ideas, the rightness of subservience to the well-born remains unquestioned. Traditional authority possessed an aura of religious sanctity, of authority confirmed by association with traditional status and of ancestral time reaching deep into the past. Those deserving deference had either inheritance to justify them or sacred functions to perform. Contemporary leaders of the emerging states, however, do not automatically possess these qualities. Indeed, by virtue of the essentially secular nature of the political activities which brought them to prominence, they are seen primarily as secular men of this world. They lack the aura of sacred legitimacy which hitherto surrounded the truly indigenous leader. Colored by the agencies of modern statehood which give them place, they may seem more like their former colonial masters than men rooted in the soil of the new country itself. States but fifteen years old—or less—lack the authoritative institutions which in themselves confer legitimacy upon individual incumbents. To be sure, to have led the independence movement through years of struggle helped confer the kind of legitimacy acquired by Nehru in India and Bourguiba in Tunisia; to have received authority from the colonial rulers strengthened D. S. Senanayake in Ceylon and Houphouët-Boigny in the Ivory Coast. To have been prominent in a successful military struggle against colonial rule helped Sukarno, as will be seen. Men previously endowed with legitimacy from the independence struggle must after a time earn it again, as the United National Party of Ceylon discovered in 1956 when it was swept out of office. It is the leaders of coups d'état who must be most concerned about legiti-

---

[2] Fred Frey, "Social Power and Economic Development," unpublished manuscript.

macy, for by their usurpation they invite others to follow their example.

Exceptional performance in tackling the most urgent and widely acknowledged problems can bring its own legitimacy, a possibility which helped Presidents Nasser and Ayub in consolidating their positions after their quite different steps to power. But this way is not easy, since administrative problems abound, skilled assistants are in short supply, and results are often disappointing.[3] Leaders of successful coups d'état pay implicit homage to legitimacy when they so promptly attempt to justify their usurpation in the name of the people, and promise a prompt housecleaning, a plebiscite, or an election.

If the legitimacy of performance is difficult, there may be another alternative. As will be seen, prominent leaders such as Sukarno, Nkrumah, and Bourguiba sought legitimacy by projecting themselves larger than life across the consciousness of their people. They attempt to evoke between themselves and their followers that charismatic relationship built on assumptions of exceptional heroism, understanding, or grace.[4] To seek legitimacy by direct personal inspiration is understandable, since other ways of acquiring it are difficult. Political leaders may also attempt to reach back to traditional religious symbolism, making their own the panoply of ancient rites.[5]

While most leaders of new states are beset with the need to acquire and consolidate legitimacy, some of the more traditional states such as Afghanistan, Thailand, and Ethiopia are beginning to experience a weakening of inherited legitimacy as increasing numbers are coming to reject inheritance and royal descent as ways of legitimizing rule, yet newer ways remain ill-formed. Afghanistan's halting experiments with representative institutions recall British experience with early parliaments. Prince Sihanouk of Cambodia inherited the role of ruler, but resigned his kingship to have his position confirmed by plebiscite. Thus far he has profited from this double legitimacy.

Regardless of its source or how it is acquired, legitimacy is a

---

[3] Shils, *Political Development in the New States*, p. 35; Seymour M. Lipset, *The First New Nation: The United States in Historical and Comparative Perspective* (New York, Basic Books, 1963, 366 pp.), p. 246.

[4] Max Weber, "Legitimate Order and Types of Authority," in Talcott Parsons (ed.), *Theories of Society* (New York, Free Press of Glencoe, 1961, 2 volumes), Vol. I, pp. 232-35.

[5] Morgenthau, *Political Parties*, p. 236.

substantial political asset. Few leaders would acknowledge the extent to which they seek such easy acceptance. Those without it are haunted by a sense of their own insecurity. Their margin for error is narrow. They have to earn their right to rule by performance which may need to be recapitulated and confirmed over and over again. Finally, time, habit, and the surrounding symbols of high estate produce for the man at the apex what he did not have at the outset. With it, the legitimated ruler can survive poor performance and catastrophes which would unseat the man who lacks legitimacy.[6]

Most of their effort to acquire legitimacy is not acknowledged. The urgent search lies within the private realm leaders may not even share with their immediate entourage. The other goals are public goals, sought not only by the regime but held and aspired to by substantial elements of the polity and society.

INDEPENDENCE AND SELF-RESPECT

The most important single public policy goal for most new countries appears to be independence. No country, not even a super-power, is fully independent; all are enmeshed in a net of relation-ships which leaves none free to go its own way. Yet there are degrees of independence, and the leaders of new countries seek to ensure greater independence for their country and their people.[7]

As the politically active see it, national independence must be enhanced and consolidated at all costs. There is nominal independ-ence and real independence, and a leader and people must be wary of not taking the one for the other.[8] National independence is not simply a matter of defending and securing the country's frontiers from exter-nal military attack, as it has been in western Europe's tradition. It is that, at a minimum, and most new states feel vulnerable to whatever great powers are nearby or consider the new country within their

[6] On legitimacy, see also Friedrich, *Man and His Government*, p. 236; Easton, *A Systems Analysis of Political Life*, Chs. 18 and 19; Feith, *The Decline of Constitutional Democracy in Indonesia*, p. 549; David A. Wilson, *Politics in Thailand* (Ithaca, Cornell University Press, 1962, 307 pp.), p. 269.

[7] A quantitative content analysis of leaders' goals, put either as explicit goals or values that are under threat, would show in all probability "national inde-pendence" as by far the most frequently referred to.

[8] See Mamadou Dia of Senegal in Paul E. Sigmund (ed.), *The Ideologies of the Developing Nations* (New York, Praeger, 1963, 326 pp.), pp. 232-37.

zone of global security. Algeria and Cambodia have expressed fear of the United States. Larger near neighbors, even if they, too, have just come to independence, can also be perceived as threatening: Pakistan fears India, India fears the new China, Malaysia has feared Indonesia.

National independence also concerns the capability of the leaders to make and implement their own decisions unaffected by influences from abroad, unless they have been freely chosen. Free choice of political institutions is necessary. Freedom to look on each problem of foreign policy "on its merits," is jealously guarded.[9] It involves the question of identity. Nehru saw his identity confirmed if he could express and act on his own views. At Bandung he declared: "If I join any of these big groups, I lose my identity; I have no identity left, I have no views left." Independence means that one must find one's own unique qualities and underline them.[10] As Sukarno put it, ". . . as I have said before, we have to return to our own personality; we want to return to our own identity. Do not let us become a carbon copy nation."[11]

Essential to identity is the need to glorify one's own historic past. Where former rulers denied the worth of one's tradition, inducing a sense of inadequacy, this line of argument is more urgent. Nehru was particularly adept at resuscitating the distant past as a way of invigorating greater self-respect.[12] Efforts in Ghana and Nigeria to popularize and glorify past African kingdoms derive from the same impulse. Yet, sustaining cultural identity is difficult. The modern communications network brings slick magazines or movies from affluent societies. The West and the Soviet Union exert the fascination of the modern, the industrialized, the changing. Young people sent abroad are pulled thereafter between the tempting foreign and the

[9] Brecher, *Nehru, A Political Biography*, pp. 215-16; Ernest W. Lefever, "Nehru, Nasser and Nkrumah on Neutralism," in Lawrence W. Martin (ed.),*Neutralism and Nonalignment: The New States in World Affairs* (New York, Praeger, 1962, 250 pp.), pp. 95, 116-17.

[10] George M. Kahin, *The Asian-African Conference* (Ithaca, Cornell University Press, 1956, 88 pp.), p. 66. In Indonesia, Feith reports: "Many of this group [around Sukarno] expected the post-revolutionary years to bring rising national welfare, but it was the nation's prestige and its sense of cultural identity which was the object of their principal concern." Feith, *Decline of Constitutional Democracy in Indonesia*, p. 37. See also Geertz, *Old Societies and New States,* p. 108.

[11] Sigmund (ed.), *The Ideologies of the Developing Nations*, pp. 61-62.

[12] See Jawaharlal Nehru, *The Discovery of India* (New York, John Day, 1946, 595 pp.), Ch. II, pp. 37-40.

all too familiar indigenous ways. Identity and distinctiveness cannot be taken for granted; they must be worked on and confirmed.

These matters appear far from the realpolitik of national independence in the strategic sense. But they are, perhaps, nearer the essence of national independence as it is perceived by many leaders in Africa and Asia.

Independence has an economic base. It is felt that the new country must be freed from its dependence upon one or two commodities or major overseas markets in Western Europe or North America. The role of foreign capital has to be carefully watched. In the past, foreign capital was protected by the colonial regime and was often seen as a supporter of that government or as an ally of ethnic minorities whose economic activities were believed to be at everyone else's expense. Chinese in Southeast Asia, Tamils in Burma and Ceylon, and Indians in East Africa all used foreign capital—as well as hard work—to gain prominent economic positions. There must be economic change if economic independence is to be achieved. Yet, as leaders and publicists see it, their peoples remain poor, capital must come from abroad, and primary producing economies are substantially more dependent upon industrial countries than the other way about.

It is important for the new leader to demonstrate that he is recognized by others as truly independent. He needs the appurtenances of high office familiar in more established states. He must be able to dramatize the independence of his decisions. His state must be accorded the status normally attributed to the larger or long-established state. However, the chances are strongly against each emerging state finding itself sufficiently recognized and reassured about its independent status on the world stage.[13]

The search for true independence goes on as cultural identity, economic independence, and international recognition fall short of aspiration. It persists as a goal in part because it is the one political goal which offers promise to nearly everyone and has proved successful in the past. Independence moved the hitherto inert masses to protest colonial rule and to act in concert. It was independence as a goal which projected most of the present leaders from relative

---

[13] Part of the impulse to rejuvenate their societies is said to be to gain the respect of the more influential and powerful states. See Taylor, *The Philippines and the United States*, p. 164; Lipset, *The First New Nation*, p. 46.

obscurity into positions of national responsibility and of diplomatic prominence.

Most threats to national independence are felt to come from abroad, from the sinister forces of neocolonialism, former colonial powers in the West, or new colonialist powers in Communist Asia and their associates who, it is held, are forever seeking new positions of control. These fears, touched again and again, are useful as a means of focusing attention on forces beyond reach and shifting responsibility for difficulties from present leaders onto former rulers or outsiders. As Mamadou Dia once put it, "We know that one of the resources of leaders struggling with domestic difficulties is to invent a foreign scapegoat. It would be a mistake to exaggerate the possibilities of this 'psychological action' that has become a method of governing."[14]

The goal of national independence can also be used by the opposition. If the opposition can demonstrate how much a regime has become the stooge of foreign forces or has risked national independence for its own special interests, a leader's reputation and political position may be undermined.

NATIONAL UNITY

Nearly all statesmen assume the virtue and the necessity of developing a unified state.

There is a range in the degree of unity necessary for a workable polity. Most leaders who seek to make new states out of old societies have taken integrated modern European nation-states as models. These evolved to their present stage of cultural unity, bureaucratic centralization, and political consensus over centuries. And even the most centralized, France, home of revolutions, still must periodically revert to quasi-monarchical rule if its chronic political stalemate is to be overcome. Had these countries come to independence in another epoch they might have taken the loose, culturally heterogeneous, semiautonomous approach of the Austro-Hungarian empire as their model, or even the federal forms and practices of our American constitution. These might have been more congenial to the cultural and political diversity of their present circumstances. In any event, apart

[14] Sigmund (ed.), *The Ideologies of the Developing Nations*, p. 233.

from India, Pakistan, Malaysia, the Cameroons, and Nigeria at the outset, which set up federal structures, nearly all are searching for a unified, indeed, centralized national entity, generally along lines of the western European model.

As the preoccupation with independence derives in part from widespread fear that it is not assured, and might, indeed, be lost, so the concern for national unity stems from an anguished sense of confusion and a desire to live within a more shapely, homogeneous whole. Nasser communicated the mood exactly when referring to Egypt's cultural diversity. In a classic evocation, he wrote:

> Sometimes I examine the conditions of an average Egyptian family among the thousands of families living in Cairo. It may be that the father is a turbaned farmer who has been born outside the city, in the heart of the countryside. The mother is a descendant of a Turkish family. The sons are being educated at an English style school, while the daughters attend schools run on the methods of the French. And all this is being backgrounded by a curious mixture of thirteenth and twentieth century ways of life.
>
> I consider all this, and feel a deep understanding of *the confusion that besets our national life and of the disorder from which we plan escape.* Then I reflect: *this society will develop form, consolidate and become a strong, homogeneous and unified whole.* But first we must make ourselves ready to survive and make growth through the period of transition.[15] (My emphasis).

Awareness of diversity and fears of its consequence have been etched on the minds of all who have responsibility, for nearly every emerging country has experienced outbursts of violence erupting out of underlying tribal, linguistic, or racial differences. Leaders in India, Ceylon, the Sudan, Indonesia, Nigeria, Congo-Kinshasa, and many others know from their own tragic observation the human cost of such antagonisms.

Moreover, nearly all leaders are aware of the sharp difference between the political culture of the modern state, which stresses inclusive interests and responds to the need for change, as compared to the traditional cultures, which claim primacy for parochial and usually mutually exclusive differences. These entities resist change and impede a host of objectives pursued by new leaders. Regional loyalties block overarching national policies in Indonesia and Nigeria;

[15] Gamal Abdel Nasser, *Egypt's Liberation: The Philosophy of the Revolution* (Washington, Public Affairs Press, 1955, 115 pp.), pp. 69-70.

racial and cultural minorities in India, Ceylon, and Burma fear for their identity if integrative policies are followed.[16]

National unity is also felt to be a prerequisite for national independence. Traditional divisions weakened pre-colonial societies, it is held, so that the Western colonial powers were able to take over. Continuing divisions after independence will be misused by the former colonial powers who, it is said, are seeking to regain control if new nations are not careful. As Mr. Nehru put it, to have ". . . supported the communal upheaval . . . would have brought on a long period of anarchic violence for no purpose. . . . India would have been disrupted and the States would have fought amongst themselves. In other words, we would have repeated that period in history in which the British power established itself in India."[17]

National unity, moreover, is felt to be necessary if developmental tasks are to be undertaken. Sékou-Touré declared: "Many nations in the world would have 100-200 million inhabitants and are centuries ahead of us, disposing of enormous riches, which we do not have, and utilizing modern methods, which we lack today. We are just beginning, and our first task to raise ourselves to the level of modern states in the world consists in our unity."[18] Joint enterprise calling for collaboration among diverse social groups is difficult because of the uncompromising, sometimes unnegotiable demands put forward by distinctive ethnic, religious, or other communal groups.[19]

National unity as a goal is particularly urgent if the leaders hope to undertake great things. Consensus on either the goals or the means to achieve them is usually lacking. Where unity of purpose and a shared sense of common destiny are absent, unity must be consciously sought to limit or overcome these differences.

The search for national unity, therefore, serves to overcome wide-

---

[16] See Clifford Geertz, on the "Integrative Revolution," *Old Societies and New States*, pp. 105-57; Lucian W. Pye and Sidney Verba, *Political Culture and Political Development* (Princeton, Princeton University Press, 1965, 574 pp.), pp. 3-26, 512-60.

[17] *Jawaharlal Nehru's Speeches: 1949-1953* (Delhi, Ministry of Information, GOI, 1954), pp. 29-30. Sékou-Touré implied the same argument when, in defending the complete authority of the party, he asked: "Without the authority of the party where would the government derive its own authority? The country would soon fall into disorder and anarchy, and rapidly lose its independence." In Sigmund (ed.), *The Ideologies of the Developing Nations*, p. 168.

[18] *Ibid.*, p. 164.

[19] Pye (ed.), *Communications and Political Development*, p. 60.

spread difficulties and to promote a number of interests shared by leaders and the polity alike. As a goal, it also has its immediate political utility to those in power.

Incumbents are likely to gain political advantage from progress toward that goal. In the name of unity, opposition can be restrained, or even quashed. To differ with the man in power can be made to seem to divide and weaken the nascent general will. To argue for greater autonomy is to reduce the power of government at the center and to promote disunity. To promote competing centers of power by voicing dissent and organizing opposition, it is argued, will threaten disruption at home and tempt intervention from abroad. The appeal to unity is a classic device of the incumbent attempting to minimize political competition and to best ensure that he will be able to remain in power.

SOCIAL TRANSFORMATION[20]

In most emerging countries, leaders often proclaim the desire to transform the society into something fundamentally new and different, far superior to what has gone before. There are many elements in this transformation. Each leader develops his unique combination. However, one can identify at least four characteristic components.

DYNAMIC SOCIETY

In the first place, the new society will be dynamic and active. By comparison, the old was passive, set in its backward ways. The new society abuilding will be bold and daring. The petty calculus of gradual change is to be disdained as essentially conservative, playing into the hands of the privileged and their foreign friends.

The style reiterates the mood of the independence struggle. It is assertive and claimant. Leaders speak as if they would collapse time and accomplish in years what others would have taken centuries to effect. Many appear to feel themselves caught up in a tidal wave carrying them forward at breathless speed. They have little choice. They are both captives of history and the agents of history. In this

[20] The term is from Manfred Halpern's *The Politics of Social Change* (Princeton, Princeton University Press, 1963, 431 pp.), Chs. 9 and 10.

sense, they are more children of European romantic radicalism than they are of the more considered and gradualist expectations of the American founding fathers.[21] This is to be expected, to some extent, since they are of the generation of nationalist agitation. Most were themselves responsible for evoking the vision of the brave new world to come. Some—though by no means all—feel that time presses them hard, as populations rise, cities swell, and opportunity lags.

This mood has appeared at different times in different countries. In India, it came immediately following independence and has gradually lost some of its momentum, except in periods of national crisis when conflict has flared with Pakistan or China. It has been characteristic of African nationalism just before and following independence. It may be fair to say that now the radical temper is less the possession of the ruling groups than it is increasingly the mood of those who have not been able to share responsibility.[22]

EQUALITY

Part of the promised transformation will be the development of an unprecedented equality. Many of the old societies are now felt to be fraught with inequity and special privilege; the new will do away with all this. Society will be reconstructed so that men shall be equal as a result of urgent efforts to equalize opportunity through the rapid expansion of economic activity and education, health, and general welfare measures. It often implies restriction if not elimination of certain hitherto economically privileged groups like the pashas in Egypt, the zemindars and princes in India, or types of foreign businessmen.

Populist ideas confirm the search for equality. Often the new men of power, particularly in Africa, are not scions of the established

[21] Hanna Arendt has an interesting discussion of this contrast in *On Revolution* (New York, Viking Press, Compass Books, 1965, 344 pp.), Ch. 1, particularly pp. 42-45.

[22] E. Shils has remarked on the need for dynamism, *Political Development in the New States, passim*, pp. 7-9; Morgenthau notes the new "faith in action," *Political Parties*, p. 238. Many other examples could be cited. Pye sees that unduly bold objectives may lead to anxieties which induce withdrawal reactions and passivity, the opposite of activity and dynamism; Pye (ed.), *Communications and Political Development*, p. 150. Some observers have noted that as objectives are set impossibly high, bureaucrats especially tend to become passive and buck responsibility for major decisions upward to their politically more secure bosses, who are closer to the leader.

families, but have come from more humble beginnings. They succeed outside the remnants of the traditional structure of power. They must find their strength through adjustment with parts of the traditional structure and by appealing directly to the more humble. Populism appeals, too, because by rejecting the privileged who, in retrospect, were associated with the West, it rejects the West and turns to the uniqueness of indigenous ways found among the simple village folk least touched by the foreigner.[23]

POLITICAL PARTICIPATION

Wider political participation is part of the expected transformation. Democracy is the stated goal of nearly every leader; and by "democracy" some measure of greater popular participation is implied. But "increased participation" may mean many things. It may simply mean attending periodic ceremonies calling out thousands to cheer in the capital. In certain parts of Africa it has come close to a self-imposed corvée of labor; this is demanded in the name of economic development and given as a sign of a new-found participation. It may represent efforts to institute local consultative bodies, largely for show, or, as in Pakistan, designed to get things done in rural areas and to develop new political links with the countryside, weakening, at least temporarily, the hold of urban-based politicians, particularly in East Pakistan. There may be direct appeal to the masses for plebiscitary approval of the leader, as in Egypt or the French-speaking African states, or a free election which is nationally dominated by one party but where regional differences generate sharp local opposition to the national party, as in India until 1967. The electorate may grow gradually or universal suffrage may be instituted abruptly.

Regardless of the form or process, however, the transformation of society implies the involvement of substantial proportions of the populace. No longer can regimes of privilege count upon public apathy; political life can no longer be the exclusive province of only the few—unless rulers make substantial efforts to discourage or divert the energies of important groups from political activity.

CHANGE IN HUMAN RELATIONSHIPS

Transformation also implies a change in the nature of human relationships to those of brotherhood, cooperation, and trust.

[23] Lipset, *The First New Nation*, p. 68; Wriggins, *Ceylon*, Ch. 6.

In most emerging countries there is an acute awareness on the part of leaders who have lived abroad that outside the small, primordial association of parochial traditional relationships distrust is the norm.[24] As leaders, they are beset by the perennial problems of faction. Prior to independence, they often felt that the intrusion of the colonial powers was to blame for this unhappy state of affairs and that after the Europeans left, there would be a new atmosphere in public life. Certain political tactics of the colonial powers no doubt did contribute some measure of mutual suspicion. The departure of the foreigners, however, has not confirmed their hopes. Indeed, in some cases, a new parochialism sharpens differences rather than allays them.

Nyerere, Nehru, and others often argued that good human relationships characterized the society before the Westerners came.[25] Now that they are gone we can become our true and good selves again. Often there is a nostalgic vision of the pure village or tribal society where differences were quietly adjusted under the aegis of universally respected elders; all worked for one another's benefit instead of his own alone. The more the real world appears fraught with faction and distrust, the more seriously one must take this notion of the idealized, reawakened, truly harmonious past society, which must now be recaptured and become universalized throughout the modern nation.

These goals of transformation are genuine enough and, if achieved, would meet certain interests of numbers of the politically active. Social transformation would serve the leader's purposes if his political need is to weaken the position of those traditionally privileged who may stand in the incumbent's way. Enthusiasm for social transformation may help release energies to reinforce the leader's influence. Present discomforts or the postponement of immediate satisfactions may become acceptable if justified in the name of a transformed future. Substantial social changes may be necessary if major policy objectives are to be achieved.

If the ruler was the beneficiary of a peaceful transfer of power, he was likely to set a moderate pace of social transformation. However, if his country experienced the disruption of protracted war of

[24] Banfield, *The Moral Basis of a Backward Society*, pp. 85-92; Carstairs, *The Twice Born*, Ch. 3.

[25] On Nyerere, see for example, "Ujamaa: The Basis of African Socialism," in Sigmund, *The Ideologies of the Developing Nations* (revised edition, 1967, 428 pp.), pp. 279-82.

independence, he pressed more radical changes. A coup d'état can accelerate or retard the pace of change, depending upon the goals and capabilities of those who take power, while rulers by inheritance will be cautious in the transformations they promote.

ECONOMIC DEVELOPMENT

A MORE PRODUCTIVE—AND EQUITABLE—ECONOMY

Nearly all political leaders in emerging countries declare their intent to promote the economic development of their countries. How can they do otherwise, when their economies are beset by so many difficulties? Their entourage and prospective opponents are increasingly aware of the way people live in developed countries at a time when their own populations are burgeoning, their unemployed are becoming more numerous, and their populace more impatient. Leaders are also more conscious of the body of economic theory and governmental practice developed abroad which holds out promise that something can now be done about their numerous economic problems.

Economic development as a goal usually implies certain more specific quasi-economic objectives closely related to the political or social goals already defined. Most leaders declare their interest in raising living standards, increasing individual income, and broadening the range of economic choice open to their people—means toward the political and social ends of a more equitable society.

As they experience growing economic cramp, some at least recognize the likely connection between shrinking economic opportunity and increasing group antagonism, thus intensifying political struggle which may make politics more explosive. If the economic pie can be made larger, and worthwhile opportunities more generally available, group antagonisms are likely to be more manageable and more widespread group cooperation may be possible. More particularly, they believe it necessary to increase the number of jobs in order to reduce chronic unemployment. Leaders are usually more concerned with unemployment in the burgeoning cities, considering this a more urgent political hazard than disguised unemployment and low productivity of the food-producing peasantry in the countryside.

Economic development may also be seen as a means of achieving greater independence. The economy must be insulated from disruptive economic forces emanating from abroad. Only if the economy is reshaped, diversified, and made more self-sustaining can the political leaders consider their country to be truly independent. More difficult to document, but perhaps as important, is the fact that many leaders in new countries experience something akin to shame that their societies are backward and their economies archaic. Only by economic development can they look the modern world in the eye, and truly believe themselves to be men of the twentieth century who are freed from ancient ways.

To achieve these only partially economic goals, a number of intermediate, more exclusively economic objectives must be pursued. The economy must be diversified by developing a substantial industrial sector. Land areas in many countries are already virtually filled and more intensive agriculture cannot productively absorb enough new hands to overcome unemployment. Only a rapidly expanding factory sector can meet employment needs. Moreover, such diversification will make it less necessary to import finished goods from abroad if new factories can process and assemble domestic and imported raw materials and components, thereby reducing the foreign exchange costs of a higher level of consumption. Agricultural output must be increased in order to improve domestic food supplies, to acquire more foreign exchange to invest in the means of economic independence, and to raise rural incomes in order to provide a national market large enough to make industrialization economic.

For those who received power from British rulers, popular political activation increased demands and made savings and investment more difficult for the inheritors. In French colonies, where political action was more restrained, this posed less serious problems. Where a war of independence took place, disruption of economic processes and relationships seriously impeded development. The remaining inherited regimes must deal with archaic and rudimentary institutions and an untrained, passive populace.

The goal of economic development has direct political utility. So long as economic development remains a general goal, it promises something for everyone. Officials will see in development an opportunity for them to play a more direct role in the economy, with larger responsibilities; the intelligentsia hope to find opportunities for their own white-collar skills and will imagine themselves as managers or supervisors. The businessmen see the promise of broadened markets for whatever they may be able to produce; they hope for government assistance in expanding their productive capacity, or foresee other economic advantages as investment programs accelerate construction or import activities. Trade unionists will expect their constituency to broaden as the industrial sector grows. The urban workers, insofar as they are politically conscious, will find new hope of betterment. Alert leaders in the countryside will see ways to enhance their own opportunities or local influence—by using the government's innovations: rural public works, new means of distributing fertilizers, tools, and seeds, or community development activities.

Economic development has the additional symbolic virtue of emphasizing that new men are now in control, men with new ideas, determined to change that which was left behind by the colonial era. Government is no longer simply to sustain law and order and develop certain limited professions like law and a civil service. But now, through economic development, the society itself is to be transformed. On a crasser level, successful economic development provides leaders with more opportunity for payoffs. Contracts can be let, salaries increased, and new enterprises established to reward loyal lieutenants or win would-be followers.

ASSOCIATION WITH SOMETHING LARGER THAN THE STATE

The leaders of new states have sought to stress national independence and unity as fundamental goals. However, they have also been concerned with the small size and weakness of their states individually and have urged the virtues of combining into larger entities. In the late 1940s and the 1950s, the goal of Asian solidarity was stressed in South and Southeast Asia. Perhaps it culminated at Bandung in 1956.[26] Since then, African leaders have been most articulate proponents of a number of experiments in seeking wider unity. In the Middle East, of course, Arab unity has been the goal of many young men since World War II, and it has become one of the most important themes in the politics of the area.[27] The more thoughtful are impressed by the impossibility of so many

[26] Wriggins, Ceylon, Ch. 11.
[27] Charles D. Cremeans, The Arabs and the World, Nasser's Arab Nationalist Policy (New York, Praeger, 1963, 330 pp.), Ch. 1.

tiny states ever achieving viability as separate entities. Many think that the world economy as presently organized is rigged against them, and that only by combination can they overcome each other's weaknesses so as to affect the world environment to their advantage. For those of this bent of mind, regional organizations, United Nations institutions, and other combinations are urgent and necessary.[28]

Certain combinations, particularly in Africa, can be understood as an effort to ensure identity and enhance the chances of independence by combining to exclude one's group from the Cold War; to demonstrate one is capable of linking up with others for mutual benefit. The Conseil d'Entente among French-speaking West African states is a case in point. In Southeast Asia, repeated efforts of the states to draw together suggest anxiety about the future role of China in the area, or the United States from without. The Association of Southeast Asian Nations is the latest and perhaps most promising example.

Thus far, it must be admitted, each of these efforts has not gone far. When there is a problem of merging elements of independent decision-making to promote greater strength, or even combining for specific purposes, the results have been limited. New leaders, like their more established counterparts elsewhere, are reluctant to concede to others primacy of place. It is almost as if there were more candidates to lead than there are regional organizations in which they can exercise that talent. The level of cooperation early achieved in East Africa declined rapidly in the face of conflicting national and individual interests. Efforts to evolve closer Asian solidarity have repeatedly foundered on contradictory national interests, competing aspirations for leadership, or a growing awareness that combining countries with parallel economic difficulties or similar social or political limitations may only compound weakness. The brief association of Egypt and Syria may not be typical of the problems, but it was a dramatic reminder of both the aspiration and the difficulties.

To pursue the goal of cooperating with friendly neighbors for specific purposes has political advantages. It heightens the domestic stature of the leader who takes the initiative. He cuts a larger figure at home as he associates with leaders of other countries.[29]

[28] See, for example, *Proceedings of the United Nations Conference on Trade and Development*, Vol. I: Final Act and Report (New York, United Nations, 1964), and Vol. VII, Trade Expansion and Regional Grouping.

[29] For more detail, see Chapter 12 below.

INCOMPATABILITY AND THE GAP BETWEEN
GOAL AND ACHIEVEMENT

These goals are not all compatible, and the preferred balance among them will shift over time. Independence and self-respect, if pressed too urgently, may slow economic development by undermining an environment conducive to acquiring external resources and by frightening away foreign skills which may be needed. National unity may be pushed so hard as to provoke the antagonism of those within the polity who treasure their own autonomy. Too rapid a transformation may undermine the power base of political associates; too much equality may bring all down to the level of the poor without permitting sufficient savings to promote self-sustaining growth. An overly rapid expansion of educational opportunity may only accelerate political defection. An undue preoccupation with economic development for its own sake may weaken present supporters, arouse sharp opposition to a government overly concerned with savings, and lead to a breakdown of a bureaucracy already overburdened.

A notable and disappointing characteristic of most emerging countries is the substantial distance between the goals officially adopted and the actual achievements. With rare exceptions, new regimes have not consolidated a sound base of their own legitimacy, and the institutional framework to confer legitimacy on successors is not yet well-established.

National independence is not the automatic answer everyone expected. Indigenous leaders now make their own policies on domestic matters; they allocate their resources in their own way instead of as the metropolitan power previously required. Constitutional arrangements, political practices, and educational and language policy are now their own affair. Yet a sense of dependence on the outside world persists. The search for indigenous solutions to complex problems is often unrewarding. Often the search for guidance still turns rulers' eyes abroad and not toward their own traditions. Economically, countries remain as dependent on the outside world as ever. Indeed, in many instances, ambitious development programs to promote economic independence in the long run have made the economy more dependent in the short run upon concessional assistance from the more dynamic economies.

National unity, in most countries, remains uncertain. Cultural diversities continue. As political participation expands, a new parochialism typically arises, sharpening ancient antagonisms. Politically relevant sectors of the society become more aware—not less—of tribal, regional, and linguistic differences. Riots and disorders from these antagonisms periodically break out. Administrative, political, economic, and other institutions transcending differences remain rudimentary. Although in most countries channels for opportunity are more open now than at any time in the past, opportunity is still, in fact, sharply restricted to those already in positions of influence, however they may have arrived there.

The quality of life has not changed much for most people. For those who generally were favored during the colonial regime, there may be a disturbing amount of unrest and disorder. A few, particularly those associated with government, now have advantages they never had before. For the most part, however, sharp inequalities persist, and men see each other rarely as collaborators in common activities unless they come from the same family, tribe or region or wear the same school tie. An awareness of a common destiny remains exceptional.

Taking all the non-communist, less developed countries of Asia and Africa together, during the period 1955-1960, their economies grew more rapidly than did those of the more developed countries. However, because of population growth rates in the former, incomes per capita grew less rapidly. During the 1960-1965 period, the economies of the developed European and North American countries grew at a somewhat more rapid pace than those of the less developed. The per capita performance of the less developed countries in Asia and Africa was comparatively even less satisfactory.[30] From

[30] Rates of Growth in Gross Domestic Product, overall and per capita: Non-Communist, Less Developed and More Developed Countries.

Rates of Growth in Per Cent Per Year

	1955-1960		1960-1965	
	Aggregate	Per Capita	Aggregate	Per Capita
Less Developed				
Africa	3.9	1.6	3.4	1.2
(except South Africa)				
Asia	4.3	1.8	4.5	1.8
(except Japan & Israel)				
More Developed				
Europe	4.5	3.6	4.8	3.7
(except Portugal & Malta)				
North America	2.2	0.4	4.7	3.1

Source: Summary tables provided by E. E. Hagen and O. Hawrylyshyn, 1968.

the ruler's point of view or from his opponent's perspective, economic development has not moved satisfactorily anywhere except perhaps in Taiwan, Thailand—taken as a whole—Turkey, and, in recent years, in Pakistan, Israel, and the Ivory Coast. Awareness of wants has been promoted by exhortations to work harder and by promises of economic development, which outpace performance everywhere.

Numerous projects have been proposed that attempt to draw emerging countries more closely together, first in Asia then in Africa. Few have gained substance beyond early enthusiasm; some begun in Africa are being dismantled. On the whole, therefore, the search for larger entities, at least in Africa and Asia, has continued to be disappointing.

Most of these goals have gained currency as communications have improved, more and more children have gained higher levels of education, and increasing numbers have been activated into politics. The extent of disappointment is a measure of the increasing pressures political leaders must deal with.

Thus, leaders give shape and currency to vaulting goals which they usually are not able to achieve, for to bring into reality the grand goals here suggested requires substantial political capability to effect the course of internal development and to cope with external relations. Political power and economic resources sufficient to achieve these goals all too often elude them. Indeed, it is concern for the equation of goals and capability, of ends and power, which underlies the predicament of leaders in new countries which this study seeks to illuminate.

Only if leaders succeed in combining the elements of social power around themselves and giving the power thus acquired a momentum in the direction of achieving these goals can they succeed in doing more than simply gaining power for its own sake.

4 Groups in Politics

Carl Schmitt, a younger German contemporary of Weber's asserted that politics is the art of identifying your friends and your enemies. There is, to be sure, no politics without struggle, and battling his opponents is an important part of any politician's task. Yet the more important and delicate assignment is that of recruiting and holding his following.

Dankwart Rustow

Confronted with his perpetual need to build winning coalitions, the professional politicians . . . seized upon the most obvious way of categorizing citizens: their ethnic differences . . . the politician devised his strategies on the assumption that whatever happened in elections could be adequately explained by shifts in ethnic blocs.

Robert Dahl

Those political leaders who succeed in remaining at the apex for some time are likely to be unusually sensitive to potential or actual sources of political power in their society. They will seek out those organizations and social groups which affect the mood and shape the action of large numbers. They will keep a particularly sharp eye out for those individuals who influence the actions of still others in key positions in the political arena. Political leaders will then attempt to enlist on their own behalf those men of subsidiary influence who bring with them the acquiescence or more active support of their followers. Out of these components of social and organizational power political leaders seek to fashion a combination which will support them. If he simply wants to stay in power, acquiescence is all the ruler needs. But if he has programs to implement, he will need the active support of those who can promote his purposes.

It is useful to look on this process of seeking winning combinations of power as building one's own coalition and attempting to weaken that of one's opponent. These are not coalitions among different political parties in the traditional sense, but coalitions combining components of organizational or social power which may lie deeper in the society than the more explicitly political parties.[1] The imagery suggests that the elements of power to be combined in support of a particular leader retain a certain autonomy. Indeed, they may have to be won over more than once. Coalition-making also suggests that there is competition between one coalition and another.

Leaders will be pulled by opposing considerations. To be on the safe side, most leaders seek larger coalitions than may be strictly necessary for winning power or staying at the summit of affairs. Unnecessarily large coalitions, however, have the disadvantage of diffusing political purpose, confusing political action if strict discipline or adroit maneuvering is necessary, and diluting the rewards available to those who organize political victory.[2]

The kinds of allies a leader seeks to include in his coalition will have an important bearing on his political strategy and set limits to his political action in other ways. Each group will require a somewhat different approach if it is to be won. Some will be mutually incompatible and cannot be combined unless their mutually antagonistic or contradictory aspirations are obscured by ambiguous promises or programs.

This chapter will consider a number of the more typical identifiable components of power or political groups which leaders attempt to build into a coalition or seek to win away from an opponent. The discussion will imply a cohesiveness and consistency of group behavior not to be found in real life. No two countries have the same group structure or political cast of characters. Each group identified will have within it significant subgroups. Influential men within them contend for leadership. Followers may consistently follow one man or a number of contenders; they may be fickle, veering from one to another. Moreover, some groups may have a crucial role in politics for many years, others may be periodically

---

[1] Parties are discussed in the next chapter. Riker has developed this view of politics at some length and substantial sophistication in his *Theory of Political Coalitions*; Dahl uses the notion in describing New Haven politics in *Who Governs?*; Zolberg uses similar concepts in discussing Ivory Coast politics, *One-Party Government in the Ivory Coast*, pp. 73, 113.

[2] Riker, pp. 33, 48, 88-89.

important, while still others may have a brief but decisive moment of effulgence before relapsing into quietude.

The general direction and phase of socioeconomic development will also affect group activity. Some groups simply do not emerge because the necessary economic or social preconditions are not yet present. Or, as they do develop, there is no guarantee that evolving groups will necessarily be politically relevant. They remain political potentials until they are stimulated to activity by dynamic leaders who may rise within them or come to them from the political arena seeking their support as additional allies in the political struggle. This approach will not give sufficient stress to the institutional framework within which political life may be channeled. The formal institutions defined by a constitution, the informal rules of the game, and the legal or customary metes and bounds of the political process may be relatively well-established in some countries. The following discussion, therefore, must be in rather general terms when in reality these matters can be fully understood for purposes of political action only in the light of the specific country situation.

Despite limitations in looking at the process of aggregating power through building coalitions out of the components of power in the society, there is probably no closer approximation to the way a successful political activist seeks to understand and deal with the essentials of his situation. The following discussion of specific, reasonably identifiable social or organizational groups provides necessary background for the discussion in Chapters 5 through 12 of the principal strategies leaders use in their attempts to build coalitions of support.

THE BUREAUCRACY

The bureaucracy is by far the most important single institution through which governments get things done. To the prime minister or president, winning its support is therefore crucial.[3] There is a great range and variety of bureaucracies. Some are oriented mainly toward political "neutrality" and are ready to accomplish whatever ends are sought by the ruler—according to Max Weber's

[3] Neustadt's book is a classic evocation of the task the President of the United States has in effecting executive authority over the bureaucracy. Neustadt, *Presidential Power.*

model and the ideals the British sought to establish in India, Ceylon, or Ghana. Others, such as Hanna reports in Indonesia, or Siffin in the Thai tradition, became organizations mainly providing welfare and other benefits to its employees, rather than services to the public at large.[4] Some may be deeply engaged in a broad range of functions, like Pakistan's or Malaysia's developmental bureaucracies. In states which have only begun to move away from traditional ways, such as in Nepal or Ethiopia, the bureaucracy will be largely the personal emanation of the ruler, very different from the complex bureaucracies of India or Egypt with heavy developmental responsibilities. There are, therefore, bureaucracies and bureaucracies. Nevertheless, certain general observations can be helpful regarding, first, the many political functions of bureaucracies and, second, the problems bureaucracies pose to rulers.[5]

The bureaucracy is the ruler's chief arm for affecting the society around him. It may be the one reliable institution capable of sustaining consistency of action during periods of great turmoil, such as Pakistan experienced during its traumatic birth and early years.[6] It usually contributes to national unity by affecting the many parts of the realm in much the same fashion. It helps maintain order and the personal safety of individuals in the populace. The full measure of social and economic transformation the leadership seeks cannot be achieved without an active bureaucracy. It is necessary if diplomatic relations are to be maintained with other countries; it also links the polity with regional or other larger groupings. In addition, many services are provided to the people such as a modicum of public order, education, health, famine relief, etc.

The leader also needs the bureaucracy to help him stay in power. Through it he garners taxes to provide the sinews of governmental activity. Without the upward flow of information in the service ministries and the intelligence and internal information sectors of

[4] Willard Hanna, "Nationalist Revolution and Revolutionary Nationalism," in Kalman Silvert (ed.), Expectant Peoples, Nationalism and Development (New York, Random House, 1963, 489 pp.), p. 163; William J. Siffin, The Thai Bureaucracy: Institutional Change and Development (Honolulu, East-West Center Press, 1966, 291 pp.), Chs. 4 and 5.

[5] For a parallel discussion see Almond and Powell, Comparative Politics, pp. 154-58.

[6] Braibanti argues this in regard to Pakistan in "Public Bureaucracy and Judiciary in Pakistan," La Palombara (ed.), Bureaucracy and Political Development, p. 374.

the bureaucracy associated with the police, rulers will be ill-informed regarding the mood of the people, their wants, and the likely sources of unrest. Good and improving government services will help to win and hold political support for the regime. In its contacts with specific organizations or groups, by its performance it may in part satisfy their demands, by its intimidation it may dampen them; however, by its disdain or harshness it may provoke them.

The bureaucracy may also play a more directly political role. The leading sectors of the bureaucracy often have well-established ideas of what can or should be done. Its staffs are the ones who define public purposes in more specific terms, particularly where economic development policy is concerned. The bureaucracy itself may become an object of acute political contention among competing interest groups. It may be one of the main channels of political struggle through which different interests are aggregated and regulated.[7] In Thailand, "politics has become a matter of competition between bureaucratic cliques for the benefits of government."[8] Jobs and promotions within the bureaucracy are a major avenue for social and economic advancement. Before taking to politics numerous political leaders have gained their experience and part of their early following while serving in the bureaucracy. By their complaisance or restrictions, civilian officials, in association with the police and the military, will influence the kinds of political contention that are acceptable and the risks men must run if they are to engage in political activity.

Because the bureaucracy performs so many critical functions in the polity, the ruler must have a close working relationship with it. As Morstein Marx put it in writing of the higher civil service: ". . . it makes a great difference whether the higher civil service happens to identify itself emotionally with a particular political leadership, whether it firmly sits on its hands when displeased, or whether it can be trusted to perform its tasks loyally and without reservations in support of the lawful government, independent of party label."[9]

---

[7] Feith, The Decline of Constitutional Democracy in Indonesia, p. 103; Wriggins, Ceylon, Ch. 7; Shmuel N. Eisenstadt, "Bureaucracy and Political Development," in La Palombara (ed.), Bureaucracy and Political Development, p. 112.

[8] Wilson, Politics in Thailand p. 277.

[9] Fritz Morstein Marx, "The Higher Civil Service as an Action Group in Western Political Development," in La Palombara (ed.), Bureaucracy and Political Development, p. 66.

The ruler is likely to find that the bureaucracy is not only difficult to master, it is even difficult to induce to active cooperation. Bureaucracies in most emerging countries are lethargic, and heavy responsibilities converge on the few at the top. This concentration of authority is compounded by traditional views of authority; it gives pride of place to the elders with long experience and ignores the younger men with new ideas. They feel their newly trained talents are being wasted or ignored, which generates discouragement at the lower levels. The administrative framework may slow the process of transformation. Over-control, mutually contradictory activities, and a tendency to repress initiative elsewhere in the society may impede the process of transformation and work against the ends the ruler seeks.[10]

The ruler and the officials use different styles in approaching their respective tasks. Impatient political leaders, newly come to prominence, have depended on the skills of oratory, political organization, and agitation. They have been active in both the more traditional society and in the more modern world. They must make their mark in a short time. The old-line officials, on the other hand, are used to a kind of security the politicians never knew. They are masters of the regulations. From hard experience they know the difficulties of translating bright or popular ideas into institutional innovation. Their training and their mood lead to caution and an effort to balance available—and limited—resources against innumerable demands sometimes made virtually unlimited by political agitation. Rapid reassignment or forced retirement may spur the bureaucracy to greater celerity, but scarce talent may be prematurely lost, and anxious bureaucrats can skillfully pass the buck, further clogging the decision process.

In the main, the leader will have to recognize his dependence upon those who may lack zeal yet have considerable competence at managing complicated bureaucratic affairs. To hold the bureaucracy it may be necessary, in some cases, for a ruler to trim his own political goals closer to those the established senior bureaucrats believe are feasible. It even may be difficult in any one instance to determine whether the bureaucracy controls the ruler in essentials or the other way about. In any event, the conventional model of the powerful sovereign with a politically neutral bureaucracy auto-

[10] Riggs in La Palombara (ed.), *Bureaucracy and Political Development*, p. 141.

matically at his command rarely represents the real world in Africa and Asia.[11]

Although the bureaucracy is a necessary ally for any ruler, too close an association with it may cause him difficulties. Among the articulate and the politically sensitive, the public service has had the reputation of being a stooge of the colonial regime. The life style and value system of many of the most experienced senior civil servants often appears to confirm this charge, since they were the ones who most fully assimilated metropolitan ways. They tend to be inaccessible, while the politically popular must be accessible. They prefer to decide "without fear or favor," while the politically sensitive often have to decide on just such grounds. Within the bureaucracy are a number of networks for mutual aid dependent upon family, tribal, or caste relationships, or schoolboy friendships rather than performance. Those who are not part of these networks resent the fact and find the bureaucracy corrupt and riddled with favoritism. Seen as a centralizing instrument, usually working against local autonomy, the central bureaucracy often continues to be looked upon as an enemy of regional interests.[12]

For these and other reasons, therefore, the bureaucracy is often subject to sharp political criticism. Too close association with it or obvious dependence upon it on the part of a leader often involves political risks where popular sentiment can be aroused against it.

To the tyrannical or deceptive ruler, the bureaucracy poses more serious risks. The senior levels of the bureaucracy are often privy to what the ruler is about; they are necessarily exempt from the ruler's propaganda. They have a need to know what the real situation is, and they, perhaps, are the only ones to be able to distinguish myth from reality if the regime is one which seeks to delude its people over a long period of time. Unless especial care is taken, those in the know may use their superior knowledge to upset the ruler.[13]

---

[11] Riggs has written on this problem in "The Heavy Weight of Bureaucratic Power," in his Administration in Developing Countries, The Theory of Prismatic Society, p. 222. See also his essay "Bureaucrats and Political Development," in La Palombara (ed.), Bureaucracy and Political Development, pp. 120-68.

[12] Maurice Zinken, Development for Free Asia (Fairlawn, N.J., Essential Books, 1956, 263 pp.), Ch. 10; Feith, The Decline of Constitutional Democracy in Indonesia, p. 567.

[13] Donald J. Goodspeed, The Conspirators: A Study of the Coup d'Etat (New York, Viking Press, 1961, 252 pp.), p. 214.

The bureaucracy, therefore, is a major source of political power, both to win support and to get things done. Ensuring its support is necessary but it is not always easy.

THE MILITARY

To the ruler the military are a necessary asset. But they also pose serious risks to his control. Indeed, in 1968, seventeen of 57 states in Africa and non-communist Asia were under direct military control or were ruled by officers who had come to power by coups d'état and were attempting to civilianize their government in some measure. In many more, civilians ruled only so long as they retained the favor of the military. The men with the guns have a certain obvious advantage. No one can intimidate as well as they.[14] A regime can survive for a time when the civilian bureaucracy opposes it if rulers resort to intensive intimidation. But no regime can survive if the military does not at least acquiesce in its rule.

If the ruler has traveled, he will have noted that no two armies play the same political role. Some as in India stand aloof, their officers schooled in a tradition of nonpolitical military service. If the army evolved from protracted guerrilla war on behalf of independence, as in Indonesia and Algeria, it will want to play a larger political role and will present a worrisome problem to civilian leadership. An army based on a tradition of colonial forces will be manned largely by those regional, tribal, or other minorities who specialized in military careers during the colonial regime. To the extent that that tradition survives, the leader is likely to be able to count on their

[14] As Manfred Halpern put it, in referring to the Middle East: "Soldiers have governed a majority of Middle Eastern countries almost continuously for at least a millennium. It is hardly surprising, therefore, that in 1961 the army ruled five of the seventeen countries between Morocco and Pakistan (namely Egypt, Turkey, Sudan, Iraq and Pakistan) and constituted the principal organizational support for the government of eight others (Iran, Jordan, Lebanon, Saudi Arabia, Yemen, Syria, Afghanistan and Algeria). Since 1930, military coups have overturned governments on at least twenty-three occasions in this area, and many other times pressures from the army or an army faction proved decisive in altering the composition of government and the direction of policies." "Middle Eastern Armies and the New Middle Class," in John J. Johnson (ed.), *The Role of the Military in Underdeveloped Countries* (Princeton, Princeton University Press, 1962, 427 pp.), p. 277.

loyalty, unless he himself is from a tribe or community looked down on by the groups these troops are drawn from.[15]

Armies differ, too, in their stratification and the political tensions these inner contrasts induce. Sharp differences between the privileged senior officers of traditional standing and those of lesser origin intensify antagonisms and make coups d'état easier, as in Nuri's Iraq and Farouk's Egypt. Such inner tensions may be less severe where social change and modernization have hardly begun or, as in the more developed countries, where channels to senior positions for the trained and able are not blocked by inheritance or social status. Where the ruler sees that there are few other channels for the energetic and ambitious apart from the army, he can expect to find there the greatest single source of ambition and energy—and possibly political danger.[16] He will also note that armies may be split by factions and made up of a bundle of competing cliques, sometimes closely paralleling the divisions in the wider society. Even senior officers may direct their loyalty more to regional commanders than to the national government, as has periodically occurred most noticeably in Indonesia.

Despite such variations, armies tend to represent certain assets to political leaders. Armies in new countries are usually the most sensitive to technical and organizational developments abroad.[17] They have the most efficient nationwide communication system and mobility. They seek to integrate their activities within a hierarchical system which leaves minimum scope for individual initiative and maximizes the reliability of command relationships. In contrast to their sister agencies, they are often models of energy and drive.

[15] Minorities may be given preference following a coup d'état, as in Syria, as more loyal to the new ruler than the generality of the army; see Torrey, *Syrian Politics*, p. 44; Indonesia has been beset by regionally based commanders. Feith in George Kahin (ed.), *Government and Politics of Southeast Asia* (Ithaca, Cornell University Press, 1964, 796 pp.), pp. 241, 247. The military-led secession of the Republic of Biafra from Nigeria in 1967 was provoked by the Ibo conviction that the Northern-dominated central government would not protect Ibos but even connived in the massacre of Ibos in the north. Audrey Chapman, "The Civil War in Nigeria," *Midstream* (January, 1968), pp. 12-25.

[16] Torrey compares the armies of Iraq and Syria as definers and promoters of social grievances; see *Syrian Politics*, pp. 44-45. See also Pye in Johnson (ed.), *The Role of the Military in Underdeveloped Countries*, pp. 83-84. See Coleman in Johnson, *Ibid.*, p. 40; and Tom Little, *Egypt* (London, E. Benn, 1958, 334 pp.), pp. 177-78, 206-24.

[17] Pye in Johnson, p. 77.

Clark Kerr et al. have characterized "the generals" in this way:

The generals influence society not through the ultimate power of the armed forces. In some societies, aside from the power at their command, they are, and are recognized to be, the best trained and most patriotic elements in the society and may also be closest to the aspirations of the mass of the people, particularly when the army is one of the few channels for upward social mobility. They often have a reputation for being less corrupt than other elements, for being more dynamic in getting things done, for being able to make decisions, for having trained staff available . . . In fact, in some societies, the definition of the ruling element is the element with the support of the armed forces.[18]

In most of Asia and Africa regional loyalties within countries remain strong, and an army can discourage frivolous secession. Political agitation is often extreme; demagogy, inflaming emotions which are believed to be just below the surface, is always tempting.[19] A military arm can discourage the irresponsible. Awareness of the growing gap between promise and fulfillment is likely to lead regimes to desire a stand-by capability to quell possible outbursts of public frustration. The symbols of independent statehood are inextricably identified with marching men and with military equipment owned and operated by the new state.

Leaders who depend on the command structure of the army for essentially political or administrative functions will usually have certain tasks simplified. The administration can change direction promptly at the ruler's command; it can remain for a time relatively aloof from the components of political power that another leader, with a different approach, would have to come to terms with. There are also cases where individual leaders fear for their lives and come to believe the men in military uniform will make the margin of difference that spells personal survival.[20]

It was natural that India and Pakistan, with military establishments deriving from a grand historic tradition and faced with major hostilities against each other in their early years, should each devote substantial resources to defense. In Asia, more generally, nearly all of the new states have had ancient rivalries with neighbors, and they

[18] Clark Kerr, et al., *Industrialism and Industrial Man*, p. 73.

[19] Edward Shils, "Demagogues and Cadres in the Political Development of the New States," in La Palombara (ed.), *Bureaucracy and Political Development*, Ch. 4.

[20] Morgenthau, *Political Parties*, p. 356.

have acted as if their own territorial integrity depended upon the ability of their forces to deal with these neighbors. The Cold War added a sense of threat from outside the Asian rimland. In Africa, by contrast, the leaders seemed to have more options, since the area was notably free of military or even police forces. However, leaders there, too, chose to build their military establishments.[21] Some seek arms to defend against or challenge the remaining areas of white supremacy or to induce a wider African unity. Some fear their more ambitious African neighbors. The calls by the impeccably anti-colonial leaders in Tanganyika, Uganda, and Kenya to the British for help in restoring order in 1964 no doubt impressed those who had hoped to depend upon police alone, as it must have underlined for others the risks of mutiny by even small local forces.

Armies serve useful purposes. But they also have liabilities. Traditionally, armies have been exploitative, living off the land, taking at gun point the peasant's animals and enjoying his women. In many countries, armies absorb a substantial share of total national resources.[22] Janôwitz has calculated that in twelve South and Southeast Asian countries, an average of 29 per cent of the public budget was spent on the defense establishment; in seventeen African countries, the average was 25 per cent. The populace—or the more alert civilians—may perceive this as officers living in comfort while they, themselves, toil in misery. In many societies, however, this still appears to be the right and customary state of affairs.

Leaders who use the military for quasi-political functions will indefinitely postpone the development of open political instrumentalities for translating demands into manageable political energies, and may tempt the military to play a more direct political role. More important, armies often represent a direct threat to civilian rulers. In the main, the generals look down on the politicians, considering them quarrelsome and undignified. Few military men appreciate the politician's role as aggregator of demands, broker and mediator between conflicting interests.[23] By comparison with other agencies of govern-

[21] Coleman in Johnson (ed.), The Role of the Military, p. 359.

[22] Morris Janowitz, The Military and the Political Development of New Nations (Chicago, University of Chicago Press, 1964, 134 pp.), pp. 20-21.

[23] For a discussion of several of these points, see M. Janowitz, "The Military in the Political Development of New Nations," The Bulletin of Atomic Scientists, vol. xx (October, 1964), 6-10. See also Taylor, The Philippines, p. 193. Pye in Johnson (ed.), The Role of the Military, pp. 79-80.

ment, the army can usually move with considerable coherence and decision.[24] Officers tend to have the self-confidence that men of politics no longer feel. Where civilian politicians have not been up to their tasks, the military may be the major agency of power, even if it can only prevent actions or intimidate into acquiescence.[25] Considering the multiple weakness in most emerging societies, it is perhaps remarkable that there have not been more military coups d'état.

Most civilian political leaders in new states, therefore, are understandably ambivalent in their feelings toward their armies. They need them for many functions; they fear they may be overthrown by them. Winning their backing is a central concern of any leader.

TRADITIONAL ATTACHMENTS

The bureaucracy and the army are essential allies if government is to function and the regime be capable of protecting itself against its internal and external enemies. Viable government however requires a broader coalition base. Regimes depending exclusively on them are not likely to reflect the underlying social power. They may survive by ignoring the structure of society, but coercive efforts are likely to be costly, and traditional or more modern governmental functions will be impeded.

The fundamental components of the social structure in most countries are the inherited groups—roughly defined in terms of family, clan, or tribe and regional, linguistic, or religious affiliations. Here are the deepest loyalties, the ties which bind men in solidarity to one another.[26] In politicians' terms, these are the elements of electoral arithmetic which make elections sure things. Without elections, it still may be indispensable to gain the support of particular traditional

[24] Wilson, *Politics in Thailand* p. 183; Halpern in Johnson (ed.), pp. 288-89, 300.

[25] Dankwart Rustow, "The Military in Middle Eastern Society and Politics," in Sydney N. Fisher (ed.), *The Military in the Middle East: Problems in Society and Government* (Columbus, Ohio State University Press, 1963, 138 pp.), pp. 3-20; Majid Khadduri, "The Army Officer: His Role in Middle Eastern Politics," in Sydney N. Fisher, *Social Forces in the Middle East* (Ithaca, Cornell University Press, 1955, 282 pp.), p. 170; Andrew C. Janos, "The Seizure of Power: A Study of Force and Popular Consent" (Princeton, Research Monograph No. 16, February, 1964), pp. 62-63.

[26] Geertz uses the term "primordial" for such groupings after Shils. See Geertz (ed.), *Old Societies and New States* pp. 105-57.

groups if public authority is not to be flouted, if separatism is to be nipped in the bud, and if critical areas of key cities or indispensable groups are to be won for a regime or levered away from an opponent.

These groupings may derive from *assumed blood ties,* such as an extended family, tribe, caste, or "community." African politics cannot be understood without a tribal calculus, in some ways similar to the ethnic calculus of American urban politics of the nineteenth century.[27] The Kashgai in Iran, Kurds in Iraq, Pathans in Pakistan, and Kachins and Shans in Burma, all pose, in different degrees, special difficulties. In India or Ceylon, few politicians run for office without carefully considering the caste structure of the constituency; political promotors will be sure that their man is of the right group before they will support him.

Each of these groups or peoples has to be dealt with, in a sense, as a distinct people. Many have developed tribal or community organizations to promote their interests.[28] Most come from an area where they form a majority. They have some highly educated spokesmen, whose local positions depend in substantial measure upon their ability to represent the interest of these peoples as they perceive them. They seek to defend autonomy or to continue arrangements long agreed on or to obtain for their people additional advantages, such as schooling or new economic enterprises. If a ruler is seen as one of them, their support is often forthcoming simply because there is satisfaction in knowing that "our boy" has made good.

To win the support of the leaders of such groups is to win the whole following, as in the patron parties of West Africa, or in the political maneuvering centering on winning the backing of the more traditional communities in South Asia.[29] To penetrate and capture

---

[27] See Zolberg on this as it applies to the Ivory Coast, *One-Party Government in the Ivory Coast,* p. 74; Sklar on Nigeria, *Nigerian Political Parties,* p. 136. Even the impatient modernizer, Sékou Touré, had to defer to the underlying tribal structure of Guinea, going so far as to represent himself as the son of a woman belonging to the largest tribe—"Guinea after Five Years," *African Report* (June, 1964), p. 4. Also Morgenthau, *Political Parties in French-speaking West Africa,* p. 249. Dahl has seen this type of calculation in twentieth-century New Haven, *Who Governs?,* pp. 53-54.

[28] See Sklar, *Nigerian Political Parties,* p. 460; Myron Weiner in *The Politics of Scarcity* has an extensive discussion of the growth of such "community organizations" representing the caste groups in India, Ch. 3.

[29] See Morgenthau, *Political Parties,* p. 337; Weiner, Ch. 3; and Wriggins, *Ceylon,* pp. 25-26.

tribal or communal organizations may make it possible to turn the whole group to one's account.

There are liabilities, however, in allying with tribal or communal leaders. If the price of winning their support is to meet their full demands, parochial attachments will be confirmed and national integration delayed.[30] The successive efforts of the Iraqi government to win or subdue the Kurds, of New Delhi to deal with the Nagas, or of Rangoon to attract or repress the Shan rulers are examples of this intractable problem. The dilemma is nicely pointed up in the following discussion of Nigeria:

> On the one hand, the tribal unions are the most characteristically Nigerian political institution of the modern Nigerian State; yet their existence is in fundamental contradiction to Statehood. Their work is more effective than that of the local organs of constitutional government, and it is work of high importance; yet the longer it continues to be done tribally the more Nigerian nationhood is retarded. In the long run it would benefit the country if community development and education were channeled through local government and not through extra-constitutional organs based on kinship and lineage; in the short run their achievements are too valuable to be lightly cast aside. In any case the question of casting them aside hardly arises, since a state with pretensions to democracy cannot suppress or control spontaneous and useful work by voluntary organizations, even if it only benefits kinsmen or co-tribalists.[31]

Many of these traditional tribal or communal groups have been mutually antagonistic for generations. To build on one group may automatically drive its opponent to join one's enemy.[32] Kautilya's apothegm concerning "my enemy's enemy is my friend" works in reverse, as the enemy of my friend becomes my enemy.

Linguistic groups may also be politically important. These appear to be particularly sharply defined in South Asia, where many leaders have sought to build their coalitions by activating people on the issue of which language shall be given official status. Official status

---

[30] On the way differences are strengthened when ethnic differentiations are used for political purposes, see Dahl, *Who Governs?* pp. 53-54.

[31] Ronald Wraith and Edgar Simpkins, *Corruption in Developing Countries* (New York, W. W. Norton and Company, 1964, 211 pp.), p. 51.

[32] Austin reports from Ghana that had the National Liberation Movement limited its political arguments to the single issue of cocoa prices, Ashanti, Colony, and Brong farmers would have joined forces. When, however, it appeared to become a movement based primarily on Ashanti interests, the other groups fell away. Austin, *Politics in Ghana,* pp. 344-45.

for one language has cultural, historical, and bread-and-butter implications, as well as reflecting a concern for the relative status of one people in relation to another. It affects school systems, government administration and a people's sense of distinctiveness from foreigners or from rival ethnic groups. Policies regarding official language may fundamentally affect a group's chances of sending its sons to the civil service.

To seek out linguistic groups and become their champion can quickly crystallize a following where before there were jealous castes and communities. In this sense, it can be a unifier of a hitherto fragmented traditional society and bring self-awareness and a sense of wider identity and self-respect which was not there before. However, because of the numerous languages typically encompassed within any one state's territory, such a move is likely to exacerbate group rivalries and make national unity more difficult. Language agitation tends to strengthen the hand of the traditionalists in a society—the keepers of the ancient word. It risks insulating the country from external ideas and from innovations.[33]

Religious identifications, too, may be politically relevant. Men and women may be moved by an appeal to their religious attachments when they would otherwise be highly individualistic and lacking in alternative modes of identifying with others. Confessional politics is critical to an understanding of Lebanon; it has played a substantial role in Burma and Ceylon.[34] In India, it was the proximate cause of the partition of the subcontinent, and it complicated South Vietnam's effort to find political identity. Religious issues have also posed major constitutional problems in certain Arab countries.

The political leader who seeks to use religious appeals usually has to reckon with several related problems. In matters sacred, most religions are led by specialists who are intermediaries between man and the deity, interpreters of texts and leaders of specific congregations. Religious agitation may enlist a following, but it may also activate the religious specialists. Indeed, it is usual for religious followers to be mobilized for political purposes through the religious

[33] For discussion, see McKim Marriott, "Cultural Policy in New States," in Geertz (ed.), *Old Societies and New States*, pp. 27-57. Harrison, *India*, Ch. 4; Wriggins, *Ceylon*, Ch. 7.

[34] Geertz, *Old Societies and New States*, p. 143; and Herbert L. Bodman, "Confessionalism and Feudality in Lebanese Politics," *Middle East Journal*, vol. 8, No. 1 (Winter, 1954), 10-26.

specialists. Some of the latter may share a leader's vision of a changing, more modern society and help individuals to make the transition by reinterpreting classical propositions in new ways, as did Iqbal in prepartition India. Others, however, may be inflexible obscurantists, or they may be seeking to return to a pure tradition now out of reach.

Politicians who evoke religious enthusiasm have not always been able to calm it down when the politically propitious time has come. Mr. Bandaranaike could not moderate the more extreme manifestations of Buddhist excitement in Ceylon, and in the end was assassinated by a monk. Jinnah and Liaquat Ali-Kahn found the Ulama intractable and the latter was assassinated by a Muslim. Gandhi, who had preached a return to Hindu virtues, as well as religious moderation, was assassinated by a Hindu enthusiast.[35]

Less easily perceived, yet perhaps even more decisive among political activists who must be dealt with, are cliques. In most emerging countries, leading individuals have around them men who follow a personal leader because of family connections, common regional origins, the shared experience of political daring, some deep and immediate personal relationship, or a past sense of indebtedness. Younger men will often seek to attach themselves to a powerful patron and become staunch lieutenants in return for assistance from the powerful. Only if one understands the intricacies of family connections, or the history of such personal relationships, can one rightly guess how men are likely to act in political crises. This phenomenon has been clearly analyzed in Southeast Asia, but it is to be found in South Asia and Africa as well.[36] Indeed, in many instances, careful examination will reveal that, in their early stages of development, political parties are little more than aggregations of personal followings brought together temporarily for a specific political purpose, such as claiming independence or winning an election. The larger a man's following, the stronger is his bargaining position within a political coalition. Hence, a good deal of time, effort, and substantial

[35] See Donald E. Smith, *India as a Secular State* (Princeton, Princeton University Press, 1963, 518 pp.) pp. 473-74; Hugh Tinker, *India and Pakistan* (New York, Praeger, 1962, 228 pp.), p. 76; Wriggins, *Ceylon*, Ch. 6; Keith Callard, *Pakistan, A Political Study* (New York, Macmillan, 1957, 355 pp.), pp. 202-07.

[36] See, for example, Wilson, *Politics in Thailand*, pp. 116, 232, 246-47; Feith, *Indonesia, The Decline of Constitutional Democracy*, pp. 107-08, 115; Taylor, *The Philippines and the United States*, pp. 157-58.

political assets go to sustaining the loyalty and support of a host of personal followings. The matter is acute in Thailand, but it can also be seen in party politics in Nigeria, the Ivory Coast, and Malaysia and in state politics in India.

Where basic political units are essentially cliques, political relations tend to be unstable, for the relationships among subsidiary leaders tend to fluctuate between coalition and hostility as their leaders' relationships alter with the changeable climate of personal likes and dislikes or calculations of the main chance. Each change in personal relationships is exaggerated by the extra weight of each man's following.

Few institutional signposts indicate this phenomenon. Much of it is inconspicuous. Most of it can be perceived only by understanding the network of personal relationships which link the politically active to one another. But no political leader has been successful who is not adroit at playing upon these cliques and, by all the political arts, ensuring they remain loyal to him while he seeks to undermine the loyalty of those linked to his opponents.

LANDOWNERS

In a number of countries, landowners remain a political force to be reckoned with. They may continue to perform traditional local functions historically associated with land ownership, while inherited social status makes them still highly respected and influential in their locality. Their tenants and laborers may feel obliged to act politically the way the landlord urges them. Although their interests may be narrow, landowners are often useful intermediaries between urban-based politicians and the peasantry. Any party in power will attempt to come to some working terms with them, unless it is determined to eliminate them. If it does do that, it will have to develop a substitute framework of authority for sustaining order in the countryside and for performing many of the economic, ritual, and other functions the landed may still perform. As a group they command substantial economic resources useful for building an electoral machine or a political party. If they produce for export, it is quite possible that their economic activities are among the most efficient of any producers in the economy and contribute heavily to foreign exchange earnings.

On the other hand, large landowning families tend to spend heavily on status consumption, and they have less for economic—or political —investment than their spacious style of life would suggest.[37] Where traditional status values have eroded, large landholders are losing their traditional legitimacy. Their preference for living in cities or towns, and for working their lands through paid overseers, adversely affects productivity for the home market and deprives them of the alternative legitimacy of high performance.

They can therefore be a political liability to a leader needing popular backing. Since they are likely to resist those tenure, rent, and other reforms necessary to improve cultivator incentives and to assuage public resentment against them, landowners can be politically costly as a conspicuous part of a coalition.[38] In Africa, by and large, huge landowners never existed. Elsewhere, as in the Middle East and India, the dramatically large landowners have been virtually eliminated by substantial reforms; but in many countries large and medium sized owners still exist and remain locally influential.[39]

Even when elected village or district councils are established, in an effort to give the lesser people greater representation, prominent local families of traditional standing often continue to be central figures in local politics.[40] Not infrequently, therefore, political leaders will criticize landlords in public and press legislation to require reforms of land tenure, establish rent ceilings, and set limits to the land area any one owner may possess. At the same time, they will nurture tacit and generally inconspicuous arrangements with individual landowners who may assure order in their area, provide essential—if sometimes costly—economic services, or supply funds necessary for a leader to hold his lieutenants. If elections are necessary, in some instances landowners may still deliver the rural vote or bring the leaders other forms of political support in the rural districts.

[37] William Arthur Lewis, The Theory of Economic Growth (Homewood, Illinois, R. D. Irwin, 1955, 433 pp.), p. 277.

[38] Halpern, The Politics of Social Change, pp. 81-87.

[39] For a detailed discussion, see Doreen Warriner, Land Reform and Development in the Middle East, 2nd edition (London, Oxford University Press, 1962, 238 pp.).

[40] Walter C. Neale, Economic Change in Rural India: Land Tenure and Reform in Uttar Pradesh, 1800-1955 (New Haven, Yale University Press, 1962, 333 pp.), p. 256.

EMERGING GROUPS AND ASSOCIATIONS

These identifiable groups are largely in the inherited social structure of a country. Students, intellectuals, businessmen, trade unionists, and press and radio people derive from changes taking place in the society. They are likely to become more important in political life in the future.[41]

STUDENTS AND UNEMPLOYED INTELLECTUALS

In most countries of Asia and Africa, students play a more important role than they traditionally have in the United States. The great Chinese and Indian civilizations confer considerable status on the scholar. Students were among the first to embrace the new ideas of nationalism and independence, and during the national struggle they developed a tradition of involvement in political agitation.

Higher education was then the passport to prominence and status. Compounded with the scholastic tradition of the pre-colonial society, colonial education often encouraged a sense of superiority, alienating scholars in important ways from their local culture and from many jobs considered beneath the dignity of the man with education. Higher education tended to stress verbal virtuosity, and did little to encourage working with others on behalf of matter-of-fact, common tasks.[42]

In the main, curricula have changed little since independence, but the numbers of students have risen sharply. Graduates of the more selective science and medical faculties have usually found opportunities for rewarding work commensurate with their talents. The rapidly expanding liberal arts institutions have not provided an assured future for those students who do not succeed in entering the civil serv-

[41] For the social scientists, they are less ascriptive, more the result of individual achievement; they tend to be more specialized, more in the nature of associational interest groups. But as Fred Riggs points out, such distinctions have serious limitations in societies which are transitional, and most of these groups themselves combine characteristics of traditional and modern institutions. The purpose here is not to draw such distinctions but to consider those aspects of these groups which affect their role in politics. See Riggs, *Administration in Developing Countries*, Ch. 5.

[42] Edward Shils, "The Intellectuals in the Political Development of the New States," *World Politics*, Vol. XII, No. 3 (April, 1960), 329-68.

ice. Their training not only has not prepared them for genuine opportunities, but has also brought them a sharper awareness of the outside
world.[43] They perceive the contrast between the reality abroad and
their country's present circumstances. The educated feel acutely the
anguish of the man pulled in both directions—yearning toward closer
identification with their own tradition while rejecting that culture
because his own values have changed. The intellectual's standards
have become more alien, yet he himself is a nationalist. He doubts
his own identity as he seeks to define the identity of his country.[44]

They are by nature oppositionists.[45] Typically they are irresponsible; they are students of traditional, often religious education, and
they are looking back to an ideal rendered obsolete by social and
political change; frequently they are the products of modern, West-
ernizing schools, and they have "no continuing commitment to any
single institution or philosophical outlook, and they are not fully
answerable for the consequences."[46] They are volatile and capable
of rapid shifts of interests, emphasis, and loyalty. In general, they
see official authority as an enemy, as a protector of the privileged.[47]
Students are usually impatient with reformist notions. They look
down on the man of politics whose life is caught in contemporary
contradictions, and who must deal with an all too contingent and
intractable real world.[48] Yet they can also be won to enthusiastic
political followership if their particular leader can promise a great
vision, or activities which provide excitement and a sense of
identity.[49]

The students, moreover, are the source of the coming generation

[43] Until recently, at least, Thailand has been an exception, where university
admissions have been consciously related to available opportunities. Wilson,
Politics in Thailand, pp. 62-63.

[44] Seymour M. Lipset, "The Political Behaviour of University Students in
Developing Nations," unpublished paper prepared for presentation at UNESCO
Conference on Students and University Education in Latin America, Bogotá,
Colombia, July 13-19, 1964, pp. 25-27, 49-50.

[45] Shils, Political Development in the New States, p. 34.

[46] Clark Kerr et al., Industrialism and Industrial Man, pp. 70-71.

[47] Edward Shils, "The Intellectuals in the Political Development of the New
States," World Politics, Vol. XII, No. 3 (April 1960), 339.

[48] Halpern, The Politics of Social Change, p. 117; Harry J. Benda, "Non-
Western Intelligentsias as Political Elites," in John H. Kautsky (ed.), Political
Change in Under-developed Countries: Nationalism and Communism (New York,
Wiley, 1962, 347 pp.), p. 240.

[49] Hoffer, The True Believer, p. 44.

of responsible men and women. From their ranks must come the political leaders, the government officials, the businessmen who will expand the economy, and the qualified teachers who will raise the level of the next generation. The quality of the training and the values the students acquire are critical to the country's future. They will also affect the leader's political future. They have the gift of tongues to influence those who have long depended upon word of mouth for learning and for authoritative judgment. They have time on their hands and, if favorable to a regime, they can be its agitators and part-time organizers.

In Turkey and South Korea, for example, students precipitated coups d'état in 1960. In Ceylon, unemployed intellectuals have been useful organizers for opposition parties which gained control in 1956 and 1965. In the Ivory Coast, student returnees have been among the regime's most intractable critics and opponents.[50] These are notable examples of the more general problem posed by the growing frustration of school graduates in a number of countries. Every year, thousands of restless men and women, without marketable qualifications, are facing apparent perpetual unemployment. This is a built-in time bomb, which the new leader will find it difficult to defuze.

The students are both a resource and a threat. Keeping them on the side of the leader, or minimizing the political risks they pose is not an easy task. But as Silvert has noted, when students are able to seriously challenge authority, it is more a reflection of the weakness of other elements of power in the society than a reflection of the inherent political strength of the students themselves.[51]

BUSINESSMEN

The political role of businessmen in Asia and Africa is difficult to assess. In general it would appear that they have had a

[50] On student disorder in India, see Weiner, *The Politics of Scarcity*, pp. 170-79. In Ivory Coast, see Zolberg, *One-Party Government in the Ivory Coast*, p. 207.

[51] "If young persons can gain sufficient influence to change on occasion the course of national political life, then it must be that other power centers are in such disarray as to elevate the relative power of *any* organized groups." From "Continuity and Change in Latin America: The University Student," unpublished manuscript by S. M. Lipset, "The Political Behaviour of University Students," p. 33.

smaller role in politics than has been traditionally the case in the United States or Great Britain. But very little has been written on the political role of businessmen or the interaction between business and politics in Africa and Asia. The following observations, therefore, are suggestive only.

Businessmen are diverse in their characteristics and their interests. The village shopkeeper/moneylender is one thing, sitting cross-legged in the midst of small heaps of wares, with his scales, black tin money box, and tea- or coffeepot all within reach. Often he or his ancestors were alien to the area, and they may still be regarded as outsiders. The man of substantial urban business may trade in commodities, organizing the purchase from farmers when the crops are in and selling high when food is scarce. He may be experimenting with a small factory, tentatively making the transition from trading to manufacturing, or he may be a sizeable manufacturer. He is likely to keep multiple books, and deal frequently with government administrators to ensure the smooth flow of permits and authorizations. In between is a whole spectrum of intermediary types.[52] Have they anything in common except their economic classification as active businessmen?

Usually they are disliked. The local shopkeeper/moneylender is distrusted because his economic power can cause the ruin of neighbors and friends. The trader is resented because he profits from the farmer's weakness; the manufacturer of new products, because at the outset quality is usually poor and prices high. Unlike the well-born, the newly rich are not believed to deserve display because they are usually self-made men who, it is held, must have gained their wealth illegitimately. Their position has been made more invidious by the prevalence of Marxist ideology, which identifies such private activities as the source of evil and economic waste. In many cases the most effective entrepreneurs are ethnic, religious, or national minorities. Hostility sparked by envy of their wealth and by the tough competition their frugality makes possible is compounded by suspicion drawn from traditional racial and national antagonisms. The businessmen therefore represent a class that is both disliked and envied. One of their political functions, therefore, is to provide a target for political hostility. As such, they may be as useful to many political aspirants as was the foreigner a generation earlier.

[52] Clark Kerr et al., *Industrialism and Industrial Man*, p. 58.

They may also play an important role in economic development. In many instances, they are a source of innovation and of venture. They often find ways to economize resources and to try new things. The lively entrepreneurs are a channel for importing better ways of pursuing familiar goals or for defining new and unprecedented economic purposes.[53]

However, not all businessmen are creative in this way. Many like high markups and low turnover; they may prefer minimum risk import business to improving local productive capacities; too many use their businesses to lay away accounts in New York or Switzerland. Many invest heavily in land, attempting to gain the status normally reserved for the hereditary old families.[54] Thus, they do not play the role of the reinvesting puritanical capitalist of the protestant ethic so vividly depicted by Weber and Tawney. Moreover, if they do perform this classical function, they often are from a minority group, which leaves them easy prey to the unscrupulous bureaucrat. Riggs has identified the "antagonistic cooperation" between these "pariah entrepreneurs" and government administrators. They help to supplement the inadequate income of the underpaid officials who, in return for under-the-table payments, acquiesce when the businessman violates the regulations in order to keep his business profitable.[55] They are, however, a potential asset in the task of development, and governments seriously trying to develop often provide incentives to induce their creative energies.

They are also a source of funds, facilitating many political activities for those to whom they contribute. As in India, some give heavily to the national independence movement. More generally, they provide support to the political parties, as Sklar reported from Nigeria. With their help, parties need not limit their slates to those candidates

---

[53] For the classical analysis of the creative role of entrepreneurs, see Joseph A. Schumpeter, *Capitalism, Socialism and Democracy* (New York, Harper and Brothers, 1947, 411 pp.). See also Zinkin, *Development for Free Asia*, Ch. 3; Gustav Papanek's discussion of entrepreneurship in Pakistan is also worthy of note, *Pakistan's Development, Social Goals and Private Incentives* (Cambridge, Harvard University Press, 1967, 354 pp.), Chs. 2, 3, and 4.

[54] P. A. Baran, "On the Political Economy of Backwardness," in Amar Narayan Agarwal and S. P. Singh (eds.), *The Economics of Underdevelopment* (New York, Oxford University Press, 1963, 510 pp.), pp. 75-92; Clark Kerr et al., *Industrialism and Industrial Man*, p. 58.

[55] In La Palombara (ed.), *Bureaucracy and Political Development*, p. 143; Feith in Kahin (ed.), *Government and Politics of Southeast Asia*, p. 256.

who can cover their own expenses, for business contributions make it easier for parties to cover the campaign costs of their less well-off spokesmen.[56]

They also are a source of political energy applied in support of specific policies, usually at the point of administrative decision. In the main, they are not averse to government initiatives in development planning or even in more direct economic activity and regulation. Domestic markets are more likely to expand when the government actively promotes economic development. Government protection insulates from foreign competition. Planning to conserve investment resources often allows a quasi-monopolistic situation to exist for some time; this favors the firm which gains permission to enter the protected field at the outset. Firms devise many methods for accommodating to and making the most of government regulation and initiative.[57]

Accordingly, a critical relationship is that which exists between management and key members of the bureaucracy who administer the economic rules and regulations. "The new industrial managers must be as much oriented toward the state as toward the market."[58] Sometimes the very survival or elimination of a firm depends upon a single administrative decision. Substantial organizations are developed to accelerate normally lethargic bureaucratic decisions as well as to ensure that the "correct" decisions are made.[59] Access to key administrators, therefore, becomes a critical business asset. Family alliances between bureaucratic and business families are highly sought after.

It is perhaps obvious that in such activities the entrepreneurs are by no means at one. Despite mythology to the contrary, they do not act as a homogeneous pressure group, except where the extreme of a national take-over of all business is in question. There are instances of close combination, where business economic interests support

[56] Sklar has many examples of the relationship between business and party politics in Nigeria, *Nigerian Political Parties*, pp. 328-31, 456-57, 343-44; Zolberg notes their relationship in the Ivory Coast, *One-Party Government in the Ivory Coast*, pp. 186-87; on Ceylon, see Wriggins, *Ceylon*, pp. 152-53; Weiner, *The Politics of Scarcity*, Ch. 5.

[57] Robert E. Lane, *The Regulation of Businessmen: Social Conditions of Government Economic Control* (New Haven, Yale University Press, 1954, 144 pp.), Chs. 3 and 6.

[58] Clark Kerr et al., *Industrialism and Industrial Man*, p. 58.

[59] Weiner, *The Politics of Scarcity*, p. 121.

each other. But as an economy develops and becomes more complex, there are increasingly numerous instances of contradictory economic interests, where the efforts of each to obtain special advantages for his own enterprise can be realized only at the expense of his competitors.

For the man in power, the resources and energies of entrepreneurs can be an important political asset. But a political leader may run substantial risks in conspicuously associating with the business community, because it is so widely looked down upon and distrusted. Where politics is an open, competitive affair, and where opposition can be politically articulate and active, leaders are likely to avoid open alliances with businessmen.

Indeed, it is most likely that the political leader will adopt public positions critical of the excesses of selfish business interests. Nevertheless, he may at the same time have tacit associations with particular elements of the business community. Businessmen need him— and he needs at least some of their resources and skills.

TRADE UNIONS

There are many types of trade unions, ranging from the least politicized—concentrating on collective bargaining—familiar in the United States; moderately politicized trade unions, typical of Scandinavia; the ideologically committed unionism in the competitive political situations of Italy and India, to the unions acting as auxiliaries of the government, as in one-party African states.[60]

Despite these differences, however, sheer organized numbers are of political utility. If the situation permits relatively free voting, unions are important because they organize large numbers of voters. While there is no guarantee that union members will vote the way union leaders desire, leadership views are likely to affect significantly the rank and file at the voting booths in factory or plantation areas. Numbers are important, too, if mass demonstrations are permitted as a way of voicing demands or challenging a government's policies. Political demonstrations may be particularly useful to promote the growth of labor organizations, for they do not involve the risks to

[60] The most systematic study of the political role of trade unions is the monograph by Bruce Millen, The Political Role of Labor in Developing Countries (Washington, D.C., The Brookings Institution, 1963, 148 pp.), pp. 11-14.

job security inherent in strikes held in economies where there are large numbers of unemployed ready to replace the strikers. Demonstrations also serve the political function of underlining public support for, or lack of confidence in, a regime.

Numbers may be politically significant by virtue of their ability to mount direct economic pressures against a government. As most developing economies are built on a narrow base, the total modern sector of the economy may be vulnerable to the actions of a very few unions.[61] Export economies can be brought to a virtual halt by control of the port or a few trucking or railway workers unions. Public services in an acutely overcrowded capital are easy to disrupt. A number of simultaneous strikes can be used to dramatize a government's inability to cope with the country's necessities. This may be a prelude to a defeat of the government at the polls, or to a change of government by other means. Alternatively, cooperation by union leaders in a government development program will accelerate economic development. Successful development, therefore, requires some modus vivendi with at least key union leaders to ensure desirable levels of worker output and to prevent undue disruption of productive activities.

Trade unions may also act as adjuncts of government. In Africa, particularly, many small trade-union movements inherited at independence have been taken over by political leadership. Under such political conditions, trade unions help to indoctrinate the workers with the government's objectives, restrain worker demands, and keep the men at work on behalf of developmental objectives. Strikes are usually forbidden. Trade-union pressures, when they are exerted, are expressed within the government itself, usually through trade-union leaders participating in the inner councils of the dominant party, as in Ghana, Guinea, and Tanzania. But if the dominant party remains in power over an extended period of time, the unions are likely to become increasingly the means of disciplining the workers rather than of expressing workers' demands within the party itself.[62] Where trade unions are auxiliaries of government, the members also can be used by government to intimidate other elements of the society. They may become a substitute for the police, protecting party men

[61] Douglas Ashford, *Political Change in Morocco* (Princeton, Princeton University Press, 1961, 432 pp.), p. 270.
[62] Millen, *The Political Role of Labor*, pp. 91-92.

at rallies. They may be the source of toughs on call to intimidate selected opponents or members of the opposition.

Trade unions perform a number of additional functions. They may provide means for resolving workers' grievances without resort to strike. By drawing together workers from different traditional groups or from different parts of the country in common effort, they can contribute to national integration. Activities within union organizations provide practice in the skills of modern purposive organization, skills which are often lacking in the society and may be applied later on to other purposes. In those instances where union structures are truly democratic, they can provide practice in democratic ways of reaching group decisions. Trade unions may also provide partial substitutes for the friendship and mutual reassurance of tribal or ethnic loyalties. An active union movement, demonstrating to the participating workers that their circumstances can improve through their own organized efforts, is likely to make Left totalitarian unionism of the communist type less attractive.[63]

Trade unions pose certain political liabilities to the ruler wanting to remain in power. They often have been the recruiting ground for political leaders and are therefore a source of threatening competitors. If trade-union leaders arise independently of one-party governments, they are likely to be removed when their popularity appears to grow too sharply, as Ben Salah, the head of the powerful Union Générale des Travailleurs Tunisiens (UGTT) in Tunisia, was removed by Prime Minister Bourguiba.[64] Trade unions have built into their own inner imperatives the necessity to increase claims on the political system. Wages must be gradually raised, working conditions improved, subsidies and other means devised to keep the cost of living down. Sometimes the demands can be used by the political leader to extract higher taxes from the wealthy, or to induce them to use their wealth in economically more productive directions. These demands may sometimes be transformed into more effective output by labor, since improved incentives may be critical to improving productivity.[65] The more usual result of union activity is to increase the net demand for immediate consumption. This may

[63] Weiner, *The Politics of Scarcity*, p. 95.

[64] Charles A. Micaud (with Leon Carl Brown and Clement Henry Moore), *Tunisia: The Politics of Modernization* (New York, Praeger, 1964, 205 pp.), p. 100.

[65] Gunnar Myrdal, *Asian Drama* (New York, Pantheon, Random House, 1968, 3 vols.), Vol. III, appendix 2, pp. 1912-19.

induce greater investment by entrepreneurs eager to profit from this increased demand, but it will complicate the government's problem of retrieving savings from the economy and channeling these into productive investment.

In a society where organizational structures are all weak, a few well-organized unions can have a substantial direct political impact. Indeed, they may precipitate a coup, as in Upper Volta, where a hard-pressed government sought to reduce wages. But it is easy to exaggerate the political importance of trade unions at this stage in the development of most emerging countries. Where unemployment is serious, strikes are difficult to sustain. Union funds are usually meager. In many countries, there are large numbers of unions, often loyal to a particular union personality rather than to a complete craft or industry. Where the union leaders are themselves men of political ambition, competition among the leaders for political advantage will lead unions to act at cross-purposes.[66] Although the bulk of the swelling population remains unorganized in the union sense, one can expect trade unions to grow in number and, in most countries, to play an increasingly significant political role.

THE PRESS AND RADIO

The aspiring political leader or one who has already "arrived" will find in the press and radio important resources—and potential threats. He will want them on his side and, if possible, opposed to his political opponents.

If they work in the ruler's favor, the press and the mass media can perform many political services. They can promote his cause by projecting a vision of the leader as he would like himself to be. They can mediate between the somewhat alienated, cosmopolitan man he typically is in fact and the man who, if he is to win the trust and sustained support of the less evolved, must be known to be deeply rooted in indigenous ways. They can also dramatize his multiple purposes and make more widespread and persuasive an awareness of the ruler's goals and how congenial or indispensable

[66] For more detail see Millen, The Political Role of Labor, Ch. 2; Weiner, The Politics of Scarcity, Ch. 4; James S. Coleman and Carl G. Rosberg, Jr. (eds.), Political Parties and National Integration in Tropical Africa (Berkeley and Los Angeles, University of California Press, 1964, 730 pp.), p. 380.

these may be to the bulk of the populace. Through the media, his sense of the need for an appropriate distribution of sacrifice and benefits can be evoked. The media can popularize his vision of how much change the society must absorb while it remains thoroughly consistent with and close to the more familiar.

The press can influence accepted notions of the rules of the political game, call a foul play when it thinks it sees one, expose corruption, or generally raise—or lower—the levels of what the reading and listening public comes to expect of political leaders. A press with considerable independence can publicize examples of bureaucratic lethargy or misuse of authority. Critical areas of unrest may be signaled through the press before the often self-serving administrators can bring themselves to report that all is not well within their area of responsibility.

The media can also diminish the status of the leader's opponent. Lenin urged that people should be filled with "hatred, aversion and contempt" for the enemies of the party.[67] The press and radio can debase individual opponents or whole groups in the population who stand in the way. The press may also transmit to those in the bureaucracy and provinces the necessary cues on what is now expected of the faithful, as well as how fare the relative fortunes of the more prominent members of the entourage.

Typically, there are several indigenous languages which the media use. If each one plays upon the particular emotions and prejudices of its narrow audience only, the media will confirm present social fragmentation. Public issues will be seen in quite different terms by each element in the society, for each lives within its own universe of discourse.[68] On the other hand, national unity may be encouraged if the media consciously seek to define issues and differences in ways calculated to transcend these traditional fissures, promoting nationwide purposes and a widely shared awareness of problems to be tackled.

But such an approach is difficult to encourage in some individual journalists. In former colonial areas, the press has had a tradition of nationalist opposition to authority.[69] Manned by writers usually

---

[67] Lenin, "Speech for the Defence," *Selected Works* (International Publishers, c. 1943, 12 volumes), Vol. III, pp. 486-98, p. 490.

[68] Wriggins, *Ceylon*, p. 253; Pye (ed.), *Communications and Political Development*, p. 102.

[69] Herbert Passin, "Writer and Journalist in the Transitional Society," in Pye (ed.), p. 102.

on the margins of ruling circles but not born close enough to feel, or be, fully accepted, the typical press man, who is seriously under-paid, and an intelligent observer from close at hand of the contrast between the ideal and the reality of political life, is not easily brought to lay aside his oppositional instincts.[70] This will be particularly, and understandably, so where leaders profess a high concern for democratic practice or for dealing with social or economic grievances when, in fact, they are seen to give little serious attention to either.

The vernacular press is particularly important in linking the central government in the capital with the bulk of the people. The independent vernacular papers, however, are not likely to promote national solidarity, for they are usually financially precarious and play upon parochial sentiments, communal jealousies, and tribal differences in efforts to retain their readership. The linguistic dis-tance of many leaders from the vernacular rubs the vernacular journalist at a particularly sore spot.

While many papers started under British and French regimes as protest and nationalist journals, in some countries they have become businesses in their own right. Where this has happened, the papers are neither forces for revolution nor compliant tools of the govern-ment, but retain enough autonomy to remain critical of the govern-ment, as in the major journals in India's larger cities, in Colombo, and the case of L'Afrique Nouvelle in Dakar. They are less easily intimidated or bought by the government than the weaker papers which have always led a hand-to-mouth existence. Where owners are less able to stand on their own and governments are more deter-mined to induce conformity, papers will be more nearly spokesmen for government views and policies. The government's control of foreign exchange gives it substantial leverage to influence editorial policy and news coverage. Increasingly, in the single-party states, the papers have become virtual propaganda instruments of their governments.

For the most part, broadcasting is controlled by individual govern-ments and should improve a regime's chances of survival. Its impor-tance is attested to by the fact that it is one of the immediate and critical targets of any coup d'état. Rarely does a state radio allow political criticism or opposition voices, although contradictory voices may penetrate the airways from neighboring states. Radio can arouse hostility against a regime's political opponents and can promote

[70] Pye, p. 79.

euphoria among its listeners by its appeal to the anxieties and dreams of the populace. Such short-run political advantages, however, do not contribute to a more poised civic sense or encourage the growth of democratic rules of the game for the political long run.

While some of the more highly educated may be skeptical of government papers and radio, those who have just recently learned to read or are hearing directly the voice of leadership for the first time tend to be more easily influenced.[71] Yet only rather simple ideas and imagery are likely to be absorbed by listeners in the early years. Useful messages may be limited to the realm of suspicions and enthusiasms. Promoting matter-of-fact approaches to the solution of intricate problems will not be easy in any event.

Where government reaches toward complete domination of the mass media, cynicism and disbelief usually come to characterize the public's reaction to them. Official media lose their persuasiveness when the picture they paint of men and affairs deviates too sharply from familiar and manifest reality. The media, therefore, can perform certain political functions in assisting a regime to stay in power, but they are of limited value in helping it to achieve its wider purposes.

There are, of course, other groups which aspiring leaders will seek to combine into their ruling coalition. In certain areas, for instance, a technological intelligentsia of "new men" reportedly is coming forward. They are trained and needed by regimes seeking to modernize, and they bring with their growth a direct challenge to contemporary rulers.[72] There may be still other groups of political relevance for the future. To discuss them further would unduly extend this one aspect of the analysis. Suffice it to point out here that each leader will find a unique combination of potential allies—and opponents—in his polity. And a substantial proportion of his efforts will be devoted to ways of enlisting them in his coalition and of preventing them from coalescing to oppose him.

[71] Pye, p. 126.
[72] William Polk, "The Nature of Modernization—The Middle East and North Africa," Foreign Affairs, Vol. XLIV, No. 1 (October, 1956), 100-10.

III

**Strategies
for
Aggregating
Power**

5 Project the Personality

If you would work any man, you must either know his nature and fashions, and so lead him; or his ends, and so win him; or his weaknesses or disadvantages, and so awe him, or those that have interest in him and so govern him.

Francis Bacon

No two political leaders approach their task of aggregating power in the same way. Yet it is possible to discern certain characteristic approaches to extending and consolidating one's own coalition and undermining that of one's opponent. These are here called strategies, for there is no other word which comes so close to suggesting what is intended.

A WORD ON STRATEGY AND PARTICULARITY

The activities of those who are successful in politics usually imply considerable forethought and sometimes even planning. Skilful political actors usually distinguish in their minds between an overall approach and particular tactical actions. Substantial activities of political leaders are within situations of conflict, associating with allies, working against opponents. They often speak of their gains and losses as if they were not unlike the advances and retreats of conventional military actions.

However, the term strategy suggests more advance planning and rational calculation of means to ends than may be entirely accurate in a field where "feel" and improvisation play such an important role. Dahl describes the process nicely when he writes:

> To achieve their goals, leaders develop plans of action, or strategies. But actions take place in a universe of change, of uncertainty; goals themselves emerge, take shape, and shift with new experience. Hence a choice among strategies is necessarily based more on hunch, guesswork, impulse, and the assessment of imponderables than on scientific predictions. Adopting a strategy is a little bit like deciding how to look for a fuse box in a strange house on a dark night after all the lights have blown.[1]

Taken as a whole, political leaders in Africa and Asia are probably no more or less foresighted in assessing their political circumstances and identifying economical means to their political ends than leaders of the established states. Differences among them will be as marked. Out of the eight components of likely strategies about to be identified, each leader will fashion his particular combination. This will be an emergent of his particular personality, organization, and political circumstances. His power requirements and approaches to aggregating power will be different, depending upon whether he has successfully mounted action against colonial rulers and displaced them, is seeking to establish a viable regime for himself after a coup d'état, or is attempting to ease the way for his preferred successor; and whether in this his primary concern is to establish state authority, integrate the nation, push the revolution of participation, or promote generalized public welfare. How he combines components of strategies will depend, too, upon whom he identifies as opponents and how he perceives their intentions, strengths, and weaknesses; whom he seeks as allies and what he believes will be required to win and hold them. He will have notions of accepted rules of the game and assumptions regarding the expected role of politicians, and the political costs or advantages of deviating from these local norms. He will be influenced by local expectations regarding trust or deviousness in

---

[1] Dahl, *Who Governs?*, p. 96. For a similar usage, see his discussion of axioms of political strategy in New Haven, pp. 94-95; Clark Kerr, et al., *Industrialism and Industrial Man*, also speaks of the strategies elite groups use to "order the surrounding society in a consistent and compatible fashion." p. 50.

political affairs, the imminence of violence, and the traditional ways in which leaders relate themselves to followers. Each one's combination will vary over time. It may change with changing social and economic conditions and his own skills and predilections. Relations with his immediate entourage are rarely fixed. Changing means of political communication, the structure, process—and relevance—of such political institutions as elections and legislatures, and the existence and effectiveness of law enforcement agencies will affect his approach to politics. All these, in their particularity and in their change, will have a bearing on the strategies leaders adopt.[2]

Moreover, some regimes may be inherently more adaptable. Some leaders will be more versatile and more responsive than others to changes in the environment, depending in part upon the personality of the leaders, the nondoctrinaire approach to public problems of the entourage or subsidiary leaders, and the openness of the class or status structure to new groups who may be drawn forward by imaginative leadership or who may be pushing upward toward new assertiveness.[3] The past decade has demonstrated some remarkable changes in approach. Perhaps Jomo Kenyatta of Kenya has been most notable in this respect. At first the most outspoken critic of British presence in Kenya, he has become the responsible, moderate statesman of the mid-1960s. Mr. Nkrumah made a gradual transition from moderate constitutionalism to increasingly radical agitational authoritarianism.[4] Indonesia swung sharply from the days when Mr. Sukarno collaborated with Mr. Hatta, who sought to solve administrative problems and promote economic development. Subsequently, Sukarno projected himself as the national father; he excited the populace into perpetual revolution, and led his country into foreign policy adventures.[5]

[2] For these matters, see, among others, Feith, *The Decline of Constitutional Democracy in Indonesia*, pp. 116-17; Weiner, "Political Integration and Political Development," *The Annals*, Vol. 358 (March, 1965) 52-64. Pye (ed.), *Communications and Political Development*, pp. 6, 42; Roger Henry Soltau, *An Introduction to Politics* (London, New York, Longmans Green, 1951, 328 pp.), p. 41; David Apter, *The Political Kingdom in Uganda*, pp. 15-16; Harry Eckstein, *A Theory of Stable Democracy* (Princeton, N. J., Center of International Studies, Research Monograph No. 10, 1961, 50 pp.); Susanne Rudolph, "Consensus and Conflict in Indian Politics," *World Politics*, Vol. XIII, No. 3 (April, 1961), 385-99.

[3] Shmuel Eisenstadt, "Modernization and Conditions of Sustained Growth," *World Politics*, Vol. XVI, No. 4 (July, 1964), 576-94.

[4] For a discussion of Ghana, see Austin, *Politics in Ghana, passim*.

[5] On the need for both "problem solvers" and "solidarity makers," see Feith, *The Decline of Constitutional Democracy in Indonesia*, pp. 24-25, 117.

Despite the problems posed by the fact of particularity and the importance of changes over time, it is nevertheless possible to identify major strategies leaders use to attack the problem of aggregating political power.

It should be clear that the distinctions to be drawn between each of these strategies are not clear cut. In certain instances they merge into each other, and some are clearly dependent upon other related strategies. No one alone is sufficient for political success. Each leader will combine them in his own way, and lay his peculiar stress upon those he employs. Nevertheless, it will be useful to discuss each of eight principal strategies in turn, with the understanding that they are not intended to be all conceivable strategies but that they appear to be the most important and widely used.

PROJECT THE PERSONALITY

> We must not fall into the error of believing that leaders whom we regard as "charismatic" are individuals whose exceptional qualities come to be spontaneously recognized by their populations. They are often persons who succeed more than others in exploiting the situation around them. They know what their people feel most strongly about, or can be made to feel strongly about. In a way, they are not "picked" by their people; it is the other way around.
>
> K. J. Ratnam

Many leaders in the emerging nations of Africa and Asia have consciously sought to project their personality across their country's stage. By the size of the shadow they cast, by the art of their imagery, by the response they evoke in the hearts of their peoples and their entourage they consolidate their position and help aggregate around themselves sufficient power to pursue their purposes.

AN EXAMPLE: THE CASE OF SUKARNO

One of the most dramatic examples of personality in politics was President Sukarno of Indonesia. Sukarno's Indonesia was just that, for many years. He was the centerpiece of political life. He did not have a solid political organization. His economic policies, if they could even be called policies, were disastrous. He was not cruel, he intimidated only moderately. The Indonesians were not content; there was much unrest. But he managed to win enough of them to his side, largely by the strength and originality of his personality, to remain at the center of power for more than a decade.

It was in part his image. Though a group of "hot heads" virtually forced him to assert Indonesia's independence as Japanese power faded, he became the personification of the independence movement, the spirit of 1945. The practical affairs of organizing the military action against the Dutch fell to Hatta and others in the civil and military services. But it was Sukarno who exhorted the troops and populace, and it was Sukarno who came to symbolize for the Indonesian people success in that struggle and the shape and direction of the new independent Indonesia.

Sukarno had the knack of persuading the Indonesian people that he understood their wants, fears, and dreams. His rhetoric could move them by the thousands. As he once put it:

"Why is it that people ask me to give a speech to them even when the sun is hottest? The answer is this: What Bung Karno says is already written in the hearts of the Indonesian people. The people want to hear their own voice but . . . they cannot speak eloquently for themselves . . . . When I die . . . write on my tombstone "here rests Bung Karno, the tongue of the Indonesian people."[6]

He could also touch the hearts of the few. When a mob, led by some of the senior military leaders, begged him to disband the provisional parliament and rule with military support, he appeared before the crowd and persuaded them he understood their wish but could not become a dictator. After talking privately with the military men for an hour and a half, they left, weeping and asking him for their forgiveness.

He was obviously master of the personal negotiation, manipulating the men in his entourage by maneuver and supple argument, understanding their mutual jealousies, sensing their private dreams and each man's weakness. Supporting first this cabinet, then that prime minister, he played leaders against each other, and, as they were successively eliminated, he set the army and the Communist Party

[6] Reported by Willard Hanna, *Bung Karno's Indonesia* (New York, American University Field Staff, 1961), WAH 13-59, p. 3.

of Indonesia off against each other. In the end, it was that conflict which precipitated his downfall.

He understood the popular wish for panoply and color; indeed, he obviously loved them himself. Like the early kings of Sumatra and Java, he traveled with a huge entourage, demonstrating his more than human energy by his tireless activities—inspecting schools, clinics, and army units; participating in local ceremonies—laying cornerstones; dancing into the night.[7] His seemingly insatiable sexual appetite may have alienated the Djakarta upper middle class. But there is evidence to suggest that the Indonesian masses vicariously enjoyed the fun and secretly admired the Bung for his virility, if not always approving of his taste.[8]

His eloquent references to Jefferson, the Federalist Papers, and to Lincoln amazed and brought plaudits from a bemused joint session of the American Congress. His world travels revealed him to his people as the equal of presidents and kings, a man who hobnobbed with the prime ministers of great powers.[9]

Sukarno's mode of projecting his personality permitted him to say something to men and women all across that vast and scattered archipelago. His paternal figure appears to have brought reassurance and enlisted enthusiasm from people in all communities and at all levels of society. The deterioration of his position in the middle 1960s should not obscure the fact that this remarkable man played a substantial role in generating a sense of self-confidence, giving to Indonesia for the first time a widely accepted focus of attention, as well as projecting himself as an object of admiration and affection. From his personality some solidarity was brought about which transcended Indonesia's numerous and deep cleavages.[10]

When the old order developed by the Dutch was thrown down and the traditional stratifications which defined for so many their role and place disintegrated under the triple pressures of Japanese occupation, a war of independence, and continued turmoil, it was Bung Karno who spoke with authority. Many hesitated, attempting

---

[7] *Ibid.*, WAH 13-59, p. 7.

[8] Ann Ruth Willner, *Charismatic Political Leadership* (Princeton University, N. J., Center of International Studies, Research Monograph No. 32, 1968, 113 pp.), pp. 84-85.

[9] Hanna, *Bung Karno's Indonesia*, p. 6.

[10] Hanna, in Silvert, *Expectant Peoples*, p. 140.

to analyze the confusion, but Sukarno acted, confidently telling all what to do next. That part of his recipe only compounded the confusion was less immediately important than the fact that he appeared to have answers. Many people listened to his advice and tried to act on it, even if they sometimes did not understand what he recommended.

Not unlike the magicians of Javanese tradition, Sukarno played with word magic. His acronyms, built from the initials of political slogans into single words lacking in familiar referents, could be infused with whatever meaning seemed to suit the present need.[11] Although by 1959 Hanna reported growing disenchantment, it was not until 1966 when the two best organized political forces—the army and the Communist Party of Indonesia—fell into open and fatal quarrel that he himself was brought down. And such was his reputation even then that the military successors dared not move directly against him, but only slowly—like a Javanese play that runs endlessly while the audience alternately naps and watches the drama with rapt attention—pushed him aside. Neither he nor his remaining supporters had occasion to raise a cry on his behalf.

Projecting the personality, so vividly exemplified by Sukarno, is perhaps the most widely used approach to aggregating power. By dramatizing the unique qualities of the indispensable leader, quite independent of his office, he is made to appear all-wise, larger than life, a giant among men. He has the answers to all problems. He understands everyone's needs. He knows what people ought to want. He embodies in his single person the country's strengths and virtues. He is the focus for diverse interests and variegated purposes. These and other qualities give legitimacy to his exercise of authority and make the acts of government acceptable. Without a central personality, colorful, dramatic, and all-knowing, few regimes in emerging countries are able to survive for long. President Nasser and Prime Minister Nkrumah have been other outstanding examples of this approach to aggregating power. In the end Sukarno and Nkrumah were pushed aside, but Nkrumah ruled for over ten years and Sukarno for fifteen in stormy times. These were no mean accomplishments.

[11] Hanna, in Silvert (ed.), p. 176; Willner, *Charismatic Political Leadership*, pp. 92-93.

THE MANY FUNCTIONS OF THE PERSONALITY

The personality performs many political functions. In most emerging countries the institutions for endowing political leaders with the authority to rule are ill-formed. Traditional ways of acquiring legitimacy no longer remain; the legal and political methods introduced by colonial regimes have been discredited in many places; and the innovations adopted after independence lack roots. By his direct appeal to a multitude of individuals or leaders of autonomous groups, the personality can gain acceptance for his exercise of power. He, personally, may thus acquire the authority necessary for at least minimum governance.[12]

In a society made up of diverse primordial groupings with parochial loyalties, a personality can be the main focus of common loyalty. The office he holds may be new, untried, or too closely approximating something depreciated during the anti-colonial struggle. It may be possible for subsidiary leaders or masses to experience some identification with the great leader, and through shared loyalty to him they acquire some sense of solidarity with others in the society. He may enlist solidarity where little would exist without him.[13]

Interests diverge, intentions conflict, and overarching purpose is rare. Indeed, where institutions for aggregating and compromising conflicting demands, i.e., the institutions of political bargaining and adjustment, such as representative legislatures, are ill-formed or not well-established, it may be only the predominant person who can define some general goals on which all can agree. President Ayub provided for a time a common purpose of economic development that his predecessors were unable to define. Prime Minister Nehru's person drew countless Indians along a single path despite their manifold differences. Often, such a function is linked to an intensive ideological effort, conducted by, or in the name of, the

[12] This function, of course, is Max Weber's third type of authority, "charismatic," the other two being "traditional" and "rational legal" authority. *The Theory of Social and Economic Organization*, edited by T. Parsons (Glencoe, Free Press, paperback, 1964, 436 pp.), p. 328. For a good recent critical discussion, see Ann Ruth and Dorothy Willner, "The Rise and Role of Charismatic Leaders," *The Annals*, Vol. 358 (March, 1965), 77-81.

[13] See Feith, for a discussion of leaders as "solidarity makers," *The Decline of Constitutional Democracy in Indonesia*, p. 117.

ruler, who may be depicted as the source of the ideology. President Sukarno and Prime Minister Nyerere invested substantial effort in this direction. The ideas may be vague and contradictory, or they may be intellectually respectable. But if they contribute to consensus on shared dangers or on what should be done, they will be adding to the assets of the ruler and assisting him in his task of coalition building.

Indeed, one of the virtues of developing solidarity through the leader-personality is that diverse elements can follow the person while concrete policy differences can be temporarily set aside. The personality, thus, at times may be a substitute for policy choice. This device may lead to administrative lethargy and even stalemate, as in Burma under U Nu, but at least it will help to sustain a minimum level of mutual acquiescence preferable to widespread civil war. In India, Nehru often was able to resolve disputes within the Congress Party and elsewhere, not merely by compromising conflicting claims but by virtue of the fact that his personal stature made a settlement acceptable, even to the individual or groups who lost in the contest. Sukarno also often acted as the reconciler.[14]

The changes taking place within an emerging society create anxiety. In transitional societies, status positions are changing. Where before, traditional modes have been sufficient, new ways must be adopted, often by people who feel ill-equipped to deal with anything unfamiliar. For many among the educated frustration is keen, as the society has too few places for them or its performance falls far below the foreign standard they learned abroad. Those who have left the countryside are often disoriented, no longer embedded in traditional social entities. Even if they have moved into the communal or tribal organizations which usually develop in the cities, they are often in frequent contact with people from tribal or ethnic groups traditionally considered hostile. By attaching themselves to the personality, they gain comfort and reassurance, as the family head, village elder, or the tribal chief gave comfort and reassurance before. As Adamafio wrote of Nkrumah: ". . . to us his people, Kwame Nkrumah is our father, teacher, our brother, our friend, indeed our very lives, for without him we would no doubt have existed, but we would not have lived; there would have been no hope of a cure for our sick souls . . ."[15]

[14] Hanna in Silvert (ed.), *Expectant Peoples*, p. 140.

[15] Quoted by David Apter in "Political Religion in the New Nations," in Geertz, *Old Societies and New States*, p. 84.

The personality often is the principal embodiment of both tradition and the future. Many, though not all, of the great personalities have been able to meld in their persons attributes of both epochs. Mr. Nehru, as a Kashmiri Brahman, combined the highest qualities of the traditional status system with a reiterated independence from traditional religion, and he articulated a suggestive conception of the kind of society and economy India should develop in the future. Mr. Nkrumah increasingly clothed himself in ancient chieftaincy ritual—while promoting the Volta River project. Few ordinary individuals can in fact encompass both the past and future. But the personality may, in his person and his attributes, come to represent aspects of both.[16]

In building a coalition, the strategy of personality in itself can provide certain subjective satisfactions to prospective allies. The personality may represent the good man above the squalor and pettiness of politics and contention. He may thus come to personify the dream of those who aspire to be freed from a contingent, expediential world where resources are scarce, ambitions great, and men competitive. He may provide warmth and reassurance in a rapidly changing and therefore perplexing world for those who place their trust in him. Their own personal stature grows larger in their own eyes as they identify their small and sometimes frightened selves with the great, confident leader.[17]

For his part, if he is skilled and fortunate, the personality can translate the subjective satisfactions he gives to his following into more tangible political assets for himself. For example, President Nasser publicly resigned when Israel defeated Egypt in 1967. He was reconfirmed by the acclaim of the masses, whose psychic rewards were more evident than the tangible benefits they may have

[16] Ann Ruth and Dorothy Willner, "The Rise and Role of Charismatic Leaders," The Annals, Vol. 358 (March, 1965), p. 87; Brecher, Nehru, A Political Biography, p. 230; Feith, The Decline of Constitutional Democracy in Indonesia, p. 594; Zolberg, One-Party Government in the Ivory Coast, p. 267.

[17] The mechanisms at work here are close to Erich Fromm's classic analysis, Escape from Freedom (New York, Holt, Rinehart and Winston, Inc., 1941, 305 pp.). See also Lucian Pye, Politics, Personality and Nation-Building: Burma's Search for Identity (New Haven, Yale University Press, 1962, 307 pp.), pp. 54-55; Frederic W. Frey, "Political Attitudes in Development," prepared for the summer seminar on "Political Development Research," held by Inter-University Consortium for Political Research, 1964, Ann Arbor, Michigan; Theodore Geiger, The Conflicted Relationship (New York, McGraw-Hill, 1967, 303 pp.), pp. 92-97.

received. On a less dramatic level, subjective satisfactions may win the support of those who can raise money, or who dispose of jobs, or whose acquiescence or more active support can help sustain his position or implement his policies.

Finally, the personality may also perform an indispensable function in personifying the new state at home and abroad, dramatizing the new equality by his dealing as an equal with leaders from the other established states. As Ben Franklin in Paris underlined the independence and demonstrated the equality of the new state at the courts of established monarchies of that day, so the leading personality, tackling distant great powers—or traditional enemies nearer home—in speeches from the platform at home, in foreign capitals, or at the United Nations, accentuates independence and raises self-respect. When Nasser met with Khrushchev; Nehru with the British Prime Minister; when Ayub talked with Eisenhower, Kennedy, or Johnson; or Bandaranaike spoke before the United Nations—the country's stature was enhanced. No mere official can do this, whatever his office. Only the personality can fulfill this role.

THE PERSONALITY MUST BE BUILT UP

The personality, then, can perform many functions. But this position is not acquired automatically; it must be worked toward. As one political promoter admitted:

> What was needed was a kind of saviour . . . "human nature" is such that it needs a kind of hero to be hero-worshipped if it is to succeed . . . . Mr. Chipembere said quite frankly that Dr. Banda's reputation would have to be built up . . . . He must not be frightened if he was heralded as the political messiah. Publicity of this sort could be used to advantage.[18]

It was relatively easy to do this if the personality took a leading role in the independence struggle. Certain famous issues may be identified with the personality and become his hallmark, such as Gandhi's salt march, Houphouët-Boigny's elimination of forced labor in French West Africa, and Sékou Touré's rejection of the French community.[19]

[18] Nyasaland Commission of Enquiry, 1959, cmnd. 814 from Thomas Hodgkin, *African Political Parties* (London, Penguin, 1961, 217 pp.), p. 137.

[19] Zolberg, *One-Party Government in the Ivory Coast*, pp. 74-75. Special correspondent, "Guinea After Five Years," *African Report*, Vol. IX, No. 6 (June, 1964), 3.

Some near-miraculous immunity may denote a special grace, such as Menderes' survival of an air crash, Nasser's taking over the Suez Canal with impunity, or Nkrumah's achieving independence from the British without a fight.[20]

Certain elements of the other strategies are necessary to promote the personality. An organization in part dedicated to promoting the stature and reputation of the leader will be necessary. Traditional symbols, ritual, and pomp from the pre-colonial period may be revived to contribute to the greater glory of the leader.[21] Political folk songs and devices in the traditional idiom will be used.

At the same time, he will usually show himself devout, dedicated to traditional shrines and ceremonially respectful of the men in whose supernatural wisdom the simple people have faith. In Buddhist areas, the personality is likely to demonstrate his moderation, his perception of, and readiness to follow the middle path. It will be known among the cognoscenti that he consults astrologers before taking major decisions. He will visit holy places to ensure political success. He thus simultaneously reinsures with indigenous deities and shows the populace that he believes as they believe, even though he rides in a car, speaks English, and wears Western clothes. In Muslim countries, he will periodically consult the Ulama, will have no truck with the religious orders of the infidel, and will regularly appear at mosque for prayers, as his Christian counterpart attends public services every Sunday.

Rumor channels, traveling entertainers, and other traditional means of communication will be used, along with modern means of glorification. The press, radio, and magazines must be enlisted to turn the spotlight on the personality, to dramatize his qualities and make his routines and his extraordinary activities familiar. President Nasser's austere personal life and physical prowess; Prime Minister Nehru's bent for reflective writing or his conciliatory skills; President Bourguiba's political thought, or President Sukarno's tireless gaiety —these will be accented. There are usually competitors, too, whose reputations must be deflated and even blackened. For most, the glamour and power associated with modern weapons in the form of parades and demonstrations will add to the leader's stature, unless the army has become a symbol of repression. The foreign travels, noted above because they dramatize the equality and independence

---

[20] Frey discusses these qualities in "Political Attitudes in Development."

[21] Apter, "Political Religion in the New Nations," in Geertz, *Old Societies and New States*, p. 81.

of the new state, also enhance the reputation of the leader. Invitations to the world's great capitals may come unsought or some means of reaching to the apex of possible host governments through diplomatic channels, well-placed friends, or the well-paid public relations firm may be required. To be sure, competitors may charge that time—or foreign exchange—is being squandered on foreign junkets. But it appears to offer political rewards at home. And if state visits should result in increased foreign assistance, so much the better.

THE PERSONALITY AS A COALITION BUILDER

Perhaps no strategy is more likely to attract an extensive and varied coalition than the strategy of the personality. The entourage is likely to be enthusiastic; important segments of the wider public are likely to be activated. Indeed, it is often possible to bypass the leaders of intermediate political groups and directly gain the support of members of these groups; this weakens if not undercuts entirely the position of subsidiary leaders, who might otherwise stand in his way. Nkrumah did this in Ashanti, Nehru did it in some princely states, Sukarno did it in the islands. Certain traditional groups; students; those concerned with national prestige, national unity and social change; traditionalists; and modernizers can be drawn to common action, or at least be induced to set aside their differences, in a rally behind the personality. Possible opponents may thus be neutralized and criticism muted.

However, there may be certain groups not susceptible to the personality. Former lieutenants are an ever present liability, since they, more than those less familiar with the personality, know how very far below the image the real person may actually stand, with all-too-human feet of clay. Also, there are those who may have been touched by the earlier magic and have been disappointed. No one sees with a more critical eye than the rejected or disillusioned former admirer.

The leading sectors of the bureaucracy and the army are likely to remain unimpressed with the personality approach to power, unless periodically the ruler manages substantial and perhaps unexpected success, such as acquiring massive foreign aid for economic development, for building up the military, or for dealing with intractable domestic problems. No doubt, for example, President Nasser's stature improved in Egypt when he obtained the Soviet commitment to build the Aswan Dam, and President Ayub's support within the Pakistani army was strengthened before he came to power and for some years thereafter by his success in obtaining military assistance from the United States.

It is an exaggeration to say that performance alone will impress the technicians, for bureaucrats, too, are anxious in the face of great difficulties and sometimes humiliated by insufficiencies, and they find reassurance and inspiration in the personality. Nevertheless, it is generally true that the civilian and military officials are drawn to a man by what he can accomplish, not by what he appears to be or by the emotions he is capable of stirring in the society at large. And this is a substantial point since, for his part, the personality is likely to be impressed by the importance of appearances, by the image of government rather than by the policy output. In this effort, he is likely to move toward the unexpected and the brilliant improvisation to the dismay of the orderly and analytical bureaucratic or military man. Thus, as Feith records, Mr. Sukarno's fascination with "expressive" politics was at the expense of "problem solving."[22] His public policies led to near despair among many Indonesian bureaucrats. Mr. Bandaranaike's efforts to reform the language of public administration created major demoralization in the Ceylon public service and precipitated the early retirement or expatriation of numerous experienced officals.

Students and unemployed intellectuals are likely to be attracted to the personality if he can offer an action program promising expanding opportunity. He can easily appeal to their frustrations and desire for an active role in affairs, so long as this does not unduly curtail their freedom to criticize. But such a modernizing action program is likely to alienate key leaders of traditional groups and hence sharpen differences. Thus, the temptation is to set aside specific programs and policies and rely simply on personal loyalty, an approach likely to alienate the argumentative, idea-oriented intellectuals.

LIABILITIES OF THE STRATEGY OF PERSONALITY

The strategy of the personality has certain liabilities. After all, it does require an unusually endowed individual leader. Yet of

[22] Feith distinguishes between "expressive" politics and "problem-solving," *The Decline of Constitutional Democracy in Indonesia*, pp. 595-96.

all aspects of politics, this is the one most subject to chance and happenstance. To have to depend on the personality to cope with the problems of aggregating power, therefore, is to maximize a country's dependence on accident and luck.

While much can be done in the way of "building an image," a preponderantly political personality cannot be fabricated out of whole cloth. Some states have suffered from this lack. Syria, for example, was dogged by bad luck in the personalities of those who took power, notably in the cases of General Husni Zaim and Colonel Sami Hinnawi and most of their successors. How different might have been the fate of Indonesia had Mr. Sukarno been more of a "problem solver" and less enthusiastic about "expressive" politics. India was twice blessed with Gandhi and Nehru, and Pakistan was favored when someone took power who was as matter-of-fact and well-placed to exert unchallenged control as Ayub; Egypt experienced a notable improvement when Neguib and Nasser replaced Farouk.

The problems of most emerging countries are intricate and the goals which have been set are so ambitious that only energetic and artful policies, adopted after analysis and promoted with great care as well as flair, are likely to lead to success. The personality is often caught by the need for quick results, inspired improvisation and a preference for the dramatic and dashing, rather than the inconspicuous, the orderly, and the step-by-step. Success will require a good deal more than the inspiring personality.

The personality is not likely to encourage arrangements to permit an orderly succession.[23] So long as he remains at the apex and in reasonable command, it will not seem necessary to develop political institutions, such as orderly and increasingly competitive elections, or to groom a possible group of experienced men from whom a successor might be chosen. The personality is prone to avoid giving others of near-equal stature opportunities to be fully conversant with public affairs in advance of his own disability or death. Members of his entourage are rarely hardened and tested by gradually increasing responsibility. The test for them is not executive or political effectiveness in the country, but the loyalty and personal art displayed in relation to the Great One. Nkrumah surrounded himself with younger men, for these could not challenge his authority, and each was deeply in Nkrumah's debt for his high estate. Rare, indeed,

[23] Ann Ruth and Dorothy Willner, "The Rise and Role of Charismatic Leaders," *The Annals*, Vol. 358 (March, 1965), 88.

is the leader like Mr. Ben-Gurion who passes on authority to another while he is still alive, conferring a portion of his authority on his successor, who in turn is able to draw on the predecessor's reserves of reputation in case of national emergency. That Mr. Ben-Gurion could not hold to his retirement till the end only underlines how rare it is.

And there is always the liability that the personality will himself become unduly impressed with his own reputation, impatient to have his way, increasingly intolerant of bad news or other views, and unable to respond realistically to what his real situation requires. In the extreme case, his posturing and self-glorification may alienate his followers, bringing government into disrepute, and only exaggerate the cynicism so often widespread in new countries.[24]

Moreover, as attention always focuses on the leader, bad news or growing difficulties may arouse feelings of resentment and even hatred against him. He may come to feel his own safety is in danger. The resentful may seek to eliminate him as the centerpiece of governance. Attempts on his life will lead to increasing isolation. Like the tyrants of Italy's city states, he may come to live in increasing fear, isolating himself from others, afraid of the hand that might be raised against him. His entourage will become smaller. Secluded by his own choice, he will lose even more, and his political days will end by a coup d'état. He will be lucky if it occurs while he is out of

---

[24] See for example, Arthur Lewis, "Beyond African Dictatorship, the Crisis of the One-Party State," *Encounter*, Vol. XXV, No. 2 (August, 1965), 3-25. Hanna put it colorfully in considering Indonesia, no doubt exaggerating:

"The two primary elements of the mystique are neither new nor unique to Indonesia. They have now assumed, however, an all-engrossing importance which makes review and interpretation imperative for any understanding of Indonesian nationalism today. Element number one is the paramount position of the charismatic leader—President Sukarno—whose emergence and re-emergence as self-designated *deus ex machina* has already been stressed. The second is a national intoxication, Sukarno-stimulated, with the symbol, the slogan, and the shibboleth. Today the two elements are almost interchangeable. Sukarno, once the living, vital symbol of the Indonesian nation in its nationalist aspiration, has become so enamored of his own slogans and has so bewitched the nation by them that for the new revolutionary nationalism slogan is spliced to slogan, and both the new Sukarno and his adherents transfix themselves in incantation of the Sukarno acronym, MANIPOL-USDEK." (Hanna in Silvert, *Expectant Peoples*, p. 176.)

the country, as happened to Nkrumah. It is perhaps more degrading to end like Sukarno.

A strategy of projecting the personality alone will not be likely to permit a man to remain in power for very long or help him to implement his policies. He must combine this with other political strategies.

6 Build an Organization

> In its struggle for power, the proletariat has no other weapon
> but organization. We require *organization* and *organization*.
>
> V. I. Lenin

Boss Tweed, V. I. Lenin, and Abraham Lincoln had this in
common: they believed in the political necessity to organize. Whether
dealing with illiterate immigrants, refugees who dreamed of being
revolutionaries, or Illinois lawyers and farmers, all three recognized
the need for some kind of organization, to give the few the means to
shape the direction and sustain the consistency of action of the
many.

Without organization there can be no coherent action; without it
energies are expressed only intermittently and not necessarily in
ways likely to promote a group's political fortunes. Given equally
attractive, energetic, and inspiring personalities, he who organizes
will succeed, while he who depends on mere inspiration will lose the
game. Mr. Nkrumah, perhaps exaggerating, declared in his autobiography that his primary aim was "to learn the technique of
organization [for] . . . I knew that whatever the programme for the
solution of the colonial question might be, success would depend

upon the organization adopted."[1] When his organization swept the electoral boards while he was still in jail, his emphasis on organization appeared to be vindicated. Without the organization of the Congress Party in India, built up over eighty years of cultural revival and anti-British agitation, it is difficult to see how even a commanding figure such as Mr. Nehru could have pressed for independence and sustained the continuity of government as successfully as he did. Particularly in the fragmented post-colonial societies, "power within the new states . . . passed, by default, into the hands of the leaders of organized groups."[2]

AN EXAMPLE: THE CASE OF BOURGUIBA

One of the more successful party builders has been Habib Bourguiba, leader of Tunisia's independence movement and of the ruling Neo-Destour party. Bourguiba nurtured the party and fought for its solidarity from the early 1930s. At that time it was largely manned by the highly educated. Bourguiba was among the early leaders who sought to broaden the party's base by attracting new middle-class men from the towns south of Tunis who were looked down on by the aristocratic families who ruled Tunisia in collaboration with the French. He sought graduates of his own modernist Islamic Sadiki and of the more conservative Zitouna colleges. He sought to enlist young artisans and peasants, and the souq merchants who resented French commercial and banking power.[3] He enlisted his toughest militants from among the longshoremen who came to Tunis in tight-knit groups that retained the solidarity of their tribal, oasis origins.[4] The Neo-Destour, in short, was opened to men from all walks of life and all parts of Tunisia, and Bourguiba was skillful in drawing them together in common action.

Modeled after the French Socialist party, the party's constitution provided for a complicated structure of centralized authority at the top and democratic bodies below. In practice, as has so often hap-

---

[1] Austin, *Politics in Ghana*, p. 40.

[2] Coleman and Rosberg, *Political Parties and National Integration in Tropical Africa*, pp. 1-2.

[3] Clement Henry Moore, in Micaud, *Tunisia: The Politics of Modernization*, pp. 80-83.

[4] *Ibid.*, p. 83.

pened, the party was more centralist than democratic. French repression and the necessity to act clandestinely confirmed this tendency, for when its leaders were in jail the party had to be directed by inconspicuous successors co-opted instead of elected.[5]

Large numbers of young men learned of politics through the Neo-Destour; they discovered the skills of cooperation and the necessity for discipline and self-restraint in coordinated political action. Local party federations were the training grounds, although the party provided opportunities for the more eager or skillful to improve their capacities and understanding as they rose in the party ranks.

Like their French models, the leaders of the Neo-Destour developed a series of "national organizations," grouping workers (in the Union Générale des Travailleurs Tunisiens [UGTT]), farmers in a farmer's union (the Union Générale des Agriculteurs Tunisiens [UGAT]), and students (in the Union Générale des Etudiants Tunisiens [UGET]), to mobilize large numbers for the independence effort. These bodies proved a mixed blessing to Bourguiba, since at times it was hard to tell whether they were the party's instrument for reaching and organizing large numbers in the population, or whether they were special interest groups with privileged access to the party's councils.[6]

Two internal crises were precipitated by leaders of such nonparty organizations affiliated with the party. Ben Youssef, leader of the party's guerrilla wing set up to fight French rule by direct action, and Ben Salah, popular leader of the party's trade union affiliate, used the popularity and organizational base they developed in these activities, as Bourguiba saw it, to challenge his leadership. In the first instance, Bourguiba had Ben Youssef exiled from Tunisia, and he died mysteriously in Frankfurt. Ben Salah was removed from his trade-union leadership and, after a period in the political wilderness, brought back in the apparently safe job of Minister of Health. He eventually gained new importance as Bourguiba's Secretary of State for Finance and the Plan.

Through the political control the party made possible, Bourguiba operated a subtle strategy of alternating direct pressure and cooperation vis-à-vis the French; this culminated in a negotiated independence in 1956. Tunisia was thus spared the casualties, destruction, and overgrowth of the army, which has left such an unhappy legacy for future orderly civilian governance in Algeria.

[5] Ibid., pp. 84-85.
[6] Ibid., pp. 86-88, 100-07.

After independence, the party remained the armature of all political power in the country. The bureaucracy early came under its command as Bourguiba's nationalist program won the support of many younger officials, and as top administrative positions were filled by the party faithful. Elements of social power were, in the main, integrated through the party's national organizations. Jobs, economic opportunity, and local and district improvements were available mainly through the party or its affiliates. And so long as Bourguiba retained control at the party apex, he retained effective control of the polity.

Bourguiba devoted considerable attention to the problem of incipient party factions. By shifting political lieutenants, disgracing those who seemed to be gaining popularity and bringing them back as chastened men, he gave little opportunity for factions to become consolidated.[7]

Bourguiba has been remarkably successful at building a party and using it as a base for his continued preponderance over Tunisia's polity. He strengthened national unity, promoted economic development, sustained internal peace, confirmed civilian dominance, and won for Tunisia respect abroad. But as C. H. Moore has pointed out, at the heart of Bourguiba's rule is a dangerous paradox concerning succession. To assure his own preponderant rule, he sought to break up all incipient factions. In this he appeared successful. But where factions cannot emerge, prospective successors cannot show themselves, test their political skills, or develop a personal following of their own on whom they will be able to rely when they have to take power in his stead. Such fragmentation keeps the system open, by permitting the leader to be accessible to diverse groups and individuals, but it inhibits the growth of stable factions which might have a stake in democratic procedures after he goes. To stay in power he appealed directly to the coming generation, but, when he dies, they may not have attached themselves to anyone in the succeeding ruling group, and they may be extremist or repressive in their own actions as a result.[8]

Bourguiba, therefore, is a dramatic example of the man at the center of a political organization which is playing a critical role in many countries. The success of his rule is, in substantial measure

[7] Clement Henry Moore, *Tunisia Since Independence, The Dynamics of One-Party Government* (Berkeley, University of California, 1965, 230 pp.), p. 119.

[8] *Ibid.*, p. 205.

the result of the organization he has built. The vulnerabilities of the system are shared by all such regimes. A more general discussion of political organizations will suggest the types of organization leaders have found useful and the limitations of these organizations in aggregating power.

MANY TYPES OF ORGANIZATION

As a strategy for aggregating power, organizing can have many meanings. The most obvious modern organization specializing in politics is the political party, and most of the discussion will be concerned with contrasting types of parties. But there are other forms of organization, too, which deserve brief mention.

The organization and manipulation of *cliques* may be central to politics, as in Thailand or the Philippines. A leader may develop an informal "organization" within the bureaucracy or army, using his position of command to adjust promotions and assignments so as to place "his" men in key positions. He may need that network of men loyal to him to push his enterprises or to support, even protect, him in time of crisis. Particularly if a regime comes to power by coup d'état, its leaders must first assure the loyalty of the army by highly discriminating promotions, transfers, and retirements of all who are in reach of command positions. Reassignments in the bureaucracy and police may also be necessary. A number of regimes have survived for some time without a more sophisticated political organization than this, including Nasser's and Ayub's during the early years and General Sarit's in Thailand. Some regimes, like Prime Minister Daud's in Afghanistan prior to 1963, concentrate their organizational activities in the bureaucratic realm, as long as other, more overt political organizations are discouraged or have not yet developed.

Some may promote *political machines*, analogous to those of nineteenth-century United States urban politics, where electoral victory or more general acquiescence is won through the systematic granting of patronage opportunities for wealth or of personal services which state institutions cannot provide or by withholding "protection" or other assets from those who do not show themselves willing to support the machine. Politics in some cities in India and the early activities of certain West African leaders are said to have been close to these practices.[9]

A *movement* can have a profound though often temporary political effect. It focuses on highly emotional appeals and is marked by informal membership, which is determined more by the individual's subjective adherence than formal criteria of affiliation. It projects a vision of a completely reformed society, which taps the flow of emotion latent in large numbers of individuals and gives meaning and order to those who participate. It differs from a party in the intensity of the feeling it evokes and by the looseness of its armature, which often results in its only fleeting effectiveness. Substantial efforts may go into organizing a movement, and a number of leaders have gained prominence and based their organizations on a movement at the outset. But its effects will not provide a steady base of power, unless it is organized into something closer to what we understand as a party.[10]

TYPES AND FUNCTIONS OF POLITICAL PARTIES

No leader has entirely free choice in the kind of party he seeks to organize. He may inherit a party, ready-made. In the main, major existing parties are the result of political agitation and organization leading to independence. A leader's political circumstances, the interests and capabilities of his entourage, and what he believes his opponents are up to will affect his organizational activities. He may feel obliged to settle on only one type of party, since in no other way can he aggregate any power at all. Yet each type serves somewhat different political purposes more efficiently; and his choice may therefore be related to the political ends he seeks. No one real party will be an embodiment of any single model; each is in fact a mixed type. At least four different types of political parties can be distinguished.[11]

[9] See for instance, Myron Weiner, *Party-Building in a New Nation: The Indian National Congress* (Chicago, University of Chicago Press, 1967, 509 pp.), Ch. 6.

[10] David Apter, *The Politics of Modernization* (Chicago and London, University of Chicago Press, 1965, 481 pp.), pp. 204-06, 210-11.

[11] For example, Maurice Duverger's *Political Parties* (London, Methuen, 1951, 439 pp.) used mainly European and North American examples; Thomas Hodgkin's *African Political Parties* (London, Penguin, 1961, 217 pp.) was a pioneering

Ethnic, tribal, or regional parties enlist support on grounds of particularistic, traditional affilations. Examples are the Dravida Munnetra Kazhagam (DMK) in southern India, the Sudanese Liberal Party, and the Ashanti-based National Liberation Movement (NLM) in Ghana. Stressing the particular distinctiveness of those who belong to one or another traditional grouping, they have been concerned above all with "boundary maintenance." They emphasize the threats to that group's autonomy from others in the nation. They call upon historical conflicts in the society to justify their continued separateness. Often, they depend upon the traditional authority structure in the locality to bring followers, but they may also appeal directly to the deeper emotions of common blood or regional or linguistic solidarity to enlist a plebeian following. The aspiring leader will have to stress traditional local virtues, and the superiority of the group he seeks to lead as compared to all others in the society. There is no easier way for a leader to identify himself with his followers. It will require little organizational skill to activate them.

His objectives may be limited. He may use the improved bargaining position his organizational activities give him to extract more autonomy, investment, services, or whatever his constituency desires from the central government than would be granted if he did not organize. He may have wider aims, however, hoping to lead a secession movement and form a new state, although often threats of secession may simply be used as bargaining devices to extract more for his people. In India, for example, the DMK in Madras threatened secession, thereby winning support from the Tamil enthusiasts who wanted to demonstrate resistance to what they felt to be the often overbearing Aryan northerner. It also served to demonstrate to New Delhi the depth of feeling in Madras against Delhi's proposals to make Hindi the sole official language. There are still some doubts about how seriously Mohammed Ali Jinnah believed in partition at the beginning. Originally he may have sought to use the idea of

---

study of parties in that continent for which there is no comparable study on the Middle East or South Asia. *Political Parties and Political Development* edited by Myron Weiner and Joseph La Palombara (Princeton, Princeton University Press, 1966, 487 pp.) adds to our understanding. For a critical report, see Immanuel Wallerstein on "The Decline of the Party in the Single-Party African State," *Ibid.*, pp. 201-16. For a critique of writing on West African parties, see Zolberg, *Creating Political Order.*

Pakistan to improve his and the Muslim's bargaining position in future negotiations with the Indian National Congress.[12]

If the leader has ambitions to play a sustained role on the national stage, such a party has the advantage of providing the prospective leader with a relatively secure political base at home. On the other hand, its imperatives will usually lead to his political isolation from many elements in the wider nation, since to maintain his position in his own area he must stress how different he is from others in the nation.

Such parties may contribute to group cohesion if their activities result in drawing together into common action still smaller entities which hitherto have acted separately. They can promote the dignity and pride of minorities. But they also perpetuate differences, sharpen group tensions, and impede national integration.

A *patron party* encompasses more diverse elements in loose association.[13] It draws together notables, respected heads of different tribes, ethnic or other traditional groups, or leaders of more modern associations who nevertheless can "deliver" the political support of their followers. A patron party does not mobilize a mass following; it settles for aggregating political followings already in existence. As such it is bound to be conservative. The leader is usually well-born himself and has at his disposal a body of followers who are "reliable" by virtue of traditional loyalties. He usually has to be personally acceptable to the leaders of other groups in the society as a result of his family status, his unusual wealth, his personal qualities, or some notable exploit on behalf of his people. He must devote great effort to accommodating the interests of those he seeks to build into a coalition. His major skill, therefore, must be quiet, face-to-face negotiations or bargaining and an attentiveness to a host of local interests.

He must be willing to put up with loose political ties wherein a segment may periodically threaten to withdraw unless its particular interests are met. New groups may have to be attracted to replace the defectors. His ambitions for aggregating power, therefore, must

---

[12] Pendrel Moon, *Divide and Quit* (London, Chatto and Windus, 1961, 302 pp.), p. 21.

[13] Ruth S. Morgenthau, *Political Parties in French-speaking West Africa*, p. 237; see also her "Single-Party Systems in West Africa," *American Political Science Review* (June, 1961), pp. 204-307.

be modest. His policy objectives must be similarly limited, since he will have to work on the basis of consensus reached among near equals. Bold policies requiring sacrifice or radical innovations are generally avoided. Such a party usually moderates confrontations and imposes on its leaders a willingness to settle for half-loaves and for many compromises. It is likely to represent the diversity of interests in the plural society and thus make for a certain stability which may be lacking where more ambitious ends are sought.

The early United National Party (UNP) in Ceylon was of this sort. It combined locally prominent notables and acknowledged leaders of the minority and majority communities in an extensive coalition. Its policy aims were moderate; it was not a mass-action party, but one where political participation was generally limited to the few at the top who dealt quietly with one another. Bargains were struck and actual adjustments between communities and interest groups made with little mass agitation—though the active political community was so small and the newspapers sufficiently enterprising for many of these activities to become public knowledge fairly promptly.[14] The Alliance Party in Malaysia has been a combination of ethnic elements —Chinese and Indian—associated with the Malay majority. In the Malay community, the Alliance represents a combination of notables, whose following can be counted upon on traditional grounds of support, and younger men in the party apparatus who have risen from humble backgrounds through education and participation in the public service. The Chinese and Indians have participated in the Alliance through their own, relatively conservative, community representatives. Most difficulties are hard-bargained behind closed doors, while the public presentation is of a noncontroversial, reassuring sort, exactly personified by the Tungku.[15]

Such a party can be politically successful against parties of similar type or where the distribution of rights and values is to remain much as it has been. However, it is not likely to be sufficiently sustained in action to compete successfully for electoral success against an integrated mass party or, if more direct political action is contem-

[14] Wriggins, Ceylon, Ch. 5.

[15] Willard H. Hanna, Eight Nation Makers: Southeast Asia's Charismatic States-men (New York, St. Martin's Press, 1964, 307 pp.), pp. 93-95. For an analysis of the Malaysian political system, see R. S. Milne, Government and Politics in Malaysia (Boston, Houghton Mifflin, 1967, 259 pp.).

plated, against a determined colonial administration or a protracted and organized insurgency.[16]

An authoritarian "mass" party can be used for pursuing more ambitious goals, but it will require greater application and effort. The leader does not need to be well-born; he is more likely to be a commoner in origin. His party will seek to escape the dominance of the notables by entering their preserves and attracting directly their erstwhile followers. It will be necessary to penetrate and eventually capture existing organizations and mold them to the party's needs. Many new party-controlled auxiliary organizations, such as youth groups, women's circles, farmers' unions, neighborhood sections, and so forth, will also have to be created if the party is to mobilize large numbers of people for party activity and prevent political opposition from growing. Political competitors will be eliminated whenever possible.

Building such a party and its auxiliaries requires a large number of enthusiastic and dedicated lieutenants who are relatively free of traditional attachments, possessed of the conviction that prolonged and detailed organizational efforts are necessary and armed with the necessary skills. The leader, therefore, must devote substantial effort to sustaining their commitment, for if their enthusiasm flags the whole enterprise may fall.

The leader of such a party is likely to promote an ideology to sustain his militants, impress the larger multitude with his superior knowledge and provide a conception of common purpose. These usually sketch with a broad brush the innovations the party intends to achieve, including rapid economic development, social equality, and dramatized independence. Since these goals taken together are rather grand objectives, great energies must be mounted to achieve them. This, in turn, involves more organizational effort and growing political pressures.

If rapid changes are to be pressed or competition from traditional leaders eliminated, tribal, ethnic, or other traditional leaders must be

[16] The contrasting types of "patron" and "mass" parties are developed most clearly in writings on Africa and are discussed by Hodgkin, *African Political Parties*, Ch. 4; Morgenthau, *Political Parties in French-speaking West Africa*, pp. 336-37; and Apter, *The Politics of Modernization*, Ch. 6. For Ceylon, see Wriggins, *Ceylon*, pp. 106-19; for Philippines, see Taylor, *The Philippines and the United States*, pp. 156-57; for Ivory Coast, see Zolberg, *One-Party Government in the Ivory Coast*, pp. 76-143; for Nigeria, see Sklar, *Nigerian Political Parties*, pp. 474-94; for Syria, see Torrey, *Syrian Politics*, pp. 51-52.

undermined. Land reform liquidated the pashas in Nasser's Egypt; Nkrumah's Convention People's Party (CPP) in Ghana penetrated the chieftains' bailiwicks for a time and turned local grievances against them, and constitutional reforms provided for local bodies with powers to perform the notables' former functions. Expropriation may eliminate substantial business interests.[17] Great ends, it appears, can be sought; compromise with outmoded social entities is no longer necessary. It seems as if one can press forward to social and economic transformation without concern for those who formerly possessed privileges in these inequitable societies, or who held influence over others on traditional grounds.

In the Middle East, the early Baathist party aspired to such an organization and role; in Tunisia, the Neo-Destour approaches it in many respects. In Africa, Nkrumah sought to make his CPP into such an instrument, as did Sékou Touré his Partie Democratique in Guinea.[18] The principal model for such mass parties has been European socialist or communist parties, usually observed in action during student days or publicized since then by communists—or by their opponents who have unwittingly provided the most persuasive endorsement of this approach to organization. To the leaders of authoritarian mass parties such organizational methods hold out the promise of eliminating competition, both within their own entourage and, by apparently destroying alternative centers of power, outside the party, too. But Nkrumah's overthrow suggests that a mass party of mobilization is harder to organize than it is to imagine, and that organizational forms are easier to establish than is the sense of inner commitment and institutional solidarity which must sustain such ambitious party building.[19]

Democratic mass parties, like the Indian National Congress, sought wider coalitions than did authoritarian mass parties. By mutual adjustment, complicated organizational efforts, and generalized ideology, Congress leaders aspired to absorb a great variety of interests into one inclusive party. Though modern in ideology and formal

[17] P. J. Vatikiotis, The Egyptian Army in Politics, (Bloomington, Indiana, Indiana University Press, 1961, 300 pp.), pp. 77, 98; Austin, Politics in Ghana, pp. 377-78.
[18] For detailed discussion, see Gwendolen M. Carter (ed.), African One-Party States (Ithaca, Cornell University Press, 1962, 501 pp.) in contrast to Zolberg, Creating Political Order.
[19] Henry L. Bretton, The Rise and Fall of Kwame Nkrumah (New York, Praeger, 1966, 232 pp.), p. 171; Zolberg, p. 98.

organization, the Congress Party was built on numberless traditional linguistic, regional, caste, and subcaste groupings. Like leaders of an authoritarian mass party, they sought to activate the masses through a set of auxiliary organizations. By the party's inclusiveness, they attempted to lure those ambitious for public careers, since for a time no other party seemed more likely to provide a way to office. Like leaders of the other "mass" parties, Congress leaders projected an image, however imprecise, of what the future of the nation could be. Among their many activities, they placed substantial doctrinal and administrative stress on expanding the economy and changing the society. But the mood, the pace and the results have been different.

Congress leaders did not attempt to make it a national monopoly party. Political opposition at the margins was permitted, allowing among other things, concern for local issues to be voiced which the preoccupation with national goals might otherwise ignore. Political competition helped to keep party militants from the privilege and sloth more familiar in single-party states. Particular regional and local challenges produced a considerable turnover in party personnel and in elected representatives. A combination of machine politics and open electoral processes was used to help deal with open dis-agreements within the party.[20]

Seeking to impose less of its own doctrinal views and not eliminat-ing, either figuratively or literally, those who disagree with it, the party leadership has tried to moderate competing interests. Compared to most regimes, intimidation has been minimized and bargaining, negotiating, and mutual adjustments have been marked.

Such parties generate less antagonism than the more doctrinaire and determined authoritarian parties; they appear to move less rapidly but, in the end, may accomplish more. Because they are being more sensitive to existing forces, they are more likely to promote gradual growth and change than to succeed in rapidly transforming their societies. Such parties do not fall to pieces after the death of their great leaders, as have the authoritarian parties of Africa, though they are weakened, of course, when a leader like Nehru goes. They represent perhaps the closest approximations to a solution to the

[20] For the best study of the Congress Party to date, see Myron Weiner, *Party-Building in a New Nation: The Indian National Congress*. For the relationship between traditional subgroups and political organization, see Lloyd and Susanne H. Rudolph, *The Modernity of Tradition—Political Development in India* (Chicago, University of Chicago Press, 1967, 306 pp.), pp. 24-29.

problem of the sustained aggregation of power, subject to orderly representative influences, to be developed outside the North Atlantic democracies. The Congress Party in India and the Partido Revolucionario Institucional (PRI) in Mexico are the principal examples. They have taken time to develop; no one community or ethnic group was large enough to presume to rule over all the diversity of either country; in the early years, and subsequently, leaders were remarkable and were clearly committed to democratic political practices. But such parties, too, have liabilities. The election of 1967 demonstrated in India, at least, that the days of assured rule are always numbered.

Each of these party types serves certain common functions. They are intermediaries between public and government. They select, groom and present leaders to a polity. They may do this in an open, pluralistic, and competitive setting, or they may do it secretly and without public participation. Except when leaders are displaced by a coup d'état, parties have been the means for dealing with the problem of succession by installing new leaders and bestowing on them whatever legitimacy the party itself commands.

Both types of mass parties perform additional functions.[21] Where the total society is marked by ethnic or tribal differentiations and wide cultural gaps among classes or other groupings, mass parties, such as the Congress Party in India or the Partie Democratique de Guinée, may enhance a sense of unity. It helps to project a common vision of national purpose, which may become part of the new political culture for the future. It brings peoples from diverse walks of life and segments of society into working proximity.[22] By linking parochial entities and hitherto passive groups to the national governernment, such parties provide indispensable communication which may be otherwise lacking. Inclusive parties may weaken the urgency of regional aspirations as they open opportunities for the ambitious, regardless of their region or community of origin, as in the example of the Neo-Destour in Tunisia and the Congress Party in India.[23]

---

[21] On the multiple functions of parties in Africa, see Hodgkin, *African Political Parties*, Chs. 5, 6, and 7; for the Middle East, see Halpern, *The Politics of Social Change in the Middle East and North Africa*, Ch. 14; also Weiner and La Palombara, *Political Parties and Political Development*.

[22] Halpern, *Ibid.*, pp. 282-83; Micaud, *Tunisia*, pp. 187-88.

[23] The Communist Party of Indonesia (KPI) is said to have performed this function. Feith, *The Decline of Constitutional Democracy in Indonesia*, p. 540.

Where parties exist in a relatively sharply stratified society, and bureaucratic and business opportunities are restricted by status, inherited wealth or family connections, a political party may be a channel for upward mobility for the ambitious and the gifted. In the mass parties, auxiliaries provide new social entities for those who no longer are part of traditional structures. Party activities directed toward influencing opinions, changing power relations, and promoting government policy can affect attitudes toward political cause and effect. They can demonstrate that organized effort makes a difference, that political events do not simply happen as a result of incantations, inhuman forces, or inherited positions, but are the fruit of individual and collective effort.

A ruling party can play a direct political role as well. It can strengthen the position of friends and allies and weaken the position of opponents as the party leaders prepare for periodic political tests, such as elections, or for unexpected challenges. If it has a near monopoly of political control, it can leave an opponent without lieutenants by offering the more able and ambitious among them politically promising jobs within the ruling party or bureaucracy.[24] Through the party, leaders may seek to ensure that the bureaucracy does not function simply for the benefit of itself but meets the needs of at least some of the populace. Successful parties can bring the leader's influence to bear to check up on bureaucratic performance, stimulating a more energetic pursuit of development goals, promoting public support for necessary bureaucratic action, or directing criticism against bureaucratic sloth.[25]

They may also bend bureaucratic procedures to make certain that some portion of bureaucratic power and assets is used for the party's advantage. The bureaucracy, after all, can set the terms for political competition by the scope for opposition it permits or the way it supervises elections. It may provide all kinds of patronage and other inducements to political "regularity," including the distribution of contracts, scholarships, import licenses, and the location of schools, hospitals, roads, and so forth.

Even such an ineffectual "party" as Nasser's Arab Socialist Union (ASU) may be useful, since it provides a visible front behind which

[24] Zolberg, *One-Party Government in the Ivory Coast*, p. 188.

[25] In India, "Ginger groups" within the Congress Party see this as one of their important tasks; similar views can be found in African party discussions. On Tunisia, see Micaud, *Tunisia*, p. 69; on the Ivory Coast, Zolberg, *Ibid.*, p. 327.

the real political game is played. Leaders of the ASU can be thrown to the wolves when things go badly. Such a lightning-rod party catches mass hostility and conducts it safely past the president, who remains unharmed by its possibly destructive energy.

The leader may see a party not necessarily as an instrument for forwarding his own interests, but as a means of establishing a countervailing power to check the bureaucracy, army, or other weighty power group he fears, as Sukarno used the PKI to balance off the army.[26]

In certain areas of Africa, parties have even taken on quasi-administrative functions of collecting taxes and administering justice and public order. More frequently, they undertake social welfare functions for their members. These are presumed to recompense party members for the risks they ran in the party's service and reflect the professionalization of political activity in the mass parties, where members have no other means of support but party aid—or what they can acquire as a result of their personal influence within the party. More generalized welfare measures by the party enhance its reputation as a body of men and women devoted to the uplift and comfort of the common man, as the Indian Congress Party stressed its "constructive work" in the early years.[27]

The prudent political leader will seek to identify new and rising groups within his society, and cast his appeals to win them to his party. But this is not an easy organizational principle to apply, since it is often difficult to determine when a particular "rising" group is sufficiently numerous, self-conscious, or possessed of enough political potential to be worth going after, if the price of winning it is to lose some allies who already may be on one's own side. Not infrequently, an effort is made to identify the appeals which will attract the emergent middle-class groups, who are possessed of more modern skills and goals but who have not yet found a satisfactory place within the transitional society. Equally critical may be individuals in key intermediary or professional roles linking the rural or urban masses with larger, national issues.[28]

---

[26] Feith in Kahin, Government and Politics of Southeast Asia, p. 245.

[27] Hodgkin, African Political Parties, Ch. 6, and pp. 142-46, p. 167; Zolberg, Ibid., pp. 119-21; Austin, Politics in Ghana, p. 378; The Indian Congress has long had special units concerned with welfare and uplift.

[28] The role of key intermediaries has been noted by Lucian Pye, "The Non-Western Political Process," The Journal of Politics, Vol. XX, No. 3 (August,

Regardless of the type of party, funds must be raised, differences within the entourage ironed out, and decisions made on who should be sought as allies or dealt with as opponents. The patron party may receive larger contributions from a few sources, who may fear a more radical party might take its place, while the mass party may raise its money by membership contributions or by the kind of intimidation which authoritatively organized numbers can bring to bear. In both cases, the most tempting means of financing party expenses is to gain governmental power and tap government resources. Indeed, it is often difficult for successful leaders and parties to distinguish between government and party in this respect. Travel expenses, salaries, and other returns presumably received by individuals for performing official functions often are directed toward covering party activities.[29]

In practice, parties usually include characteristics of both patron and mass party types. Parties are living institutions which change as their leadership gains experience, as their tasks alter following independence and as challenges develop from competing political leaders and parties, or from internal tensions. Few are the patron parties which do not make some effort to cope with the realm of ideas and induce certain social and economic innovations; some develop complex sets of party auxiliaries. Few are the authoritarian mass parties which succeed in sustained mobilization of the masses, exerting firm discipline and fully encompassing the individual members. Nearly all the mass parties aspiring to unitary structures must come to terms with leaders of certain traditional groups or with dominant local personalities in the regions. They thus often have within them segments which bring them nearer to the patron party than they care to admit. Chiefs in the districts in Ghana had a place in the Convention People's Party, major ethnic groups have had to be recognized in the Partie Democratique in Guinea and within the

---

1958), 468-86; Wriggins, Ceylon, pp. 337-48; a new "middle class" is increasingly being identified by scholars, see Halpern, The Politics of Social Change, Ch. 4; Sklar, Nigerian Political Parties, pp. 487-94.

[29] See for example, Coleman and Rosberg, Political Parties and National Integration in Tropical Africa, p. 80; Wilson on Thailand, Politics in Thailand, pp. 238-39; Wraith and Simpkins, Corruption in Developing Countries, pp. 52-53; The latter pioneering study of a very difficult subject points out that British practice in most of the eighteenth and nineteenth centuries closely paralleled much that can be seen in emerging countries today; Zolberg, One-Party Government, pp. 193-94; on Syria, see Torrey, Syrian Politics, p. 51.

Tanganyika African National Union Party (TANU) in Tanganyika. The Indian Congress Party, long aspiring to be a democratic mass party, has been dependent in many districts on local notables and on ethnic, caste, and other groups which lend—or threaten to withhold—their bloc support.[30]

LIABILITIES OF PARTY ORGANIZATION

Each of these different party types has its own liabilities. The ethnic party is too narrow for any but parochial political purposes. The patron party may not have enough organizational solidity or may be so dependent upon power groups in the society that it is unable to press for, or even adjust to, social change. It is particularly vulnerable to growing political mobilization as improved communications arouse political awareness, and new groups jostle staid political actors as they press to enter the political arena.

The authoritarian mass party, however tempting it may be, also has its difficulties. Sustaining political zeal and commitment to the ideology is difficult.[31] The ideal of intense and universal participation on behalf of party objectives is beyond reality, inducing leadership impatience and mass disenchantment. The party's pretension to authority and centralized control is most likely to evoke resistance among major power groups embedded in the regional, traditional, or more advanced sectors of society. As claims to inclusive authority rise, resistance will also mount. It is difficult to find enough dedicated and committed activists to man the party's proliferating organizations.

Indeed, the leader of the mass party is often caught in a vicious circle of interacting pressures; he frequently has to project ever more ambitious ends in order to enlist his lieutenants, further raising, in

[30] Hodgkin, *African Political Parties*, p. 90; Philip Whitaker, *Political Theory and East African Problems* (London, Oxford University Press, 1964, 116 pp.), p. 68; William J. M. McKenzie and Kenneth Robinson (eds.), *Five Elections in Africa* (Oxford, The Clarendon Press, 1960, 496 pp.), conclude that where elections are serious, "all African Parties tend to become tribal parties," p. 484; on India, see Harrison, *India*, Ch. 7; Hugh Tinker, *India and Pakistan*, Ch. 5; Myron Weiner, *Party-Building in a New Nation: The Indian National Congress, passim*.

[31] R. Michels in Talcott Parsons (ed.) *Theories of Society* (New York, Free Press of Glencoe, 1962, 2 vols.), p. 604.

turn, popular hopes and requiring more dramatic changes if such hopes are to be realized. These sharpen the antagonism of those who are reluctant to change or to make more effort, and they also require ever more sacrifice from the populace. In turn, these steps increase friction and require still more party discipline and energy.[32]

Party auxiliaries, originally developed to activate and bring under wider party control large numbers of nonparty people, may make demands of their own.[33] Labor or student unions come to shape and press their own claims for scarce resources. At first, they may forward these claims within the party's inner councils. But as they gain coherence, numbers, and capacity, they may make their claims in public where none were made before or were made to less effect. Korea's student movement began as an auxiliary support of Syngman Rhee's regime. On call to demonstrate popular acclaim, it ended up by precipitating the overthrow of the regime. Ambitious lieutenants may use the prestige they have developed in the auxiliary to challenge the central leadership—as Bourguiba feared in the case of Ben Salah, and as Nkrumah took his Youth Organization out of the United Gold Coast Convention (UGCC) and used it to build his own political career.[34] If it successfully achieves a monopoly of power, the authoritarian mass party will lose the stimulus of competition. Its leader is likely to become increasingly authoritarian. Lieutenants are more chary of differing with the leader and are likely to become increasingly arrogant toward the people. Such a party risks becoming flabby and corrupt, and early mobilizational activities degenerate into ritual and mere talk, as Arthur Lewis observed in Ghana.[35]

The more consensual, democratic mass party also has difficulties. The need to work within an extensive and inclusive consensus may lead to policy stalemate; the nexus of conflicting aspirations and diverse views regarding political means and ends may block decisions and promote policy timidity. Because alternatives remain open for specific power groups in the society which a mass party seeks to eliminate altogether, important elements of the coalition can

[32] Douglas Ashford, The Elusiveness of Power: The African Single Party State (Ithaca, Cornell University Press, 1965, 31 pp.), p. 17.

[33] Coleman and Rosberg, Political Parties and National Integration in Tropical Africa, pp. 302-03.

[34] Ibid., pp. 271-72.

[35] Arthur Lewis, "Beyond African Dictatorship: The Crisis of the One-Party State," Encounters, Vol. XXV, No. 2 (August, 1965), 3-18; Zolberg, Creating Political Order, pp. 34, 98; Bretton, Rise and Fall of Kwame Nkrumah, p. 66.

bargain again and again with the leader, inducing levels of corruption which are likely to rise as the party continues in power. The original zeal of the early movement days may give way to increasing dependence on patronage and place seeking. And once a party dependent on patronage loses an election through factionalism, public anger against its particular policies or inability to cope with a local crisis, it has difficulty in rebuilding, because it has lost control of the source of its patronage—the public treasury, job assignments, or bureaucratic discretionary decision.[36] Up through the party may come contenders to challenge the leader, which historically may be good for the party but which the leader himself may not appreciate.

No matter what the organization, time spent in organizational matters is often time taken from policy problems, and vice versa, so that Prime Minister Nyerere had to leave government in order to rebuild his party organization; U Nu stepped down in 1956 to "cleanse" the party; the Tungku Abdul Rahman temporarily resigned his prime ministership to prepare the United Malays' National Organization (UMNO) for elections in 1959. Those who have been ministers for some time often find their party support eroding, for they have not had time to devote to organizational matters. In India, the Kamaraj Plan was said to have been designed in part to meet this need by relieving a number of cabinet members of their posts presumably so that they could return to their states and rebuild the party base.[37]

Party organizations may begin to make claims on both the leader and the political system, pressing specific party interests on the leadership or providing to members the perquisites and profits accessible in many societies only from positions of ministerial and administrative responsibility. Parties may thus become more a source of direct pressure on the leader and of exploitation of the system than they are reliable instruments of the leader's will.

All groups can be affected in one way or another by different organizational strategies. Army and bureaucracy can be influenced by the ruler's efforts to build his "organization" of personal followers

[36] Weiner, *Party Building in a New Nation*, Ch. 1.

[37] On the Tungku's resignation, see Hanna, *Eight Nation Makers*, p. 112; on India, Michael Brecher, *Nehru's Mantle, The Politics of Succession in India* (New York, Praeger, 1966, 269 pp.), p. 9. On Burma, Louis J. Walinsky, "The Rise and Fall of U Nu," *Pacific Affairs*, Vol. XXXVIII, Nos. 3 and 4 (Fall and Winter 1965/66), 269-281.

into these critical institutions. Traditional elements in the society are more easily drawn along in a patron-type party which, by its nature, seeks to accommodate and not to mobilize these elements, at least so long as they do not actively attempt to bring the ruler down. They will generally resist efforts of a mass party to mobilize them or to modernize their bailiwicks. Landowners can be approached through a patron or through a mass democratic party like India's National Congress. As seen through an authoritarian mass party, by contrast, they are likely to appear more as appropriate targets for elimination than as useful intermediaries to the rural populace and regular sources of party revenue.

Students and intellectuals are more likely to be drawn to an authoritarian mass party, at least at the outset, for they are attracted by the promise of its vaulting goals and the excitement of participating in its manifold activities. But their critical abilities make them unreliable allies for a party presuming to exert authoritarian control, and the leader may find, as did Nkrumah, that the less well-educated and finicky may be more amenable and useful. The talents of the more highly educated, however, may be lost to the regime.

Businessmen are more likely to prefer a patron-type party, which leaves more room for their initiative. But since their activities require access to governments with increasingly detailed regulatory powers, rulers can expect them to accommodate in one way or another to any mode of political organization except those which seek outright liquidation of their assets and absorption of their functions. The main target of businessmen's "political" activities will be the bureaucrats who actually administer the regulations. However, if the party is clearly responsible for specific decisions affecting them, businessmen are likely to attend to the needs of the party as well.

Trade unionists can also be influenced through most organizational forms. Since they usually have the strength of numbers on their side and are organized around worker grievances, they are not likely to work closely with the ruler for long unless he turns the economy to their exclusive—and usually temporary—benefit. The authoritarian mass party provides the most inclusive framework for mobilizing them, although in order to gain control a leader must either win union leadership to his side, quietly replace it with more cooperative leaders, or precipitate a fight and capture existing unions—steps which may alienate rather than consolidate a labor following. The democratic mass party may set up its own competing unions, but these are caught in the dilemma of winning adherents by opposing government policies or by being "responsible" and losing adherents. Only in rare cases can a government provide enough rewards to fully win them.

Despite the liabilities parties may have within them and their limitations as instruments for mobilizing and sustaining an assured following, the strategy of building a political organization of some kind is second only to that of attempting to project the personality. Few political leaders succeed in gaining power by methods other than a military coup d'état unless they have invested substantial effort in developing a political party. Few can stay in power for any length of time if they do not have something akin to a political party, unless they control the state through army and bureaucracy alone. Utilizing a political party is also a major component in most of the other strategies to be discussed.

7 Promote an Ideology

The creation of a doctrine has often been one of the very first steps along the road to power.

Barrington Moore, Jr.

Creating a doctrine may be one of the steps along the road to power, as Barrington Moore maintains. It is also one of the preoccupations of leaders once they gain power. The doctrine or ideology they promote will vary with the individual, the time, and the place, but few leaders are prepared to do without the effort to develop and to popularize an ideology.

By "ideology" we intend something both more and less than "a systematic scheme or coordinate body of ideas about human life and culture."[1] The notion here is more than ideology, because we are concerned with the realm of emotional and intellectual commitment, a definition of purpose and an orientation toward action. It is something less because often ideologies propounded by the leaders of emerging countries are anything but systematic. Ideologies in this sense are the means in the realm of ideas by which political leaders

[1] Cited by Sigmund, *The Ideologies of the Developing Nations*, p. 3.

129

and their entourage attempt to affect the perceptions, the goals, the attitudes and, ultimately, the actions of political followers. They are also the prism through which political leaders peer at their reality, sometimes distorting it, sometimes illuminating it with a particularly sharp light. One type may be likened to a "political religion," all-encompassing, unchallengeable, somewhat mysterious.[2] Another is the more logically elaborated ideologies of western European revolutionary politics, romantic perhaps, but intellectually developed. There are ranges in-between.

AN EXAMPLE: NYERERE OF TANZANIA.

One example of a leader who has devoted considerable attention to developing and promoting his own ideology is Julius Nyerere, President of Tanganyika African National Union Party (TANU) for many years, and President of Tanganyika since independence in 1961. He has been a prolific writer and speaker, projecting his ideas on the nature of the good polity, the proper political organization, the tasks and rights of the citizen, and the necessities of the state. However rich and varied his ideological output, it has not provided the guide to the state of mind and political action for which he appears to have hoped. But his ideas have affected the style, the sense of priorities, and the rules of the political game in Tanzania.[3] And the subjects which he found it desirable to discuss are characteristic of the articulated concerns of other rulers in Africa and Asia.

Like many other leaders, Nyerere extolled the virtues of the traditional society and argued the desirability of combining these with constructive change, economic growth, and diversification. In the old days, he held, the villagers were contented, their small societies had means for resolving local disputes and for hearing the views of all before decisions were made by village or tribal councils. They were socialist in essentials—all worked hard for the benefit of the village;

[2] David Apter, "Political Religion in the New Nation," in Geertz, *Old Societies and New States*, pp. 57-104.

[3] Henry Bienen, *Tanzania: Party Transformation and Economic Development* (Princeton, Princeton University Press, 1967, 447 pp.), pp. 205, 250.

all were cared for if necessary.[4] Now that foreign rule is finished, these virtues can be reaffirmed.[5]

At the same time, national unity and an expanding economy have to be promoted. In Nyerere's view, "African Socialism," if reborn, could point the way to improving the quality and scope of brotherhood, represented by the traditional extended family, and to encouraging rapid, humane economic growth. His prescriptions for economic development remained vague.[6] They underlined the necessity for equality, hard work, and change. They stressed first the need for industrialization to bring self-confidence and prosperity and, later, agricultural improvement to meet the urgent food needs of a rapidly growing population.

Nyerere's ideology encompassed a view of Tanzania's place in the African world. He feared the "second scramble for Africa" in which outside powers would seek to regain positions of influence by arming one African state against another. He pressed for closer cooperation with his neighbors of East Africa.[7] It proved easier to appeal for unity than to sustain it, however, for in the event, Nyerere was one of the first to threaten to withdraw from the East African Common Services Administration.

For Nyerere, the single party held the key to national unity and economic development. Without it the multiple tribal divisions would become sharpened; with it these would be overcome as the spirit of brotherhood would gain strength. Open to all and not forced to gird for constant struggle against other parties, the single party was "more democratic" than parties in Western democracies. Such parties had to be disciplined and centralized to fight their opponents, and that discipline weakened the individuality and freedom of the party members.[8] Because TANU included everyone and there were no

[4] Julius Nyerere, "Ujamaa: The Basis of African Socialism," in Sigmund, The Ideologies of the Developing Nations (revised edition, 1967, 428 pp.), pp. 279-82.

[5] Fred G. Burke, "Tanganyika: The Search for Ujamaa," in Wilhelm H. Friedland and Carl G. Rosberg, Jr., African Socialism (Stanford, California, Stanford University Press, 1964, 313 pp.), pp. 206, 218.

[6] Bienen, Tanzania, p. 213.

[7] Julius Nyerere, "Nationalism and Pan-Africanism," in Sigmund, The Ideologies of the Developing Nations, pp. 205-11, p. 208.

[8] Government of Tanzania, Report of the Presidential Commission on the Establishment of Democratic One-Party State (Dar es Salaam Government Printer, 1965), p. 15, referred to in Bienen, Tanzania, p. 241.

capitalist exploiters permitted by the new regime, trade unions had no need to assert their political independence, as in capitalist countries, but were to be responsive to the political guidance of the party, like every other identifiable group.[9]

While the assertions appear totalitarian in aspiration, he was at pains to distinguish his party from the "doctrinaire socialists" and "Leninists." And in practice, TANU was not totalitarian. Nyerere himself was a liberal, moderate man. He urged brotherhood and unity, and in his political action he called for compromise, for including all rather than drawing sharp and exclusive lines separating the chosen few from the rest. At the same time, the reach of his ideology and his organization was limited.[10] The distance between the central government and the bulk of the tribal, rural people left plenty of room for traditional differences and familiar ways to persist.

Nyerere invested considerable time and energy in promoting his ideas. He wrote a number of books; he organized and instructed a special commission to study "Democracy and the Party System."[11] He spoke hundreds of times, often in excellent English which, along with his books, gave his ideological arguments a wide international audience. More often he spoke in Swahili, reaching across the distance separating him from the masses of the people. They hardly understood the niceties of his argument. But they applauded him as the "great teacher" or the "giver of truth," and appeared unprepared to have his ideas publicly challenged.[12] More important, as Bienen argues, the central government is in fact so far away from the urban and rural populace that: ". . . the political development of Tanzania consists largely in the center establishing contact. The frames of reference for looking at problems have a tendency to preempt the very political programs themselves."[13] And for many of the middle-level party and bureaucratic leaders in the districts and towns, their

---

[9] Julius Nyerere, "The Role of the African Trade Unions," in Sigmund, *The Ideologies of the Developing Nations*, pp. 202-05.

[10] Burke in Friedland and Rosberg, *African Socialism*, pp. 202, 204.

[11] For a further discussion of the party, see Rupert Emerson, "Parties and National Integration in Africa," Joseph La Palombara and Myron Weiner (eds.) *Political Parties and Political Development* (Princeton, Princeton University Press, 1966, 487 pp.), pp. 283-87. For an assessment of Nyerere's reach, see Bienen, *Tanzania*, Ch. 6.

[12] Bienen, *Tanzania*, p. 211 and *passim*, where it is pointed out no one directly challenged his views.

[13] *Ibid.*, p. 250.

frames of reference have been influenced by the ideology of Nyerere. It is these frames of reference which have so much to do with the way problems are presented, the priorities that are set, and the type of contact which is in fact established.

Nyerere was not able to convince many of the more authoritarian, radical and impatient in Tanzania and the newcomers who were accepted into the ministry and the bureaucracy when Zanzibar joined Tanganyika in 1964. Nor did his ideas take among all the middle-level leaders whose attitudes are of such importance in shaping Tanzania's future.[14] Younger cadres in particular have been impatient with his respect for tradition and his pragmatic, nondoctrinaire approaches to political action.[15] The fact remains, nevertheless, that Nyerere is a vivid example of the articulate, serious-minded leader who sought from the beginning to promote his ideology as a way of consolidating his political following, providing guidance to his lieutenants, unifying his new nation, and giving shape and direction to the government's activities.

It is easy for foreign scholars to exaggerate the real political role of political ideology. Publications have traditionally been the most authentic source of materials. Statements of doctrine, particularly of ideals and exhortations, are easiest for regimes or journalists to compile and disseminate and for scholars to collect. Elaborated ideologies may conceal and divert attention from the political reality more than they provide insight. Apparently addressed to the nation as a whole, ideologies may, in fact, be heard only by the few in the immediate circle, the intellectuals and the half-educated, who often talk more to each other than they speak to the condition of those who in fact control the levers of power. Despite these general cautions, ideology is an instrument of political power, and can perform many functions.

THE MANY FUNCTIONS OF POLITICAL IDEOLOGY

Perhaps first and foremost, ideologies are a means of deepening identity. Most politically relevant ideologies underline the people's unique history, the distant, glorious past, the years when the Solomons ruled over peaceful and extensive domains; when men

[14] *Ibid.*, p. 251.
[15] Burke in Friedland and Rosberg, *African Socialism*, p. 196.

were good, power benign, and the realm admired by all. The more recent, evil days of foreign rule are stressed. The ideology will define the devils who brought it about and the angels who sought to save and to restore the pre-colonial glory. The historic drama may be punctuated by ancient myths and folk tales which point up the lesson in an idiom familiar to those remaining within the tradition. Since the colonial era is seen as a period in which their own identity was gravely weakened by a false desire to emulate the ruler's culture and by faltering self-confidence among those who did not become accommodated to those foreign ways, the more the people's unique and honorable past can be evoked, the more self-respecting and confident they can now become, as Nyerere's efforts demonstrated.[16]

An ideology may contribute to greater unity. The search for a new solidarity, transcending traditional parochialism, may induce an effort to affect perception and idea. Somehow, the diverse and narrow loyalties of traditional social entities must be overcome by dramatizing and justifying a larger reality. An attempt is made to show that in identifying with the national realm, with something wider and stronger than the now familiar family, tribe, or regional identification, individuals and groups will be reassured against anxiety and become more prosperous in their endeavors and respected by their peers and former rulers. These arguments have been used by Nehru, Sukarno, Nasser, and others. Policies of "cultural management" designed to affect the content of school curricula and communications media on behalf of unity and purpose depend on ideologies for their substance.[17]

In single-party states, this new sense of identity and common destiny is to be experienced through unquestioned loyalty to the all-inclusive single party which, in its essence, allegedly embodies the single nation. For these, social differences may be ignored and their political relevance magically removed by the easy device of denial. Bourguiba and Nyerere often sought a way out by this device.[18] Leaders in other types of political systems are not so demanding or exclusive. But nearly all leaders, including Ataturk, Nehru, Nasser, Ayub, Sukarno, Nkrumah, and Sékou Touré, sought

---

[16] *Ibid.*, p. 206.

[17] See Marriott, "Cultural Policy in the New States," in Geertz, *Old Societies and New States*, pp. 27-56, for a discussion of cultural management.

[18] Ashford, *The Elusiveness of Power*, p. 25.

to confirm the identity of their people and develop a wider consciousness of solidarity and common destiny by reiterating a set of ideas presumed to have particular applicability to their own citizens.

Sometimes in this process, external scapegoats are picked out and reviled. The new self, in its fragile solidarity, may be depicted as beleaguered and near to destruction by its many enemies and as requiring the fullest loyalty of all if it is to survive. Devils and angels, then, are of the present, not merely from the past, giving cues as to who are friends and foes in the here and now.

Ideologies may confirm the legitimacy of those who rule. As pointed out in Chapter 2, the absence of legitimated authority besets new rulers, who lack either the authority derived from royal inheritance or from established electoral or other more modern practices. The mass parties, particularly those which are demanding wide-ranging change and imposing unfamiliar sacrifices and disciplines, require exceptional authority. This authority must be legitimized in some way. Since their goals are usually beyond the realm of possibility, the legitimacy derived from performance does not come often. Legitimacy, therefore, may be sought by an all-inclusive political religion. This calls for a cessation of quarreling and strife, an end to criticism of the leaders who personify the state and society. The new regimes, being newborn, are purified of the unhappy past.[19] To challenge them is made to seem like an impure act, if not impiety. The leader's indispensability is dramatized, the world without Sukarno, Nkrumah, or Sékou Touré rendered unthinkable. Political ideologies may also draw on traditional religions, as Sukarno, U Nu, and Nkrumah used Koranic, Buddhistic, or tribal imagery and style.

Prince Sihanouk has said that "an ideology of a regime can be inspired by a religion—and above all, by Buddhism."[20] In Southeast Asia, particularly, Buddhism has provided a base of ideas and identification supporting those who rule—or useful to those who aspire to rule. In Ceylon a Buddhist revival assisted Mr. Bandaranaike to gain power. In Burma, U Nu sought to use Buddhism as an inclusive, unifying ideology which would draw the disparate Burmans and other peoples into a cohesive national whole. The effort failed, in part because it exacerbated differences with the 25 per cent who were

---

[19] Apter, "Political Religion in the New States," in Geertz, Old Societies and New States, p. 83.

[20] Schecter, The New Face of Buddha, p. 68.

not Buddhists, most of whom were also ethnically non-Burman. In Thailand, Buddhist ritual and tradition serve to confirm the position of the king. And in South Vietnam, Buddhist activists have sought to use Buddhism as a vehicle of protest. In Pakistan's early independence years, the ideas and symbolism of Islam provided sustenance to Pakistani distinctiveness.[21]

Even those leaders who ask less of their followers than did Sukarno or Nkrumah justify their continuation in power by virtue of the historic struggles for independence they may have led or by evoking ancient dangers persisting in the present. Apter has noted that in Africa "events occurring fifty years ago can sometimes have the freshness of the contemporary and can continue to be borne as current suffering and grievance in the assimilated heritage of misfortune."[22] Similarly, grievances predating the coming of the British still serve to inflame Indo-Pakistani differences today and recollections of ancient antagonisms between Sinhalese and Tamils contribute to ethnic conflict in Ceylon.[23] External opponents are identified with ancient antagonism, and leadership is legitimized by the vigor with which it fends off or humiliates these historic enemies.

Individuals torn loose from traditional entities or who have participated in protracted revolutionary struggle, may be feeling lost, beset by anxiety, and searching for some new meaning to their lives. Such men are likely to be more susceptible to ideological appeals than those who are still within the traditional groups or those who have moved into the more matter-of-fact world of modern man. Seen from this point of view, ideological constructs may be a kind of substitute for traditional affiliations, as Ashford reports from Tunisia or Feith from Indonesia.[24]

Leaders attempt to use ideology as a means for providing guidelines to the populace on appropriate political behavior. In the jargon, ideology is a means of political socialization. These often draw on traditional views of authority, attempting to transfer the deference

[21] On Ceylon, see Wriggins, *Ceylon*, Ch. 6; for Burma, see Donald E. Smith, *Religion and Politics in Burma* (Princeton, Princeton University Press, 1965, 350 pp.); on Thailand, Burma, and Vietnam see Schecter, *The New Face of Buddha.*

[22] Apter, *The Political Kingdom in Uganda*, p. 463.

[23] Robert N. Kearney, *Communalism and Language in the Politics of Ceylon* (Durham, N. C., Duke University Press, 1967, 164 pp.), Introduction and Ch. 1.

[24] For a discussion of how ideological constructs may substitute for primordial affiliations, see Ashford, *The Elusiveness of Power*, p. 22. Feith, *The Decline of Constitutional Democracy in Indonesia*, pp. 119-20.

earlier shown toward ancient rulers and chiefs to contemporary presidents and prime ministers. In general, citizens are exhorted not to be critical, independent, freely choosing voters but rather to join the new body politic and follow the leader's lead. Ideologies may also give cues to appropriate rules of the political game, what means of contention are legitimate, how differences are to be resolved, and how opponents are to be dealt with.[25]

Ideologies may help define the goals of public activity. These tend to dramatize the purposes described in Chapter 3. Before independence, ideology defined the objective of winning independence. It now evokes a design for national unity, social transformation and relations with other states. It alerts followers to injustices and to qualities in the society which should be modified if not eradicated, as Nehru's "Socialist Pattern of Society" criticized casteism, poverty, inequality and religious backwardness.

In fragmented societies, to define a bundle of purposes which will give some sense of direction to endeavor, and yet not be so specific as to sharpen antagonisms, is a difficult task. Goals which are too general will not move men; those which are too particular will divide. It is no wonder that to an outsider political objectives appear to be formulated in an ambiguous way, not too unlike the political purposes defined in. public rhetoric in the United States at election time. A variety of interests must be combined, common effort must be made to appear compatible with most men's aims and interests, and purposes must be acceptable to a variegated and diverse following.

In the realm of economic activity and social organization, an industrialized future is generally assumed; with it come greatly improved living standards and an end to exploitation. As to the realm of political purposes, the nature of the good polity is usually suggested. Democracy, the near universal positive symbol, is usually associated with civilian rule through representative institutions with widespread public liberties permitting public debate and diverse organization.[26] Deviations from the norm of competitive democracy are explained as necessary in time of national emergency as economic development must be pressed at top speed or because political

---

[25] For a contrast see Lane's discussion of the implicit American political ideology, in Robert E. Lane, *Political Ideology* (New York, Free Press of Glencoe, 1962, 509 pp.), particularly sections I and III.

[26] Shils, *Political Development in the New States*, p. 48.

competition now would deepen social fragmentation or open the way to neocolonialism.

One can also discern a trend toward debunking this ideal altogether, attempting to show that it is inherently inappropriate to emerging countries which must find their unique form and quality of democracy. Sukarno argued for guided democracy to replace the disruptive "free fight liberalism." President Ayub held that Pakistanis needed democracy, not that which is to be sought in the "theories and practices of other people alone . . . [but] . . . it must be formed from within the book of Pakistan itself." In Africa an elaborate theory has developed justifying the flight from competitive to single-party systems.[27]

Some leaders will stress the vision of harmonious solidarity within perpetual revolution, as in Indonesia; others will press the concept of a secular, democratic, and economically developing state, as in Nehru's India. These contrasting visions of the future will play back into political life, influence the direction of effort, and affect which group's scope and responsibility will expand or contract.

Ideologies may carry ideas of historical cause and effect, guiding men's hands to the levers of history and showing the way to cope with economic change, bureaucratic inefficiency, internal political enemies, or threats from abroad. Ideologies may presume to isolate root causes, identifying revivals of past decisive enemies, as in neocolonialism, interpreting economic facts, and defining ideas concerning class conflict, historical communal strife, or the more immediate political enemies of those who propound ideology.

Ideologies may be essentially apocalyptic and romantic, implying or promising change and renewal by great historic cataclysm or by the near magic of the right political rituals, the correct formulae, or the ideal leader, who, by his mere appearance on the stage of history will set all to rights. They may, on the contrary, suggest incremental change and piecemeal innovation leading eventually to something new. When leaders and followers take seriously the ideologies' notions of cause and effect, ideologies will affect leaders' and entourages' approach to their problems. Their tasks will be eased or complicated, depending upon whether the ideology accurately reflects or distorts political, social, or economic dynamics.

[27] Sukarno, "Lecture to the Students of Hasamuddin University;" in Sigmund, *The Ideologies of the Developing Nations*, p. 60; Ayub, "Pakistan Perspective," *The Ideologies of the Developing Nations*, p. 113. For Africa, Carter (ed.), *African One-Party States, passim.*

Ideologies may affect directly the distribution of political power by demeaning and diminishing the standing of domestic political opponents, laying on them blame for all difficulties, and charging them with treasonously consorting with external enemies or willfully disrupting the national enterprise at home. The enemies thus picked out may be the wealthy or the dispossessed, the leaders of trade unions or particular minority parties or communities, or spokesmen for traditional values. To the extent that the regime's opponents can be made to seem like appropriate objects of aversion, the regime's political interests will be forwarded. A number of political leaders in emerging countries successfully follow Lenin's example in arousing hatred and contempt of political opponents; in the process they sometimes reduce human resources available for creative economic activity or intellectual life that can ill be spared.

An ideology may devote considerable attention to the larger entity beyond the nation, of which the polity is but a part. Pan-Arabism, Pan-Africanism and the concept of greater Indonesia, are examples.[28] Ideas of the larger entity may infuse pride in the polity's great historic mission. They may be used to rally support behind a particular leader, support which might not be forthcoming otherwise. The opposition may use it to demonstrate to the populace how a particular regime may be insufficiently attentive to the polity's wider destiny abroad. Whatever the motive for evoking such visions, they turn attention outward, seek to transcend present national frontiers and may have substantial effects upon a regime's approach to its foreign policy.

In certain countries, ideologies may give intellectual respectability to personal rivalries. Pye reports a notable contrast in Burma between the intensity of refined ideological debate and the regularity with which individuals ignore ideological differences as they form and reform in political alliances. He suggests that where personal political maneuvering is intense and where personal confrontations are felt to involve serious personal risks, ideological differences may provide a respectable screen for intensely personal competition.[29] They may also fit societies where sacred texts are refined and reorganized over and over again in the search for the one true meaning.

Thus, ideologies perform a variety of important political func-

[28] Von der Mehden, *Politics in the Developing Nations*, p. 138; Joseph P. Nye, Jr., *Pan-Africanism and East African Integration* (1965, Harvard University Press, 307 pp.), particularly Part I; Wriggins, *Ceylon*, Ch. 11.

[29] Pye, *Politics, Personality and Nation Building*, pp. 155-56.

tions. Particularly in single-party states, the strategy of ideology is a central aspect of political activity. But even in states where leadership does not seek to establish a monopoly of power, ideology can be used to help a leader give cues to his entourage and the populace, enhance identity and convey ideas concerning cause and effect. In these latter states, ideology is an important tool of an opposition seeking to unseat present leaders.

THE LIABILITIES OF IDEOLOGICAL POLITICS

While ideological politics are widespread, they invite certain risks and involve costs. Ideologies define objectives, evoking a vision of where the polity is going or how it should evolve. It may even suggest less abstract, more proximate actions, such as Nyerere's "self help," Nehru's "socialist pattern of society," or Nasser's "Arab Unity." But to translate the concept into those achievements necessary to realize the ideology in action is usually acutely difficult.

It is the realm of ideology which projects, larger than life, the new Utopia abuilding. To attract and hold the militants it may be necessary to offer ever more exciting promises in single-party systems. Competition between leaders seeking to lure the voters to support them inflates the images of the new society in competitive systems. Regardless of the system, it would appear, promise and purpose may grow beyond possible performance. Irresponsible aggrandizement of public purposes is a seedbed of discontent and a future challenge to present leaders.[30] This may lead to widespread disenchantment, defection of believing militants, and mounting unrest or a return to apathy among key sectors of the populace.

Particular ideologies may not be appropriate to the circumstances for which they appear to analyse and prescribe. Many of the most articulated ideologies derive, in fact from western European political experience. They often presume the existence of social entities, like classes, for example, which in some instances scarcely exist. They define inherent and inescapable conflicts which do not at all reflect the major tensions in countries where traditional loyalties and affinities are still important. Groups assumed to be class enemies in

[30] Eisenstadt discusses the problem of "squandering resources" for symbolic or ideological reasons. "Breakdowns of Modernization," *Economic Development and Cultural Change*, Vol. XII, No. 4 (July, 1964), 345-67, 362.

European ideologies could be potential allies in the colonial world if dealt with properly. Some of these ideologies presuppose an intellectual formation of European background possessed by only the few. This contributes to the political alienation of those with the elaborated ideologies, as it has weakened the political energy and divided the ranks of Ceylon's and India's communists. Moreover, ideologies may have within them such conceptual richness and varied nuances that members of the entourage become absorbed in increasingly unreal exegesis. Unless events force upon party ideologues regular and hard-bargained encounters with immediate realities, early misconceptions may become increasingly serious and the ideology increasingly irrelevant as a guide to efficient action.[31]

Ideologies often have a double or manifold form. Nyerere's Ujamaa may be formulated in rounded counterpoint to include the best of tradition and of paced, humane change. But outside the immediate entourage, its qualities change among the masses, "it takes the shape of slogans, stereotypes, shibboleths and folk argument."[32] This may be necessary if the ideology is to gain popular political clout. But in the process, it may lose its balanced and subtle nature, becoming the rationalization for the actions of party cadres or of those who wish to promote their own privileges by the use of official-sounding symbols.

Ideological politics always run the risk that individuals will become attached to ideological niceties, compounding traditional differences and inherited rivalries with an overlay of precious or passionate argumentation. This may make political activists doctrinaire, unable to cooperate with one another, and set in a matrix of ideologically defined differences which separate potential long-run allies and make for inflexibility. There have been three or four Marxist parties in Ceylon, including the world's largest and most venerable Trotskyite party. Their potential influence has been seriously weakened by persisting ideological—and personal—differences.

Where elaborated ideologies extend the inclusive scope of politics, certain key concepts may politicize nearly every act. Where all aspects of life are looked on as politically relevant, the power implications of acts, ideas, and relationships become more salient. Otherwise politically unimportant disagreements and differences are perceived as having critical political import. There is no rest for leaders, no

[31] Halpern, The Politics of Social Change, p. 290.
[32] Burke in Friedland and Rosberg, African Socialism, p. 204.

areas of activity which can be ignored.[33] Such political ideologies lead to overinvolvement of government, producing fatigue and boredom in the populace. People stop listening. Political activity becomes passive conformance; private resistance replaces the enthusiasm to which the ideological effort originally aspired.[34]

Ideology and political passion are related to each other. In many emerging countries, political passions are often deliberately intensified. If the "correct" appeals can be defined, mass emotions can be excited on behalf of the leadership's purposes.[35] Many leaders appear to believe that public opinion is rather like water in a faucet; the flow of popular excitement may be turned on and off at will and directed and redirected as the leader wishes. Demagogy is all too tempting.[36] This is suggested by the frequency of demagogic political discourse and the way leaders seek to manipulate the level of hostility popularly expressed toward local or distant antagonists. Such an approach to politics is not surprising, since it was often the ability to provoke and channel mass passions which had much to do with the success of the independence movement, and which led the older leaders to their positions of prominence in the independence struggle. No wonder, then, that certain leaders may consider the pent-up emotional energy of their peoples, particularly in the urban centers, as a major asset if it is properly tapped. Communist polemics often seek to distinguish between "principled" politics, based on "correct" ideological doctrine, and "demagogic" politics, which are not based on proper doctrine. Insofar as ideologies help to identify enemies and provide an apparently sophisticated justification for this enmity, they contribute to the conviction of rightness which supports the manipulation of these hostilities.

But passions, too, may get out of hand. The frequency and extent of urban riots, the susceptibility of populations to communal, language, tribal, or other open conflicts and the priority given to the development of police forces would suggest that leaders also fear the unexpected outbursts of mass emotions.

Ideological politics also presuppose people skilled in the words

[38] Apter, The Political Kingdom in Uganda, p. 59.

[34] For this in Ghana, for example, see Bretton, Rise and Fall of Kwame Nkrumah, pp. 157-64.

[35] Manfred Halpern is impressed by the distracting effect of unduly passionate politics in the Middle East, The Politics of Social Change, p. 290.

[36] Pye, Communications and Political Development, p. 69.

and symbols which evoke and sustain an ideology and a faith. The originators and guardians of the ideology themselves must be either identified with the regime or willing to work on its behalf. Yet they are often difficult to count on. Lenin disdained intellectuals; he felt they were unreliable and not steady in a crisis.[37] Universities may be the original source and seedbed of an ideology. But faculties and students are likely to be perfectionist and feel deceived if a leader cannot live up to his early promise. They become bored with an ideology before a leader can switch to a new set of ideas. They may not understand the dicey and contingent necessities of politics, and are often oppositionist by political bent and tradition.[38] Often, they lack opportunities commensurate with their skills, and their activities may result in unrest and disorder.

Religious leaders are perhaps more "reliable." But even these may not be as helpful as the leaders originally hope. At one point, Mr. Bandaranaike reached a moderating compromise with Tamils in Ceylon, but Buddhist leaders would not permit him to implement that agreement. Muslim Ulamas in Pakistan created substantial difficulties for the pre-Ayub regimes.[39] In Vietnam, elements of the Buddhist priesthood refused to passively accept some of the regimes that emerged during the difficult years of 1964-1967.[40] Moreover, religious leaders or enthusiasts may be profoundly conservative and opposed to change. They may stand in the way of economic development policies, or administrative or social innovations desirable on other counts.

Perhaps the most reliable instruments for promoting ideology are the organs of the leader's political party. If the ideology is right, it will attract followers and induce in them both loyalty and commitment. And if the party is effective, it will provide an organization capable of promoting the ideology. Political organization and ideology thus interact and reinforce each other. Since it will usually be the leader himself who is presented as the originator, interpreter and guardian of the ideology, personality, organization and ideology

---

[37] Betram D. Wolf, *Three Who Made a Revolution—A Biographical History* (New York, Dial, 1948, 661 pp.), p. 162; Adam Ulam, *The Bolsheviks* (New York, Macmillan, 1965, 590 pp.), pp. 210-11.

[38] Shils, *Political Development in the New States*, pp. 34-36.

[39] Keith Callard, *Pakistan, A Political Study* (New York, Macmillan, 1957, 355 pp.), pp. 208-15.

[40] Schecter, *The New Face of Buddha*, Chs. 8, 9, and 10 for a detailed discussion.

will all three work together. Bourguibism, Nasserism, Nkrumahism are all examples.

But if the leader depends entirely upon his party to generate and promote the ideology, the inspiration of the followers is likely to become undermined by the necessary expediency of party activity. Party organizers will find ideology increasingly less relevant as the pragmatic challenges of achieving immediate organizational objectives become more absorbing. They are likely to deal with the ideology in a routine way, thus diminishing its appeal to the intelligent and alert elements of the society. Party workers, therefore, even if personally reliable, are not likely to be effective proponents of the ideology for the longer run, as Nyerere experienced in Tanzania.[41]

In sum, it can be said that ideologies perform a number of political functions, and leaders will attempt to use them in their efforts to aggregate power. But ideologies may divert attention from real problems, misrepresent reality, and complicate the use of means to ends. They may provoke more disunity than they provide agreed purposes. Too much dependence upon the specialized men of ideas may trap a regime into becoming a victim of their judgments or their passions.

Yet without ideologies defining purposes, projecting a higher vision of the meaning and end of it all, political life may come to appear—as it may indeed become—simply a game of jockeying for position, a crass and cynical struggle for the spoils. Where there is no vision, the polity may well perish.

[41] Bienen, *Tanzania*, pp. 252-54.

8 Reward the Faithful and the Susceptible

To secure the services of subleaders, leaders must reward them in some fashion. . . . the range of rewards seems to be as broad as the spectrum of human motives. However, some kinds of rewards are easier to manipulate than others.

Robert Dahl

No political leader has been successful who does not devote considerable ingenuity and resources to rewarding the faithful and attempting to withhold advantages from those who oppose him. Support of the entourage must be sustained by rewards which fit their needs and aspirations.[1] Unless leaders feel strong enough politically to destroy other men capable of wielding power in the society, they will want such men to collaborate with them. As a lesser good, they will attempt to prevent such men from working against them.

To achieve these ends, leaders will generally use the means their present power affords to affect each man's calculus of where his advantage lies. Insofar as the leader has effective control over government, a certain proportion of government activities will go to rewarding those specific individuals or groups whose support he

[1] Dahl, Who Governs?, p. 96.

wants. There will be political costs if an undue proportion of governmental activities is devoted to this end. But some inevitably will be.

The "range of conceivable rewards is as broad as the spectrum of human motives."[2] Personal safety, income, and deference are among those inclusive values to which men aspire, and successful leaders have usually manipulated the granting or withholding of these advantages in order to promote their own political position.[3] This section is concerned mainly with rewards which are divisible, i.e., which can be relatively easily allocated to specific individuals, such as jobs, perquisites, contracts, and the like, in return for desired political behavior.[4] Later, a discussion of economic development will deal with the problem of providing more satisfaction and opportunity to much larger groups, indeed to whole segments of society.

Individual, divisible rewards may be as persuasive in anticipation as when they are actually granted. To hold out the promise but delay the favor may extend the period of a man's political "loyalty," for so long as the favor is not yet granted it can still be withheld. Yet, if such a play of promise and withholding is too blatant, potential followers will be humiliated, and thereby repelled. Men may be rewarded and won, but only within the range considered acceptable by them as individuals or by what the particular political culture indicates is reasonable.

THE REWARDS OF OFFICE: JOBS FOR THE FAITHFUL OR THE SUSCEPTIBLE

The most obvious reward, and one which carries with it many additional returns, is that of office. All regimes reward some of the most important among the faithful by appointing them to high office, either in the government or in the party. Cabinet offices are generally the most highly prized, but senior administrative positions just beneath the cabinet level are often opened for the leader's closest followers. In systems where British traditions are sustained, political lieutenants are not likely to receive appointments within any of the administrative units beneath the cabinet level, but civil servants who have assiduously supported the incumbent's interests

[2] *Ibid.*, p. 96.

[3] Harold D. Lasswell, *Politics, Who Gets What, When, and How?*, p. 3.

[4] Dahl, *Who Governs?*, p. 96.

may find themselves rapidly promoted over many of their bureau-cratic seniors.

In single-party states, promotion within the party or assignment to senior party positions may bring all the opportunities for power, status and enrichment that may elsewhere inhere only in ministerial positions. In certain countries, as in Ghana under Nkrumah, and Guinea, positions in the party may be preferred over positions in the administration because of their greater scope, more direct po-litical role and wider economic opportunities.

From the point of view of the leader, strategic offices must be in the hands of men whose loyalty is beyond question. Those minis-tries commanding the army and the police and the Ministry of Fi-nance, usually controlling the civil service and the flow of financial resources to other ministries, are the commanding heights, and these will be filled by loyal lieutenants.

Cabinet positions are also the reward of those not immediately in the entourage, but who have been of substantial political assist-ance. In Thailand, it has been reported that "many cabinet positions are a form of political patronage as rewards for services rendered or as inducements to future loyalty."[5] What applies to Thailand ap-plies as much to many other countries.

Cabinet positions sometimes are made available to leading political competitors who may be neutralized, if not completely won, by the opportunity of office. Their opposition activities may be stopped while they hold office and policies they oppose may then be more easily implemented. Their reputation for political principles and consistency may be seriously damaged if they can be shown to be thus susceptible to the lure of office. On the other hand, like the leader's lieutenants, the competitor may be able to build a more secure political future for himself from that prominent position. For example, while Minister of Local Government in Mr. D. S. Senana-yake's cabinet, Mr. Bandaranaike sustained and improved a net-work of supporters who were helpful some years later when Ban-daranaike brought down the party Senanayake had led. If a leader gives a prominent cabinet position to a longstanding opponent, his own loyal followers may resent this preference shown to a com-petitor they may have been battling for many years. He will thereby increase his own difficulties within his entourage. Accordingly, a

[5] Wilson, *Politics in Thailand*, pp. 158, 259.

leader will weigh carefully the advantages and disadvantages of attempting to draw a competitor into his own cabinet.

In addition to top cabinet and other senior administrative positions or positions in the party, there may be numerous elected positions in national legislatures, regional councils, and so forth. The leader may win the support of followers by promoting their names on electoral slates, and by supporting them in elections with his own exalted presence or with the resources of his organization. If the election is a sure thing, such an offer will have all the more attraction to a possible incumbent. If it is to be hard fought, the man who is offered the opportunity to run will have to weigh the financial and other liabilities of the campaign against the possible rewards of an uncertain victory.

Accepting the offer of an appointive, elective, or party office may bring rewards to the recipient. It will provide opportunities for gaining experience in the ways of governance and politics. It gives an unparalleled opportunity to build an independent political following by the offices the incumbent can dispense, the decisions he can influence, or the advantages he can steer to this or that group in the populace.

The personal perquisites are often highly coveted. In many emerging countries, few men have higher standards of living than cabinet ministers. Official houses, automobiles, entertainment allowances, travel opportunities, and various side benefits which can be used for direct political advantage to enlist one's own personal entourage or, particularly in Africa, to meet one's obligation to one's family— all these advantages may come with ministerial or electoral office.[6] Wraith and Simpkins believe that in West Africa, at least, it appears to be expected that the leader, his key ministers, some elected members, or key party figures should lead a life of dramatic display and panoply, as inflating to the ego of the man at the center as it is satisfying to those who prefer political circuses to hard-won real, though often matter-of-fact, accomplishment.[7] On the other hand, a political personage's net return may be considerably less than his receipts, since he will often be expected to contribute substantially to the party's coffers or share his returns with his lieutenants or hangers-on.

[6] Wraith and Simpkins, *Corruption in Developing Countries*, pp. 41-42; Zolberg, *One-Party Government in the Ivory Coast*, pp. 192-93.

[7] Wraith and Simpkins, pp. 40-41.

As government takes on more and more functions, particularly in regulating and managing the economy, the numbers of potentially lucrative and powerful positions greatly increase, quite beyond a mere handful of cabinet posts and electoral offices. There are now countless boards, commissions, government corporations and regulatory bodies which must be manned. In Indonesia, many of Sukarno's faithful filled such posts.[8] In India, the opposition often alleged that Congress used government corporations and regulatory bodies as convenient sinecures for the party faithful who lost out politically or for those who threatened to cause Congress trouble.

One obvious political virtue of expropriation is the job opportunities it opens as the foreign managers and operatives are forced out.[9] Here, too, the leader is likely to weigh carefully the political qualities as well as technical qualifications of those who are appointed, for these can be powerful instruments of political leverage in countries of economic scarcity or tight economic regulation. They are also positions from which, as in the cabinet or senior party positions, the incumbent can enrich himself by the special inducements he may obtain in return for his convenient discretionary decision.

A job may be assigned not so much for the sake of the individual who has been appointed as for the symbolic value of that appointment to his own followers. Men may be appointed to high position because of their ethnic background, or of the community of which they are a part, on the assumption that many followers will feel that a particular leader or government is on their side. Such men may be appointed in order to demonstrate a favorable official attitude toward a depressed or other minority. Thus, in India, Ambedkar, leader of the untouchables, was honored by the Nehru administration; a Muslim, Mahlana Azad, was often at Nehru's side not only out of longstanding friendship between the two but to symbolize Nehru's concern for the secular quality of the Indian state. In Guinea, principal party leaders were drawn from the four major regional peoples. In the Ivory Coast and in Ceylon, the tribal, caste, or communal structure of the constituency is carefully matched by party slates.[10]

As Dahl puts it:

[8] See, for example, Feith, "Indonesia," in George Kahin (ed.), *Governments and Politics of Southeast Asia*, p. 251.

[9] Feith, *The Decline of Constitutional Democracy in Indonesia*, pp. 487-89.

[10] On India, see Brecher, *Nehru, a Political Biography*, pp. 106, 148, 176, 217; on Guinea, see Morgenthau, *Political Parties*, p. 249.

Benefits conferred on an individual member of an ethnic group are actually shared to some degree by the rest of the group, for every time one member makes a social or economic breakthrough, others are likely to learn of it, to take pride in his accomplishment, and to find it easier themselves to achieve the same sort of advance. The strategies of politicians are designed to confer specific benefits on particular individuals and thus to win the support of the whole group.[11]

Using the grant of office to enlist and hold a following is particularly useful immediately following independence. At that time, old offices are being vacated by colonial officials and can easily be filled by the faithful. The scope of government is rapidly expanding, and new jobs are being created almost as rapidly as people can be found to fill them, if not more rapidly.

Thus, granting offices to build or hold an entourage or to diminish opposition has many advantages. But there are obvious liabilities to it, too.

LIABILITIES OF REWARDING THE FAITHFUL WITH JOBS

Usually, there are only a certain number of offices to go around.[12] One favor may make one friend, but alienate all those who hoped to get it and were passed over. There are often more disgruntled lieutenants than there are those who have received rewards. This may not be serious if economic development is opening new job opportunities, or if the disappointed candidates have no one to rally behind. But if they can organize without undue risk, it may be possible for the disgruntled lieutenants to form the core of future opposition. In Syria, for example, successive coup leaders were brought down in part by others in the army who were not adequately rewarded.[13] South Vietnam was beset by the same problem before the temporary stabilization under Thieu.

One cannot go too far in rewarding loyalty if, at the same time, the faithful are incompetent. In traditional governments which did not claim to perform many governmental functions, loyalty was a prime virtue, and little substantive competence was required except to ensure that the ruler's opponents did not gain in influence or daring. In Daud's Afghanistan or Haile Selassie's Ethiopia, loyalty was the

[11] Dahl, *Who Governs?*, p. 53.
[12] Hodgkin, *African Political Parties*, p. 147.
[13] Torrey, *Syrian Politics*, pp. 139, 205.

indispensable quality. As governments take on increasingly technical functions, loyal lieutenants may bring the leader down by virtue of their incompetence. Miracles of social and economic transformation are often promised—and half expected—yet as Pye suggests, the ceremonial functions of government are often felt to be as important as the more "efficient" policy aspects of government.[14]

Nevertheless, obvious incompetence will cumulate and lead to increasing confusion and ineffectualness, which is likely to prove politically costly. This will be particularly true where a government's activities are subject to scrutiny and criticism by representatives selected through reasonably free and competitive elections. It will be more serious for a regime which claims to be promoting economic development than for one which does not. Since it is easier for leaders to assess the short run political value of a possible appointee than to estimate the longer run political costs of his incompetence, leaders all too often settle for the loyal but incapable.

There is an inflexibility about this type of reward. It can usually be granted only once in a year or two. Too frequent changes in top positions will bring disorder into the management of affairs and, if there is any public expression permitted, will provoke criticism and invite charges of incompetence and lack of consistency on the part of the ruler. However, a shrewd leader may retain substantial influence over senior aides who are retained in office for a considerable period of time by measuring out confidence and the subtle signs of being close to the center of affairs, so that minor increments of favor or disfavor can be communicated to the incumbent. And there is always the suggestive hint of higher office sometime in the future. If, however, a lieutenant comes to office with any following of his own or can use his office to develop one, such minor signs of favor or vague hints of future benefit may not be sufficient to keep him regular.

Finally, the great occasion of independence comes only once, although a thorough-going revolution may provide analogous opportunities, albeit usually in greatly worsened organizational circumstances. Later on, many positions are already filled with earlier lieutenants or by appointees of one's predecessor. To remove present officials may disrupt government. Displaced former officials, being knowledgeable in the ways of government, can become the informed nucleus of opposition.

[14] Pye, *Politics, Personality and Nation-Building*, pp. 150-55.

REWARD BY GOVERNMENTAL DECISIONS

Because using office to reward the faithful has real limitations, other types of reward must be found. Moreover, there are many men of influence who want to have an effect on what the state does but who do not wish to spend full time in government employ and party activity. For them, the rewards of public office are not sufficient to lure them away from their positions of tribal or caste leadership or their professional or business lives. Yet these, too, may be politically influential in mobilizing political support—the support of traditional followings, of money, and of professional bodies which can give advice or which, through their activities, can generate a loyal backing. For these, rewards may be in the form of governmental decisions. It is difficult to write precisely of instances where the powers and policies of government are used on behalf of political rewards, since these matters are rarely admitted. Some observations can nevertheless be made.

The range of rewards a government can deliver to a supporter by a favorable decision is as broad as the scope of government itself. There are now more varied ways of inducing political cooperation than ever before. Particularly in one-party states, where there is no political competition, the use of administrative decisions in economic, educational, or other spheres can mean powerful incentives toward regularity.

The host of new economic agencies, corporations, boards, and councils, all with some governmental authority over the allocation and use of economic resources, provides political parties with sharpened means of inducing political conformity. Contracts may go only to the party faithful as a reward for political support. Or they may go to close friends of the party faithful, perhaps in return for a generous kickback enriching the party member for his intercession in high places. As Austin reported on Nkrumah's Ghana: "The CPP was now a very profitable source of wealth for those who held power within it. It had always been corrupt; but it had also fought for self-government. Now, however, that the political kingdom was complete, the opportunities for private gain were very great. . . ."[15]

In some countries, "commercial patronage" has been developed to a high degree. As Sklar summarized findings in Nigeria before the

[15] Austin, *Politics in Ghana*, p. 404.

coup in early 1966: "In sum, commercial patronage, including government loans, marketing board licensing, and government contracting, is channeled through public agencies that are quasi-political in nature and composition. In all regions, these agencies serve the political interests of the government party only."[16]

In the Philippines, Taylor reports that people who have close connections with those in power are able to "evade payment of taxes and customs dues, block investigations, break competitors and ruin political opponents. More money can be made in a shorter time with the aid of political influence than by any other means. . . ."[17]

Feith reported from Indonesia that under Sukarno, overregulation on the statute books required that businessmen who wanted to expand their activities had to remain politically discreet, in friendly touch with officials high and low, in order that the regulations would be so administered as to permit some semblance of business activity.[18]

Tariffs, import regulations, the allocation of foreign exchange, the methods for distributing food supplies or collecting and storing harvests, and rural lending institutions—all present opportunities for inducing good political behavior among those with influence or economic interests. They may also open channels for incumbents to improve their own or their party's finances by the gifts which may precede favorable governmental decision. As the official Santhanam Commission put it in India: ". . . we heard from all sides that corruption has, in recent years, spread even to those levels of administration from which it was conspicuously absent in the past. We wish we could confidently and without reservation assert that at the political level, Ministers, Legislators, party officials were free from this malady. . . ."[19]

When it becomes obligatory for foreign enterprises to transfer a proportion of the management positions to local nationals or when foreign firms are nationalized, the distribution of the most desirable jobs and enterprises may serve a political purpose. Feith reports an extreme example in Indonesia. When the port facilities were taken

---

[16] Sklar, *Nigerian Political Parties*, pp. 452-53.

[17] Taylor, *The Philippines and the United States*, p. 157.

[18] Feith in Kahin (ed.), *Governments and Politics of Southeast Asia*, p. 256.

[19] Government of India, Ministry of Home Affairs, *Report of the Committee on the Prevention of Corruption* (New Delhi, 1965, 304 pp.), pp. 12-13. See also Weiner, *The Politics of Scarcity*, pp. 120-21.

over, ". . . the procedure was a classic example of spoilsmanship. Each of the main government parties [then in the coalition] had its own association of warehousing firms, many of the firms being fledgling units established after the promulgation of [the authorizing regulation], and the government simply divided up the plants among the warehousing associations of the different major parties."[20]

Schools, dispensaries, and roads are frequently distributed according to the political loyalty of the leaders in the particular district; the faithful lieutenant receives what he asks for his district, the recalcitrant is by-passed for yet another year.[21]

Educational opportunities are of critical importance to many parents, since social mobility seems to depend upon the schools and universities a boy or girl attends. Foreign schools cost foreign exchange, for which scarce resources may have to be allocated by specific government decision. It is probable that considerable political regularity is induced among ambitious parents by the careful screening of travel grants and foreign exchange requests so that only the children of the politically reliable have the opportunity for experience abroad.

Where ethnic, tribal, or other antagonisms are serious, leaders may win support by openly attacking the rivals of those they seek to enlist. Leaders may gain credit in Malay areas, by attacking Chinese; in Tamil-speaking areas of India, by charging Hindi imperialism; in Accra, by criticizing Ashanti separatism and backwardness; in northern Sudan, by charging treason on the part of Nubia. In all these and other instances, the reward offered is the satisfaction of seeing one's enemies or rivals attacked by the central government.

REWARD BY SOCIAL RECOGNITION

In highly status-conscious societies, where the elite is small and "everyone knows everyone else," where there are few alternative means of underlining one's standing, access to the precincts of power may be highly prized. Invitations to levees, ceremonies and other state affairs, or semiprivate functions of the mighty can deter deviation on the part of those who are "in" or who feel it important

[20] Feith, The Decline of Constitutional Democracy in Indonesia, pp. 478-79.

[21] Zolberg reports such discretionary decisions in the Ivory Coast, One-Party Government in the Ivory Coast, p. 194.

to be "in." Usually this is not mere social snobbery but carries with it informal access to the influential. Royal favor has always been a source of wealth and power. Where bureaucracies do not function on reasonably objective criteria but discretion is highly personal, as it is in many emerging countries, to be "in" carries with it real influence. To be "out" implies a serious loss of direct access to influence which may carry with it loss of local influence, income, safety, or opportunity. Even if the individual who is seen to have access gains little real influence on the politically powerful, the fact that he is known to have access will strengthen his position with his own followers. When a traveling official accepts hospitality in the district or village, the local position of the man who offers hospitality is enhanced. Even a visit, therefore, can be a form of reward.

Outright bribery on a large scale may also be useful if a major group with substantial power is to be won. Massive bribery is said to have helped the Ngo Dinh Diem regime to win the support of leaders of the religious sects, a first and critical step in Diem's efforts to consolidate his regime at the outset.[22]

The army will require special attention. Top military leaders will need to be rewarded with substantial perquisites and privileges, such as housing, recreational facilities, and so forth. They may prefer above all the latest equipment to satisfy their professional self-esteem; foreign training can help them improve their skills and may be a coveted reward. Too much attention to the senior officers may awaken the jealousy and resentment of junior officers not so favored, unless some of their hopes are catered to as well. The civilian bureaucracy will also pose problems. It is usually substantially underpaid. It may have grown rapidly after independence, at a rate beyond the economy's capacity to pay it adequately. Civil service clubs, credit unions, and other such devices may help supplement its low pay. But the temptation will be to turn a blind eye to widespread instances of individuals obtaining a private rake-off for accelerating a decision which otherwise was dragging or for using official discretion to favor a particularly generous citizen.

These examples are sufficient to suggest that there are other ways in which incumbents may use government power to reward the faithful, apart from the selective distribution of jobs. Such means have short run virtues and are no doubt tempting to those who are

[22] Bernard Fall, *Two Vietnams, A Political and Military Analysis* (New York, Praeger, 1964, 498 pp.), pp. 245-46.

new to power. But there are major, debilitating consequences of such action.

LIABILITIES OF THE POLITICS OF REWARD

As with jobs, so with some other rewards: the supply is bound to be limited; demands are greater than can be met. Particularly where the government has been profligate in squandering its resources of effectiveness and management skills, it becomes increasingly difficult to provide the kinds of rewards so freely given right after independence. There are, in fact, fewer jobs and perquisites now than there were shortly after independence.[23]

There has been an increase in the appetite and the number of those who feel themselves entitled to good jobs. On the other hand, there are many in this generation who find themselves blocked in their advance by the men who, at a relatively young age, climbed into the driver's seat after independence and, in many cases, still remain, fifteen and even twenty years later. Unless a system of political reward can be sustained or alternative channels for satisfying ambition can be opened, the younger men can be expected to become increasingly restless and are unlikely to remain politically regular.

Rewarding the faithful by jobs or by special government policies favoring their own interests has a wider consequence. No doubt, some of it can be accepted as normal to the transitional society, where nepotism is still taken for granted. But beyond a point—and this point will vary among societies and over time within any one— privileges for the leader and for his entourage may become too blatant. Particularly if his tenure is extended, the leader's and entourage's privileges risk becoming increasingly resented by those who do not have access to such advantages. The system can become overloaded. Resentment may increase and turn into bitterness and active hostility unless a certain habituation to such excesses sets in or intimidation deters the expression of protest. Even in countries which have seemed to accept with equanimity an excessive diversion of resources for personal reward, the exposure of these tactics after the leader departed has evoked anger and bitterness. After Sukarno's

---

[23] Feith, *The Decline of Constitutional Democracy in Indonesia*, p. 572.

gradual decline in Indonesia and Sarit's death in Thailand, their excesses were highly publicized and public displeasure manifested. Yet it cannot be said in either case that corruption was even remotely a cause of either regime's abrupt end.

Providing the army with exceptional personal perquisites or improved equipment may temporarily win it to a regime. Such rewards may at first draw to the services the most energetic and ambitious young men, perhaps to the detriment of the other professions. More seriously, like any special preference, it may in the end raise the appetite of the military leaders, and sharpen resentment among the lower ranks who do not share in the benefits. It may improve the ability of the army to overawe the populace but the military's potentiality for overthrowing the regime will be much enhanced by the very equipment provided to ensure its loyalty.

Irregular "rewards" to the civil service tend to dramatize the power of the man with wealth, since he alone can pay the necessary fees clandestinely required. Bureaucratic corruption is usually regressive, falling more heavily on the poor who are forced to pay out of very small incomes modest sums for small favors while the wealthy may pay substantial sums which, in the end, provide handsome returns. This way of keeping the bureaucracy regular tends to encourage delay until the impatient citizen pays "speed money" to promote necessary action.[24]

In many new states, the cost of corruption is not so much economic as it is moral. The resulting loss of self-respect and an increase in cynicism lead to a slowdown of effort, an unwillingness to strive for the earlier vision—the wider nation. Instead, a reversion to earlier loyalties is provoked, where one's own interests and those of one's family, clan, and caste come first.[25]

When laws, presumably set for all, are flouted too openly and regularly by the select few, the laws themselves are brought into disrepute. As rewards become more difficult to distribute and the law increasingly disregarded, more coercion may be required if public order is to be sustained. The terms of political life gradually shift from the arts of persuasion and reward to coercion. Particularly in single-party states, corruption of the law increasingly risks iso-

[24] For a discussion of these and other aspects of corruption, see Myrdal, *Asian Drama*, Vol. II, pp. 937-58.

[25] For a discussion, see Wraith and Simpkins, *Corruption in Developing Countries*, pp. 16-17.

lating the leader. His own apparent political support becomes increasingly built on delusion and falsehood.[26]

In many developed countries, corruption has been substantial in earlier periods of development. However, rarely were these embryonic governments the central focus of ambition and presumptive source of innovation and energy they are in most emerging countries today. This critical role of government makes it all the more important that men associated with it should sustain and improve the quality of public life.

In every polity, there is an optimum level of corruption. Too little of it will prevent the development of that core of loyal and energetic lieutenants who need to be rewarded if their zeal and enthusiasm are to be sustained. But too much of it renders the regime repellent to those not within reach of those rewards; it promotes cynicism and brings the law and the notion of probity into disrepute.

To set limits to corruption where it has been restrained but where there are many cultural and political pressures on its growth is difficult enough. To pare it down when the entire bureaucracy and much of the political system are now dependent upon it, as in Indonesia and the Philippines, is a heroic task. The history of such Western polities as Great Britain and France recalls how very corrupt these polities once were and how much corruption has been overcome. No outsider can presume to advise on how it should be accomplished in these or other contemporary instances. But without daring effort, this form of political decay can be expected to grow further, regardless of who is in power, unless the politics of reward is used with great restraint.[27]

[26] For some consideration of this point, see David Apter, "Some Reflections on the Role of Political Opposition in New Nations," in *Comparative Studies in Society and History*, Vol. IV (1961-1962), 160.

[27] For a discussion putting corruption into historical perspective, see Wraith and Simpkins, *Corruption in Developing Countries*, *passim*; David H. Bayley assesses the positive as well as negative aspects of corruption in "The Effects of Corruption in a Developing Nation," *Western Political Quarterly*, Vol. XIX, No. 4 (December, 1966), 719-32.

9 Intimidate the Opponent and the Wavering Ally

Men do with less remorse offend against those who desire to be beloved than against those who are ambitious of being feared, . . . [for] fear depends upon an apprehension of punishment, which is never to be dispelled.

Niccolo Machiavelli

"INTIMIDATION"—AMBIGUITIES AND LITTLE HARD EVIDENCE

The reverse of reward is intimidation. It connotes to render timid, to inspire with fear, to overawe by threat of serious sanctions or deprivations. In strict usage it implies to do this by threat of violence. Yet, there are forms of threatened sanction short of violence quite as compelling as the threat of violence itself. For our purposes, then, intimidation implies exacting conformity to the leadership's will by the threat of a sanction considered serious, whether violent or not.

All governments use intimidation in this sense in efforts to deter individuals from engaging in certain types of acts.[1] Indeed, one way of distinguishing the political system from other institutions is its

[1] Finer, *The Theory and Practice of Modern Government* (New York, Henry Holt, 1949, 978 pp.), p. 11.

159

legitimated right to use heavy sanctions.[2] Sanctions against theft, murder, and treason are severe in almost all countries. Where the legal order is well-developed, these crimes calling for severe sanctions are defined; the procedures for judging when sanctions should be applied are well-known and reasonably predictable.

But in most polities in Asia and Africa, as in developed states during times of war, turmoil, or rapid political change, intimidation is not so clearly delimited, and the definition of crimes for which sanctions can be properly applied is not so restricted. The procedures for deciding when they should be applied in many countries lack predictability and acceptance.

There are, of course, major differences between countries in this respect. Some, like India, have a highly developed rule of law. Most others are not so blessed. In some cultures, it is debasing to persons to feel themselves coerced by intimidation; in others it is normal and not felt to be inappropriate. In some the ruler's prerogatives are constrained by acceptance and by law. In others, intimidation is as much a prerogative of the top man as it is to ride in a car when others walk or to eat sufficiently while others eke out a bare subsistence.

Where that broad underlying consensus on fundamental practices and purposes of government is more tenuous than in the well-established states, one should expect a higher level of intimidation if a regime is to survive. Intimidation may be used to defend the state against secessionists and those who appear to promote national disintegration. Even in well-established states, some intimidation may be necessary if certain regulations are to be conformed to or policies carried out. An extreme of intimidation may induce a kind of anarchy, as in Haiti.[3]

It is not the purpose of this chapter to judge when intimidation is used beyond what is reasonable for that particular historical situation, but to examine it as a means of improving the chances that an incumbent remains in power.

There are difficulties in exploring the matter of intimidation. Few cases are documented. Gossip is rife but reliable evidence is scarce.

[2] See Easton, *The Political System*, pp. 130 ff.; Harold D. Laswell and Abraham Kaplan, *Power and Society* (New Haven, Yale University Press, 1950, 295 pp.), Ch. V.

[3] Leslie François Manigat, *Haiti of the Sixties, Object of International Concern* (Washington, Washington Center of Foreign Policy Research, 1964, 104 pp.).

Scholars find it far from the ideal of politics and are inclined to avoid it. Critics see it where it may not in fact exist. Moreover, since effective intimidation is largely in the mind of the person intimidated, it is difficult to find unambiguous examples of it. A few cases of exemplary sanctions may render men timid who were not intended objects of government intimidation. Does intimidation then apply only when government intends it? If sanctions are threatened by implication but never actually applied, can one say that intimidation was used? In some regimes the level of anxiety is high and intimidation seems ubiquitous. Even without identifiable instances of intimidation men may tiptoe carefully to avoid disturbing the sleeping giant of the sovereign's wrath. In others, it is easier to associate intimidation with specific political acts.

AN EXAMPLE: NKRUMAH OF GHANA

Ghana under Kwame Nkrumah represents an interesting, illustrative case. To be sure, intimidation in Ghana may have received more prominence than has been entirely justified. As Zolberg has pointed out, other African regimes, particularly in French West Africa, were not so well endowed at independence either with legal protection for individuals or for political oppositions, with a free press or with a tradition of an independent university. These institutions posed special problems to a leader who aspired to rule through a mobilizing single party. His successive steps to bring the activities of these institutions under his control have been well-recorded by attentive observers both within and from outside Ghana.[4] Despite these reservations, the trend of intimidation in Ghana was so clear that it will serve as an introductory example for our discussion.

After five years as Leader of Government Business, Kwame Nkrumah was named first Prime Minister when Ghana received its independence in 1957. He came to power under the aegis of open, competitive political practices within a constitution designed along British parliamentary lines. Quite typically, as the colonial power withdrew, underlying social and political differences came to the surface. His regime was quickly confronted by a situation in which competitive politics along Western lines would mean in fact intensifying inter-tribal rivalries. Major tribal groups like the Ashanti

[4] Zolberg, *Creating Political Order*, p. 79.

pressed for maximum autonomy and resisted any change which would work against the very conservative interests of the chieftaincy families. It was therefore not entirely personal *hubris* that led his regime over the next decade to narrow and then eliminate altogether the scope for authorized opposition and bring to focus all power in the hands of the *Osagyefo*, or victorious leader. Intimidation thus became an important instrument in effecting this change and in sustaining the regime until a coup d'état by a small group of soldiers brought it down in February 1966.

A number of legislative measures, beginning shortly after independence, rapidly narrowed the scope of opposition. A Deportation Act of August 23, 1957, intimidated those in the opposition who were not citizens. The Avoidance of Discrimination Act of December 1957, was turned against leaders of tribal and religious parties. Exhaustive investigations of the workings of certain opposition local councils intimidated members of other councils. Investigations of chieftaincy appointments or the propriety of the activities of specific chiefs who had opposed the Convention Peoples Party (CPP) induced good behavior on the part of other chiefs who feared removal—or destoolment.[5]

Preventive detention legislation gave the regime power to jail for five years without trial anyone whose activities it considered posed a threat to state security. Other states in the Commonwealth had similar emergency powers, drawn from the colonial tradition. But few successor regimes used them to such direct political effect. Preventive detention was "one of a series of measures which the government used against its opposition to ensure political control."[6] "Parliament was cowed by the simple device of lifting or threatening to lift the immunity of Members."[7]

Voting in early elections had often been irregular, with the CPP demonstrating its unambiguous desire and ability to have its way.[8] Enthusiastic bullyboys, organized by the CPP, intimidated opposition candidates and voters. Voting in the 1960 plebiscite was allegedly "fixed" in certain key districts, after the first day's returns showed

[5] Bretton, *Rise and Fall of Kwame Nkrumah*, pp. 45-46; Austin, *Politics in Ghana*, pp. 378.

[6] Coleman and Rosberg, *Political Parties and National Integration in Tropical Africa*, pp. 279-80.

[7] Bretton, *Rise and Fall of Kwame Nkrumah*, pp. 51-52.

[8] Austin, *Politics in Ghana*, p. 388.

unexpectedly weak support for Nkrumah's party.[9] The opposition fielded Dr. J. B. Danquah, the man who originally asked Nkrumah to return to Ghana to enter politics. But Danquah "could not make himself heard, let alone seen, in most parts of the country, and his partisan supporters could not secure access to polling places."[10] He was later arrested and detained without trial. Detention became so frequent and arbitrary that a former Minister of Interior was moved to complain that "anybody can go and cause the detention of anybody."[11] It is no wonder therefore that a number of political leaders chose exile, Dr. Busia being among the first to go.[12]

The courts were intimidated and brought under Nkrumah's personal control as members of the judiciary who rendered decisions contrary to his wishes were removed from their responsibilities.[13] Newspaper owners and editors were displaced and their papers closed or taken over for state purposes. Attacks by the state-controlled press became the signal that a man's career was about to be blighted by his being fired, detained, or exiled.[14] Security forces, including the secret police, the President's foreign-trained personal guard, and a special forces unit of the army were expanded, and all came under Nkrumah's direct personal control.[15]

Intimidatory steps toward one-man control had some justification, it could be argued. Chiefs and others whose loyalties were still to their parochial tribes resisted centralization and sought to maintain district autonomy, in part in an effort to prolong their own local political influence. Well-off intellectuals, professional men, and cosmopolitan businessmen defended their privileged economic position as they spoke out for political liberties on the British model. Early political competition had shown political violence to be very near the surface.[16] The competing National Liberation Movement had also used tough tactics. Indeed, the more the opposition sensed the tightening grip of the CPP the more desperate it became. The regime argued that economic development required austerity and a cen-

---

[9] *Ibid.*, pp. 392-94.

[10] Bretton, *Rise and Fall of Kwame Nkrumah*, pp. 49-50.   [11] *Ibid.*, p. 57.

[12] Coleman and Rosberg, *Political Parties and National Integration in Tropical Africa*, pp. 279-80.

[13] Bretton, *Rise and Fall of Kwame Nkrumah*, p. 51; *The New York Times*, Dec. 12, 1963, p. 13.

[14] *The New York Times*, Jan. 10, 1964, p. 3.

[15] Bretton, *Rise and Fall of Kwame Nkrumah*, p. 103.

[16] Austin, *Politics in Ghana*, p. 250.

tralized allocation of scarce investment resources, while continued open competition gave scope and voice to parochial special interests. Since opposition was felt to be akin to treason, the CPP militants saw no harm in destroying the opposition. Nkrumah's ambitious mobilizationist goals called for a level of effort not likely under normal practice. Such considerations, understandable enough in themselves, permitted and in part justified Nkrumah's growing one-man rule. Too late, however, party militants discovered that when all checks on the leader's power were destroyed, they had no protection either.[17]

For a time President Nkrumah's intimidatory steps appeared to consolidate his rule. Chiefs no longer made demands on behalf of local autonomy or tribal interests. The voices of the intellectuals and professional men of the early opposition were stilled, at least at home. The resounding declarations and mobilizationist talk were no longer challenged. The crowds still turned out to cheer Osagyefo. The civil servants quietly went about their development tasks; the army appeared to stay loyal.

But the very measures Nkrumah took to ensure his regime increasingly isolated him, even from those who had supported him before. When there was no more opposition, the politics of intrigue succeeded the politics of open competition for power. Quarrels between Nkrumah and members of his immediate entourage became more frequent, leading to the dismissal, detention, or exile of some former associates.[18] Increasingly harsh repressive measures provoked more resentments. A number of assassination attempts led to further security protection. Barricaded for safety's sake in Christianborg Castle, Nkrumah became increasingly dependent upon information which came to him through his numerous and competing intelligence services and his few remaining colleagues.[19] The civil service found itself increasingly ignored. Moreover, as the risks of displeasing the ruler appeared to increase, advice tendered became more and more tailored to what the remaining officials thought the ruler wanted to hear.

Since all channels of legitimate political action had long been closed, Nkrumah's regime ended in the only way it could short of his demise—a coup d'état. Intimidation had left the party without apparent supporters. The "vaunted one-party state evaporated almost

[17] Ibid., pp. 37, 48.   [18] Ibid., p. 48.   [19] Ibid., p. 418.

without a trace."[20] And after fifteen years of Nkrumah's rule, no channels for legitimate popular political action remained; power lay entirely in the hands of the bureaucracy and army.

Nkrumah's use of intimidation illustrates some of the processes, advantages, and liabilities of attempting to consolidate and sustain a regime by such a strategy. The following more general discussion suggests other functions, forms, and liabilities of intimidation.

THE TEMPTATION TO INTIMIDATE

Nkrumah's example suggests the temptation to use intimidation and to press toward authoritarian rule in emerging countries. To get the lethargic populace to move the way the leader wishes seems to require unusual pressure. Only strong measures can induce the divided populace to pull together. The self-satisfied bureaucrats may need the goad of fear if they are to pursue the ruler's ambitious goals. Open, competitive politics, it may be argued, will give parochial leaders opportunities to block change or exacerbate existing differences. Members of the leader's entourage see little merit in limiting their own opportunity to make the most of their positions while they are in the precincts of power. It is no wonder that ambitious and impatient men are tempted to resort to intimidation.

Normally, a regime which emerges through a coup d'état requires a substantial dose of intimidation, even if its goals are modest. A civilian regime which achieved independence through political means or one which has organized and sustained close links with a multitude of political groups in the society since independence requires less. Even if a coup group seizes power, it may need little intimidation for success if the regime it displaces was dramatically corrupt, ineffectual, or repugnant for other reasons. On the other hand, if a regime's opponents use desperate measures in efforts to bring it down, it may have to use substantial intimidation against its enemies to survive. The temptation and the need to use intimidation, therefore, depend upon how a regime comes to power, the goals it sets itself, the organizational links it has with major political groups in the society, and, of course, the steps its opponents take in efforts to displace it.

[20] Bretton, *Rise and Fall of Kwame Nkrumah*, p. 171.

THE TARGETS OF INTIMIDATION

Possible political competitors are the primary targets of intimidation. These may be acknowledged political opponents who may be deterred from dangerous political activities in a variety of ways. However, members of the leader's entourage often are also objects of intimidation, since close associates may be as much of a threat as outright opponents. Ben Bella, after all, was displaced by Colonel Boumedienne, a close associate. General Ayub replaced General Mirza, with whom he had worked closely.

Individuals in the supporting organizations may also be held in line by some degree of intimidation. Members of the bureaucracy, the army and the police, or the single party may be induced to loyal performance through a measure of intimidation, often combined with reward.

Special attention is likely to be devoted to the press to ensure that stories unfavorable to the regime are held within bounds defined by the leader or his entourage. Efforts to induce cooperation by the business community may also be necessary, if the regime has economic or political objectives which the business community might not otherwise support and if its resources are not to go to the support of opponents. Students, trade unionists, and the other components of possible coalitions may be in part intimidated into acquiescence as they may be in part rewarded.

A SPECTRUM OF INTIMIDATION

Rewards are as varied as all those things that men desire. Similarly, intimidation can be directed to deprive men of all those things they dream of, depend on, or hold dear.

If self-respect and honor are of primary concern to the individual, *the threat of disgrace and public degradation* will serve to keep a man in line. Show trials, whether in Moscow, Baghdad, or Cairo, strip honored men of their aura of dignity and respect. When the hitherto admired and distant figure is reduced to the role of suppliant, his hold on his personal following is likely to be destroyed. Trials are also warnings to those in the entourage or further from the throne who may harbor ideas of opposition, dramatizing the fate which awaits those who deviate into active opposition. Show trials were one of Stalin's instruments of power. They have been used in Iraq to degrade the opponents who lost; Nasser used them to underline the dangers of consorting with the wrong foreigners.[21]

It may be possible so to control the newspapers or other media that, when the leader is ready, the private lives and loves of potential or threatening associates may be exposed.[22] It is not inconceivable that a leader may even plant within his entourage temptations to financial corruption and morally repugnant pleasures in order to gain a hold on his followers so as to ensure their continued good behavior. One or two associates may be sacrificed on the altar of moral rectitude as a means of ensuring the continued loyalty of the rest, the threat of public degradation being more than a man may care to risk, even if he considers a policy ill-advised. This tactic will be particularly useful in societies where mutual suspicion is widespread or where there is a wide gap between what the elite has come to permit itself and what the bulk of the populace believes to be appropriate behavior. These are characteristics of many societies in transition. In other more established societies the consequences of overstepping accepted bounds can also be severe, as Mr. Profumo in Great Britain discovered when his private life became exposed to an indignant British public by journalists and political opponents.

There may be an implicit *threat that economic benefits otherwise forthcoming will be withheld.* Subtle economic intimidation can be the obverse of reward. Loyalty improves the chances of being favored with a contract, a subsidy, an allocation of foreign exchange, or an interest-free loan. Suspected dissidence risks being deprived of these advantages. Just as the bureaucratic state opens countless opportunities for discretionary decisions rewarding the faithful with the allocation of scarce economic resources, permissions, licenses, and so forth, conversely, so does it extend the scope of potential intimidation by the threat to withhold such advantages.

The importance of foreign exchange to most of the politically active has been mentioned. Most are likely to be political competitors of present leaders who have tasted the fruits of foreign education

[21] On Iraq, see Benjamin Shwadran, *The Power Struggle in Iraq* (New York, Council for Middle Eastern Affairs, 1960, 90 pp.), Ch. 5; On Syria, Patrick Seale, *The Struggle for Syria: A study of post war Arab politics, 1945-1958* (London, Oxford University Press, 1965, 344 pp.), p. 279; on Egypt, Little, *Egypt*, pp. 200, 222-34.

[22] *The New York Times*, Jan. 10, 1964, p. 3.

or living standards. They know the rewards from education or medical treatment abroad, and they are particularly vulnerable to the threat of being deprived of foreign exchange.

Intimidation can derive from *more severe economic sanctions.* Deviant behavior may invite the bureaucracy to apply tax laws strictly, when they never have been enforced before. A factory, once started, requires imports of raw materials or semifinished goods to keep it running. A temporary—or protracted—delay in the issuance of an import license, a revision downward of tariff regulations by administrative decision, or an unexpected recall of a loan, these and other devices may be used against a businessman who appears to be consorting with the opposition or expressing unduly critical views. Ethiopia's businessmen reportedly experience similar economic sanctions.[23] Party-run trade unions may call a strike at the enterprise of an entrepreneur who does not toe the line. All others may be spared for a time. Government marketing organizations can buy or sell through local friends of the regime, gravely damaging the economic interests of opponents. Thus, the economically well-placed can be intimidated in efforts to ensure that they do not provide funds to the regime's opponents, to induce generous contributions to the ruling group, or to promote active business cooperation in the government's development plans.[24]

The press may be similarly "influenced." Nothing so blatant as censorship is necessary. Since the government allocates foreign exchange and newsprint is often in large part imported, a month-by-month allocation of newsprint among competing papers may be the only government action needed. A few months of delayed deliveries following some unfriendly articles, delays allegedly due to unavoidable administrative difficulties, will prove persuasive in most instances. The cost of newsprint may be managed; papers cooperating with the government will pay as little as 10 per cent of the free market price, and even become suppliers, at substantial markups, to papers not approved by the government. Where newsprint is not so easily diverted, government advertising can be an alternative lever. Government is by far the largest enterprise in most countries

---

[23] For the problems facing successful businessmen in Ethiopia, for example, see Levine, *Wax and Gold*, p. 188.

[24] Nigeria's experience has been particularly well-documented in *The Report of the Coker Commission of Inquiry into the Affairs of Certain Statutory Corporations in Western Nigeria* (Lagos. Federation of Nigeria, 1962), 4 vols. FDP 3225/163 (62)/2000. See also Sklar, *Nigerian Political Parties*, p. 501.

in Africa and Asia. Notices of contracts to let, public service examinations, and new laws and regulations are a substantial source of income to newspapers, nearly all of which are hard-pressed. These can be manipulated to serve the leader's short run purposes. Trade unions can be encouraged to strike a critical press and leave others alone.[25]

If the leader presides over a party which succeeds to a substantial extent in encompassing the total life of the members, such as the Neo-Destour party in Tunisia, *expulsion from the party is a kind of excommunication*, a descent into outer darkness. Renewed avowals of loyalty may be rewarded if, after appropriate suffering in outer darkness, the excommunicated is generously taken back and given a post where he can do little harm. Others feel sorry for him, admire the generosity of the leader—and are careful to avoid following in the footsteps of the punished man. It will be recalled that Bourguiba dealt with Ben Salah in this way; President Nasser has also imprisoned and then rehabilitated former lieutenants.[26]

Opponents may be *falsely incriminated in apparent antistate activities* in fact organized by the rulers. It has been reported that in Thailand, for example, "rebellions" may be initiated by the ruling group for the purpose of suppressing troublesome or rival elements or as an excuse for further tightening security and reducing the political activity of all opponents.[27]

Political activity of selected opponents may be curtailed in various ways. Former politicians may be deprived of their political rights, as in Pakistan's Elective Bodies (Disqualification) Ordinance, 1959. This ordinance gave former politicians the choice of either foregoing political activity until 1966 or undergoing examination by special tribunals whose intent clearly was to expose to public view the malpractice of many who had been politically active. Perhaps a hundred of the most prominent chose the course of temporary political retirement rather than face this kind of scrutiny. Numbers of officials were also removed for corruption or other malfeasance. President Nasser had introduced much the same measures in Egypt in April 1954.[28]

[25] International Press Institute, *Government Pressures on the Press, Part Two* (Zurich, IPI, 1955, 130 pp.).

[26] Moore, *Tunisia Since Independence*, pp. 82, 89, 95, 101.

[27] Wilson, *Politics in Thailand* p. 260.

[28] von Vorys, *Political Development in Pakistan* (Princeton, Princeton Uni-

The threat of house arrest can induce political quiescence in many others. Under such treatment, the individual cannot leave his home without permission, and only a limited number of approved persons may visit him. More subtle are examples where all who visit a former politician are interviewed by the police for a quiet review of their talk with the fallen political figure. In the course of the discussion, the police may mention back taxes not paid in full, or a request the visitor has pending in a government office. Gradually, the politician's friends will fall away; he himself will not wish to complicate their lives. He becomes isolated, harmless for political organization although, if a popular figure, he may remain as a symbolic focus for opposition as a possible alternative leader one day.

In India, house arrest under preventive detention was used to restrict the movement and political activity of the controversial Sheikh Abdullah, whose political base is in Kashmir. Periodically, communal enthusiasts are detained. After the outbreak of the Sino-Indian conflict in 1962, leaders of the Peking-oriented wing of the Indian Communist Party were jailed for a number of months.

Political activity may become personally risky to all who would oppose the leader. It has not infrequently occurred that political opponents seeking office have faced physical intimidation—or worse. Organized youths, more or less toughs, can be assigned to harass specific individuals. They may be beaten up, their cars overturned, servants frightened, etc. Indeed, one important function of youth movements in certain African countries is said to be to deal with opponents or possible disloyal followers.[29]

Sklar reports that in northern Nigeria, political activities by those opposed to the ruling party were felt to be risky because of the close links among chieftaincy, traditional courts, and party affiliations. Indeed, "4 of the 9 persons elected to the Northern House of Assembly in 1956 on the platform of the NEPU . . . have been convicted by Alkali [traditional local] courts . . . the knowledge that conviction by a native court may entail arbitrary punishment, indignities and lashes of the cane, whether 'symbolic' or otherwise, cannot be reassuring to the opposition."[30]

To take an example on the outer margin of the area, Syngman

---

versity Press, 1965, 341 pp.), p. 190, puts the figure at 6,000, but that seems very high; see Vatikiotis, *The Egyptian Army in Politics*, p 92 for Egypt.

[29] Hapgood, *Africa: From Independence to Tomorrow* pp. 138-39.

[30] Sklar, *Nigerian Political Parties*, pp. 362-63.

Rhee's principal political rival in 1949 was assassinated. His opponent in 1952, a former Minister of Agriculture, spent most of the nine-day campaign hiding from the police. In 1958, opposition members of the South Korean National Assembly were herded into the basement of the legislature while the faithful voted legislation curtailing political activities of the opposition.[31]

In Ghana, electoral intimidation is reported to have been substantial. In a 1959 by-election, for example, the assistant general secretary of the principal opposition party was reportedly attacked by thugs from the ruling CPP and narrowly escaped bodily injury.[32] In the referendum of 1960, the government openly warned those who opposed them of the consequences of opposition, implied the secret ballot no longer could be secret, and underlined the ability of the CPP to enforce its authority. Some of the most important political figures who opposed Mr. Nkrumah were placed in preventive detention several weeks before the referendum and were out of circulation during the whole campaign. Menderes's efforts in Turkey to restrict the political activities of his opponents were not dissimilar.[33]

Political opponents may be *exiled abroad* where they can do no harm. After a successful coup d'état, exile is, typically, the happiest fate of the losers. This is a characteristic technique in Thailand. Embassies may be largely staffed by those of uncertain political loyalty, whose presence at home could be a focus of opposition or a source of unrest.[34] Abroad they are relatively innocuous. Special measures may be taken to ensure their surveillance, but since their contacts with nationals are more limited abroad than at home, surveillance is much easier.

Exile as an ambassador or senior embassy official may not be

[31] Richard C. Allen, *Korea's Syngman Rhee* (Rutland, Vermont, Tuttle, 1960, 259 pp.), pp. 150, 223. For Ngo Din Diem's intimidation, see Bernard Fall, *Two Vietnams*, pp. 268-78.

[32] *Ashanti Pioneer*, Kumasi, Ghana (Oct. 1, 1965) in Austin, *Politics in Ghana*, p. 385.

[33] Austin, p. 388; See Walter Weiker, *The Turkish Revolution, 1960-61 Aspects of Military Politics* (Washington, D.C., The Brookings Institution, 1963, 172 pp.), pp. 10-11; on Iran see Cuyler Young, "Iran in Continuing Crisis," *Foreign Affairs*, Vol. XL, No. 2 (January, 1962), 275-92.

[34] Exile is characteristic after a coup in Thailand, see Wilson, *Politics in Thailand* pp. 256-57; on Ghana, Coleman and Rosberg, *Political Parties and National Integration in Tropical Africa*, pp. 279-80; on Ivory Coast see Zolberg, *One-Party Government in the Ivory Coast*, p. 332.

unpleasant, unless it is to a more isolated and unhealthy post. Exile without official position, however, may be more serious. Ways may be found to permit the exile to take assets with him, so that he need not live in penury. Indeed, he may have used his former position of political prominence to accumulate assets abroad for just such a contingency.

Nevertheless, the fear of the futility and loneliness of exile may lead many to accommodate the ruler and not oppose him, even if they do not support him with enthusiasm.

Imprisonment provides in itself a wide range of possibilities. On the one extreme, there is the confinement—with sufficient food and exercise to ensure health and books and paper to provide the means for developing a future political following—experienced by Britain's Nehrus and Kenyattas. On the other is the harsh, punitive imprisonment which leaves a man broken in body and spirit. Obedience to the leader may be exacted by a subtle process of gradually increasing pressure imposed by prison authorities, with periodic interventions by the benign leader to ease the pressure, perhaps shortening long sentences and, finally, commuting the sentence altogether so the man can return to his family on condition that he remain politically passive. A few examples may be sufficient to induce the run of men not to overstep the bounds laid down by the leader or his entourage.

Ultimately, of course, there is *liquidation.* If the means of communication are well-controlled and the police efficient, the opponent can simply disappear and nothing be heard of him again. If control of communications cannot be assured there is always the fatal airplane crash, the automobile accident, or the arrest and shooting of the victim as he was "trying to escape." Only a few such incidents are necessary to induce political passivity on the part of most men. However, if the victim has a popular following already, and if more than a few need to be involved to do away with him, the risks of such means are considerable. He may in death become a martyr and his death haunt the future of the man who caused it more than his continued life would have complicated the leader's political present.[35]

[35] Successful political liquidations are not reported for obvious reasons. For an example of a successful attempt by anti-government elements to liquidate the leadership of a regime see Maung U Maung, *A Trial in Burma, The Assassination of Aung San* (The Hague, M. Nijhoff, 1962, 117 pp.).

INSTRUMENTALITIES

Intimidation requires prior organization. As we have seen, political parties and even the economic bureaucracies can effect a certain amount of intimidation, often highly refined. Nevertheless, the police remains the principal instrumentality. It is the one element of the bureaucracy which concentrates on deterring or preventing certain types of activity by its known capacity and readiness to use force if necessary.

Like other elements of the bureaucracy, the police normally· serve as a service agency as well as an instrument of control for the political leader. In this role, the police's task is to ensure that small minorities of individuals are prevented from preying on the bulk of the populace for their own individual gain: property should be protected from theft; men and women from assault and murder; travelers should make their way safely; houses should be secure. Crowds must be allowed to demonstrate. But skilled and disciplined police may make the difference between orderly, benign crowd control and bloody repression or riots which threaten the personal safety of countless individuals or risk disrupting the fragile polity altogether. Where political institutions are not well established, mob excitement may lead to an overflow of passion that results in communal political or tribal slaughters, as have occurred in India and Pakistan at partition or in Indonesia after the abortive communist coup. If the police are used strictly within the metes and bounds established by the legal system, their actions are relatively predictable and their behavior subject to appeal and correction. But if the ruler is using his police for intimidatory purposes beyond the legal bounds, that very uncertainty will broaden the scope of intimidation—and make the regime the more repugnant.

But whatever the scope of police activity, the ruler requires a specialized organization. It needs to be well-trained and equipped for acquiring and sifting accurate information and for demonstrating the presence of potential force. If force actually has to be used, it must be discriminating, restrained yet sufficient. Since the police is often the most widely scattered element of the bureaucracy associated in the people's eyes with the ruler, it must deal with the populace correctly and with consideration. Harsh and whimsical police officials can bring a regime into popular disrepute. Clumsy pursuit of lawbreakers or indiscriminate search for disrupters can generate hostility to a regime. Just, protective, and efficient police may lend a good reputation to a regime, particularly if it has replaced a repressive or indiscriminate predecessor.

For these functions, the police need specific skills and a reliable chain of command. And of prime importance from the leader's point of view is the necessity for assured loyalty. The prime minister will want to be more sure of the loyalty of his top police (and military) officers than of any other elements in the bureaucracy. And he must select those officers who have the assured respect and obedience of the rank and file of the force. Potential opponents may be brought into camp with the Ministry of Cultural Affairs or even that of Education. But the key cabinet posts for control, the ministries of interior (or home affairs) and defense, must be filled only by the really loyal.[36]

Virtually all the measures of intimidation discussed here require that the ruler be sure of these critical parts of his bureaucracy. And for this, the key men may need to be generously rewarded. Intimidation of them will not be useful, as a rule.

THE INSECURITY PRINCIPLE

The "insecurity principle," however is one way they can be influenced. Rulers may systematically encourage a sense of insecurity among their senior officials. Ministers may be transferred from prominence and power to obscurity at the leader's whim. Where loyalty is uncertain or where a ruler's position is sufficiently unsure that any member of the entourage who uses his political position to strengthen his own political base may become a rival, regularizing insecurity may be the only way of holding an entourage without being overturned by it. All lieutenants are then so afraid of descending into obscurity that they will be doubly careful not to make obvious political capital of their positions and are likely to consult the leader on every major decision in order to avoid his displeasure. This method was used in Renaissance Italy. It can still be found today.

For example, in Ethiopia, Levine reports that Haile Selassie has found it prudent to rotate officials in office every year or two, in some cases as frequently as every six months, presumably to prevent the official from developing links with people in his area of respon-

---

[36] For a detailed discussion of the role of the police in Indian public life, see the forthcoming study of David E. Bayley, *The Police and Political Development in India.*

sibility which might produce a political following. He has also appointed mutual enemies to adjacent administrative positions, so
that they can each report something incriminating on the other to be
used by the monarch, if necessary, to ensure continued good behavior.[37] The last of the Viscontis in Milan used the same device.[38]
Prince Sihanouk is said to reassign his top generals frequently, presumably to prevent them from building their own following among
the troops they temporarily command or among the populace in any
one military district.[39] Sukarno effectively used the notion of "retool-
ing" to keep upper level civil servants unsure of their position.[40]

Such a policy has the advantage of deepening a lieutenant's dependence upon the leader by generating an anxious sense of insecurity, but it destroys initiative and greatly weakens the ability of the
government to pursue its many functions.

THE PROBLEM OF SURVEILLANCE

Detailed surveillance is an important element of a strategy
of intimidation. Surveillance must produce early warning of dangerous political activity. The intelligence services must be improved
as intimidation makes political activity increasingly circumspect and
secretive, and therefore more difficult to observe. But the surveillance
must go further, for the leader desiring to use intimidation against
specific individuals must know the strengths and weaknesses of his
colleagues and opponents in order to economize both threats and
rewards. Police and other forces of intimidation must be kept loyal
so that the ruler can count on the right people being subjected to
intimidation and be assured that those in custody do not escape to
tell their tale and awaken opposition against the regime. In such
matters effective control of critical elements of government precedes
the use of intimidation through the government apparatus.

Governments may use intimidation against possible opponents or
threatening associates. However, the rise of Fascism and Nazism in

[37] Levine, Wax and Gold pp. 187-88.

[38] Jakob C. Burckhardt, The Civilization of the Renaissance (New York, Harper
and Row, 1958, 2 vols.), Vol. I, p. 54.

[39] Roger M. Smith, "Cambodia," in George Kahin (ed.) Governments and Politics of Southeast Asia, pp. 595-675.

[40] Feith in Kahin (ed.), pp. 242-43; Flor Trujillo has described these processes
as used by her father in the Dominican Republic. Look (June 15, 1965), pp. 40-46.

Western Europe, the communist seizure of power in Eastern Europe, and Viet Cong insurgency in Vietnam suggest that there are means of intimidating government servants and political figures even before an aspiring group has achieved power, Private armies, party organizations with toughs on call, are familiar means of intimidation before one has control of the governmental apparatus. Appeals to the mob are a means open to government or well-organized anti-government forces, too. Hindu and Muslim use of mass action prior to independence challenged British rule. Mob action in Baghdad and Cairo has intimidated foreigners and specific minority groups concentrated in easily identifiable neighborhoods. In Indonesia, mob actions have been directed against specific embassies, Dutch economic installations and the Chinese community in Java.[41]

ADVANTAGES OF INTIMIDATION

Intimidation may be repugnant. But every government must have some capability to threaten severe sanctions if its position is challenged or its policies opposed in certain ways. This is particularly true in many new nations.

As has been pointed out in other parts of this study, many polities in Africa and Asia face special problems of diversity and contention; they often experience little agreement on how priorities and policies should be determined, or on how disputes should be settled. One can expect that the level of intimidation will have to be higher in such regimes than in more developed polities where political institutions are well established, procedures accepted, and consensus on major issues more easily evoked. Where differences are acute and mutual relations are suspicious, it is difficult to develop a broad coalition of sufficient solidarity to sustain a regime, and may require a degree of political art which will be rare. Under such circumstances, some degree of intimidation may make it possible for a regime to survive on a narrower base of support than would otherwise be feasible. When the voices of opposition are inhibited, the level of overt contention will be less and fewer active supporters will be required to sustain a regime.

[41] Hugh Tinker, *Ballot Box and Bayonet: People and Government in Emergent Countries* (London, Oxford University Press, 1964, 124 pp.), pp. 81-82.

Intimidation may nip in the bud demagogues whose activities might otherwise provoke widespread disorders. Few would argue that the use of the Preventive Detention Act by India against communal extremists in the past has not been in the best interests of India, since the tinder of communal fires appears to lie so close at hand. Special problems were posed to the authorities in the early days in Pakistan by religious puritans who aroused public hostility against those who disagreed with them.[42]

General strikes, persistent labor trouble among competing and often politically oriented unions, outrageous examples of tax evasion and official corruption or profiteering may be dealt with by a limited number of exemplary sanctions. This helps reduce disruption on the economic front and promotes greater effort for economic development. Minorities who lack a sense of solidarity with the larger nation may seek to secede if they are on the frontier. Sometimes a regime may be strengthened if dissident minorities leave the polity and join a neighboring one. But short of this, potential dissidents may be restrained by selective intimidation, thus either saving the state from disintegration or avoiding the creation of apples of discord likely to provoke future conflict between neighboring states.

Moreover, certain political cultures are more prone to violence than others. The contrast between pre-Cardenas Mexico and contemporary Great Britain is dramatic in this respect. And certain parties, communist and others, systematically organize to use violence. As Hugh Tinker puts it:

> Communist parties in southern Asia provide striking examples of the exploitation of direct action, physical force and violence as a deliberate alternative to the pursuit of power by way of the ballot box. Underground revolts, industrial unrest, and rural campaigns of terror have alternated with attempts to gain control of local state and central governments by constitutional means . . . But the Communists are by no means alone in their opportunistic approach to constitutionalism . . . [and] attachment to 'the cult of violence.'[43]

Where political opponents threaten assassination of key officials, destructive and well-directed mob violence, politically directed general strikes to bring the economy to a halt, or other forms of disrup-

[42] For a vivid account, see *Report of the Court of Inquiry to Inquire into the Punjab Disturbances of 1953* (Lahore, Superintendent of Government Printing, Punjab, 1954).

[43] Tinker, *Ballot Box and Bayonet*, p. 79.

tive violence, a regime must be able to mount counterintimidation to deter such activities. Only a regime prepared to deal vigorously in such coin can be expected to deter or restrain the promoters of violence, let alone accomplish indispensable governmental functions beyond mere survival.

LIABILITIES

Recourse to intimidation has liabilities, however. Beyond a certain point, it may provoke antagonism and lead to reprisals. Particularly in emerging countries, where the state apparatus is not sufficiently developed to induce a totalitarian reign of terror, the inefficiency of partial intimidation may be its saving grace and make it tolerable despite the occasional examples designed to induce conformity to the ruler's will. On the other hand, because it falls short of an effective system of terror, it may leave just enough hope of impunity to tempt men to bold reprisals against an intimidatory regime.

Intimidation usually has other costs. As open political activities are repressed, it becomes progressively more difficult for the ruler to have direct knowledge of the demands and wants of his people and of competitors. He becomes increasingly dependent upon information filtered through his own intelligence services. The surveillance agencies must be expanded. The watchers must themselves be watched, and the ruler must have a number of channels of information, else he will become the creature of only one. Intelligence and police services take an increasingly important share of economic resources and scarce human talent.[44] The intelligence services themselves become a focus of political contention within the regime, since each faction seeks to gain more access to the flow of information in order to influence the leader on its own behalf and to undercut the position of its rivals.

More serious for the polity as a whole are two other by-products. In the first place, if intimidation penetrates much of the system and serious sanctions are expected to be the result of political activity, alternative leadership will be discouraged, and possible successors will never have a chance to become knowledgeable in public affairs or to experiment with skills of developing political coalitions of

[44] On the increasing costs of surveillance, see Apter, *The Politics of Modernization*, p. 386.

support. Under these circumstances, parties skilled in clandestine operations, such as the communists, are favored. Their competitive position is likely to improve as it did in the Sudan under the Abboud regime.[45] Alternatively, the army and surveillance services may become the principal sources of successors to an intimidatory regime. These may recruit very capable persons, and men of high dedication and concern for the public welfare. But the skills of their professional advancement are not likely to be those which are necessary in an open, civilian polity.

Secondly, the level of mutual distrust will rise still further. In the emerging polity, distrust is already a marked characteristic of relationships. Intimidation will make it all the more prevalent. The nature of political contention changes from open discussion and argument to secretive intrigue and the undercover search for the protection of the ruler's favor. The leader himself becomes increasingly alone and suspicious, as occurred in Ghana.[46] Unless he is unusual, he will become more and more preoccupied with his own personal safety. Governmental actions toward necessary accomplishment on behalf of the society as a whole will become less important.

Thirdly, intimidation is likely to postpone the growth of a group of potential civilian leaders who have developed the art of enlisting a following and collaborating with others similarly engaged. It may prevent or postpone undesirable disruptions, but in itself it will not promote public consensus, a broadening of responsibility, or a resilient and adaptable institutional framework for exploring policy alternatives and for conducting political life for the future. Finally, a regime based on military coercion is itself the more easily taken from within by a military coup d'état, since power is already concentrated in a few hands and can easily be seized, while possible alternative sources of power in the society have become politically passive or are dispersed.[47]

Intimidation, then, has certain short run advantages. It requires a tight and well-directed organization to be effective and discriminating. But too much of it beyond what is deemed appropriate in the political culture can provoke resentment and can itself intensify pressures against the regime that the intimidation is designed to protect.

[45] T. E. Nyquist, "The Sudan: Prelude to Elections," *The Middle East Journal,* Vol. XIX, No. 3 (Summer, 1965, pp. 263-73), 269.

[46] Austin, *Politics in Ghana,* p. 48.

[47] Dankwart Rustow, "The Military in Middle Eastern Society and Politics," in Fisher (ed.), *The Military in the Middle East,* pp. 3-20.

10 Develop the Economy

> No society can surely be flourishing and happy of which the far greater part of the members are poor and miserable.
>
> Adam Smith

> If any goal stands out as the one most frequently acknowledged and extolled for nations to pursue, it is the goal of economic development.
>
> Kingsley Davis

By now most governments of emerging countries have committed themselves to develop their economy. Most regimes hold that their development efforts are for the benefit of the whole population and are laying the base for a happier and more prosperous future for all. At the same time, leaders assume that development provides political benefits to the regime, or at least helps them to avoid certain political risks or liabilities. Economic development policy, then, is another means by which regimes attempt to improve their power position and enhance their chances of survival.

It is remarkable that in the extensive literature concerning economic development or systematic comparative politics, little attention is devoted to the political impact of alternative modes and rates of economic growth.[1] The terrain is admittedly difficult. The quanti-

[1] The works of Albert O. Hirschman, *The Strategy of Economic Development* and *Journeys Toward Progress, Studies of Economic Policy Making in Latin America* (New York, Anchor Books, 1965, 397 pp.); Seymour M. Lipset, "Some

tative methods and the high level of abstraction useful for national macroeconomics give an apparent precision to economic development analysis which cannot be so easily assumed in political affairs. Students of politics are loath to enter highly specialized precincts staked out by economists. Moreover, there are already more ambiguous variables than any of us can easily deal with in either economic or political analysis. When both realms of reality are combined, one enters what appears to be a hopelessly uncertain realm.

Nevertheless, men in political life must act in the midst of such uncertainty. They are not permitted the luxury of postponing decisions until all the evidence is in. Similarly, this study cannot avoid some observations on this matter, even though empirical data are generally lacking.

AYUB OF PAKISTAN: ADVANTAGES AND LIMITATIONS OF DEVELOPMENT

When President Ayub and his coterie of soldiers and central bureaucrats took power in 1958, replacing a series of short-lived civilian regimes, Pakistan's economic difficulties were serious. Agricultural production was stagnating; consumer prices for nearly all items were rising sharply; tax evasion was widespread and obvious. There was a chronic shortage of foreign exchange at a time when numerous businessmen were illegally building up personal deposits abroad. Politicians, their families, and a handful of prominent trading houses and industrial families appeared able to exploit to their own advantage the detailed physical controls of the administered economy.[2] The Ayub regime justified its take-over largely in terms of the "economic mismanagement" of its predecessors. Economic stability and

Social Requisites of Democracy: Economic Development and Political Legitimacy," *American Political Science Review*, Vol. LIII (March, 1959), 69-105; Charles Wolf, *Political Effects of Economic Programs: Some Indicators from Latin America* (Santa Monica, Rand, 1963); George Rosen, *Democracy and Economic Change in India* (Berkeley, University of California Press, 1966, 350 pp.); Warren Ilchman, "The Political Economy of Foreign Aid: The Case of India," *Asian Survey*, Vol. VII, No. 10 (October, 1967), 667-68.

[2] For a discussion, see Herbert Feldman, *Revolution in Pakistan: A Study of the Martial Law Administration* (London, Oxford University Press, 1967, 342 pp.), Ch. IV; Gustav F. Papanek, *Pakistan's Development: Social Goals and Private Incentives* (Cambridge, Harvard University Press, 1967, 354 pp.).

then development became central planks in the new government's program.[3]

The new government first gained legitimacy in the small man's eyes by rolling back consumer prices and attacking obvious corruption. Intellectuals and civil servants were impressed by the pursuit of notoriously corrupt officials and those prominent businessmen who were salting away scarce foreign exchange abroad. Forgiveness of some past business activities resulted in at least a portion of the illegal holdings being brought forward, freeing these hitherto clandestine resources for legitimate development investment. Prompt land reform measures, however modest, took some 2.5 million acres in West Pakistan from the largest landholders, whose preponderating political influence in rural districts and the legislature had been notorious. To be sure, a single family could still retain 500 acres of irrigated land, a generous remainder hardly calculated to bring a landed family to ruin. But the measure did weaken the influence of the largest owners and put them all on notice that their continued extensive holdings were no longer automatically theirs by right, but depended in part upon their contribution to the national economy. Reform of tenancy arrangements, lowered land rents, and improved share-cropping terms affected many more individual farmers, particularly those near the bottom.[4]

The civil servant technicians and their foreign advisors, who had been shaping their ideas under the previous governments, proved ingenious in recommending policies which substantially accelerated economic growth. The Ayub regime implemented their advice with consistency and vigor. Government investment in irrigation, roads, electric power, and other infrastructure rapidly expanded to lay in many of the requisites of rapid growth.[5]

The system of physical controls accumulated under previous regimes, and intensified during the first months of martial law was gradually loosened. Private incentives were brought to bear on developmental goals. The remarkable industrial growth, begun under the acute consumer shortages and high profit margins of previous regimes, was sustained under the Ayub regime, even though profit

[3] Papanek, pp. 6, 86; Mohammed Ayub Khan, *Friends Not Masters, A Political Autobiography* (New York, Oxford University Press, 1967, 275 pp.), pp. 56, 81.

[4] Feldman, *Revolution in Pakistan*, pp. 47-49, 53, 61-63; Callard, *Pakistan, A Political Study* p. 67.

[5] Papanek, *Pakistan's Development*, p. 141.

margins were reduced.[6] An Export Bonus Scheme simplified import procedures, encouraged exports, and brought foreign exchange into government hands. These measures, substantial profit margins for a rapidly growing entrepreneurial class, pioneering investment by government-run development agencies, and a policy of indirect controls, contributed to sustaining a rate of industrial growth as high as that of any country in the world.[7]

In the countryside, agriculture had stagnated under the previous regime's effort to use government procurement, fixed prices, and United States food supplies provided under Washington's Public Law 480 (PL 480) to keep urban food prices down. The new regime gradually loosened procurement requirements and accelerated the distribution of fertilizers and seeds through the less cumbersome, more dynamic private traders. Credit was widely available for middle- and large-scale farmers to sink tube wells and install pumps so that they could control the flow of water on their own fields. During the 1950s, the internal terms of trade worked against agriculture, but during the 1960s more industries developed to compete against each other, and substantial foreign assistance and expanded exports eased import restrictions. As a result, prices for many manufactured goods declined while farm prices and output rose. PL 480 imports temporarily helped keep urban food prices steady, but this program was so administered as to avoid forcing down the prices paid to local farmers for their products. Fertilizer production increased rapidly and additional imports of fertilizer and high-yielding seeds gave promise, by 1968, of a genuine resolution of Pakistan's food problem in years of normal weather.[8]

This level of performance in part resulted from and in part contributed to sustained resource transfers from the World Bank consortium, underlining international confidence in the Government of Pakistan's ability to implement policies designed to expand the gross national product (GNP). Other countries were experiencing difficulties, but Pakistan seemed able to absorb and transform into growth whatever resources were made available from abroad.

In sum, Pakistan experienced a notable growth of industries in the fifties; this growth continued into the sixties, when agricultural ex-

[6] Papanek, Ch. 2.

[7] Papanek, pp. 30, 116-44.

[8] For a detailed discussion, see Papanek, Ch. 6.

pansion was added. The balance of payments position improved markedly. Reported GNP results confirm these observations.[9]

Economic development contributed to the regime's political position in a number of ways. In the first place, the morale of senior civil servants improved; this is of considerable importance in a polity where the bureaucracy plays such a critical role. Development success reflected well on their judgment and their skills. A number of retired civil servants and military officers also found opportunities as directors of government-sponsored or private industries.[10] To be sure, junior levels probably resented the fact that many of the specific physical controls they had handled under the previous regimes were now released, depriving them of both power and income. And regardless of official policies, Bengali civil servants felt they were getting short shrift in a service where they were poorly represented at the highest levels. Over all, however, economic success helped keep civil service morale high, particularly at the upper levels where it counted most.

Secondly, the resources made available both domestically and from abroad were directed toward investment and other activities which brought indirect political benefits as they contributed to development. For example: heavy construction in the Indus Basin works, the world's largest integrated irrigation system, provided numerous construction jobs for the West Pakistani unemployed and opportunities for labor, construction, and transport contractors of varying sizes. Industrial credits from government and international sources to individual enterprisers assisted numerous middle-sized and some large firms to build manufacturing capacity at interest rates much lower than they could have obtained on the local capital

---

[9] GNP Growth Rate

	1950-51	51-52	52-53	53-54	54-55	55-56
GNP	3.7	0.1	2.9	6.3	0.5	0.3
Per Capita	1.3	−2.2	0.6	3.9	−1.9	−2.5

56-57	57-58	58-59	59-60	60-61	61-62	62-63
5.1	0.8	1.4	4.2	5.2	5.9	3.5
3.6	−1.3	−1.0	1.9	2.5	3.4	0.9

63-64	64-65	65-66	66-67
8.3	4.5	4.6	5.2
5.6	1.8	1.9	2.5

Source: "Statistical Bulletin of the Government of Pakistan," Economic Affairs Division, Dec., 1967.

[10] Khalid B. Sayeed, The Political System of Pakistan (Boston, Houghton Mifflin, 1967, 221 pp.), p. 153.

market if, indeed, any capital would have been available at all except to trading or landed families who already had resources. Government efforts to promote agriculture by improved farm prices and accelerated inputs helped the large landed families to forgive the land reform and increased the income of middle-sized holders. The tenancy and other reforms, as well as improved farm income, probably helped the small man somewhat, though this is more difficult to assess. In West Pakistan, Ayub had the initial advantages of firm authority over both the army and public service, by virtue of his prior position as respected Commander in Chief of the armed forces and Minister of Defense; his place of origin near the border separating the Punjab from the Northwest Frontier Agency, where Pathans and Punjabis mingle, gave him at the outset ethnic support among both. His economic measures gave the landed and the new entrepreneurial classes a stake in the continued stability of the regime. Relatively few, except perhaps the growing urban population of Karachi and Dacca, could logically expect a sharp change to be to their economic advantage.

Pakistan's special problem of national unity, the geographical, ethnic, and economic division between East and West Pakistan, was also affected by economic policy. East Pakistan suffered grievously at partition when the jute producing areas of East Bengal were cut off from the jute mills long established in the Calcutta area. Economic activity had not been systematically dealt with under the previous governments. While industrial growth surged forward in West Pakistan, sparked mainly by the Muslim trading communities which migrated to Karachi from the Bombay area, East Pakistan development stagnated, and Bengali spokesmen persistently argued that the east wing was not receiving a fair share of investment. Ayub's economic development programs laid greater stress on accelerating investment in East Pakistan. Government-run development agencies which proved successful in the west wing were duplicated in the east. In recent years, larger government allocations have been assigned to industrial development in East Pakistan than in the western wing. Indeed, there was a noticeable trend toward government-sponsored investment in the east to promote activities taken up by private enterprise in the west. But despite these efforts, the pace of industrial development in the east continued to lag behind that of the west.

Thanks to the rural development administration of the civil service and the Basic Democrat structure of Union and Town Councils, resources were made available directly to Union Councils for local allocation. Only a minimum of supervision by East Pakistan Provincial authorities was required. Local bodies defined their needs, designed the works, and arranged for their construction, largely by local labor supervised by local officials. Additional payments to cover wages to local laborers, many of them otherwise unemployed for months at a time, and to farmers for clearing irrigation channels, building protective dikes, sinking tubewells, and building farm-to-market roads were obtained in part by selling on the open market flour obtained from the United States through Public Law 480. In this sharply decentralized fashion, local works were accomplished and local roads built at very low cost to the central treasury. In addition, local village councils gained experience in allocating resources for local needs with only a minimum of official supervision to slow things down, and individual unemployment was reduced.[11]

Economic development programs were encouraged in this way. As a by-product, the regime developed a set of political links to the rural populace through the civil service and the Basic Democratic Union Council structure. Previously, East Bengal's rural population had been linked to provincial and national politics tenuously, mainly through the urban intelligentsia of lawyers, doctors, and small businessmen concentrated in Dacca. [12] The new activities and programs short cut the Dacca intermediaries and went directly to rural areas. This appears to have brought the regime unexpected support in the 1965 election. But the long run consequences were harder to calculate, since in subsequent by-elections the regime did not do so well in those areas of East Pakistan where the development impact had been greatest.

Ayub used additional strategies in his efforts to legitimize and consolidate his regime and pursue the longer-range objectives he set for Pakistan. But the emphasis he placed on development policy and the economic success which accompanied these efforts represent a clear example for our purposes.

Certain questions, however, remained. Could the bureaucracy con-

---

[11] Papanek, *Pakistan's Development*, pp. 157-62.

[12] Wayne A. Wilcox, "New Elites of India and Pakistan," *Trans-Action* (September, 1967, pp. 43-50), 46.

tinue to implement those policies which harnessed private incentives
to the needs of Pakistan's future economic growth? Would the inequities in a mode of economic growth which gave substantial place
to the freewheeling industrial magnates remain politically tolerable?
Would Pakistan's foreign policy and the trends of world politics
outside Pakistan assure sufficiently large inflows of foreign resources
to permit development to continue unabated? The rising force of
the opposition to Ayub, once his vigor had been weakened by ill
health in 1968, suggested the limitations of economic development
as a political strategy. The regime could not permanently repress the
political groups active before 1958. They were bound to reassert
themselves unless the regime eliminated them altogether by liquidation or exile, which it refused to do. His emphasis on rural development coupled with rapid industrialization carried out, quite
typically, by a small number of entrepreneurial families, created
bitterness in urban areas that overall growth statistics could not assuage. Corruption in the form of gross privilege and profit for his
son came to taint his own name, too. It was an efficient regime, on
the whole, run by guardians of the vice-regal tradition. But it was
deadly dull; it lacked zest and color. Would the very processes of
economic change which are now beginning to gain momentum make
it impossible for another guardian to succeed Ayub? If not, what
changes in the political infrastructure occurred during his rule to
improve the chances for a more effective representative regime in
the future?

SOME GENERAL CONSIDERATIONS

A number of preliminary considerations must be examined
before we look at economic development as a political strategy in
countries other than Pakistan.

In the first place, the economic characteristics of a country will
set severe limits to choices open to political leaders. There are
markedly different economies, and few generalizations in these matters can apply across the board. Economies can be looked on as
representing different stages of economic growth, as in the Rostow
models. Geographic differences and differing priorities can be high-
lighted by oversimplified comparisons.

African economies, for example, tend to be the most backward, with a relatively small proportion of the populace in the market economy, and only one or two cash crops produced mainly for export. Characteristically, they have had to depend almost entirely upon outside resources for investment. By comparison with others elsewhere, African countries probably possess less of the social and economic structures on which development depends. Rarely is population pressure yet a serious problem. In the Middle East, among the most developed are Turkey, Lebanon, and Egypt (and, of course, Israel). The other major countries, apart from Jordan and Syria, have large oil revenues as a base of sustained and high-level foreign exchange earnings. But with few exceptions, such as Lebanon, political institutions are notably brittle or embryonic, productive entrepreneurship unusual or confined to a few, and government economic activity subject to frequent abuse.

South and Southeast Asia face contrasting problems. In India, Pakistan, Ceylon, and Java population presses hard on limited land resources; in Burma, Thailand, Malaya, Vietnam, and most of Indonesia outside of Java, there are favorable man-land ratios. But, in all, ancient civilizations long predate the European colonial intrusion of three or four centuries. Adapting these cultures to more efficient economic activity is a long and demanding process, and one fraught with political pitfalls, as important groups may oppose what government leaders want to introduce.[13]

Secondly, alternative approaches governments adopt carry different political implications. A government may be dedicated to rapid investment in industry. This is an apparently attractive course of shortcut industrialization that promises rapid structural change in the economy, provides certain, though usually limited, jobs to the urban workers, and meets the subjective needs of those aspiring to modernity. The marginal productivity of labor is increased, urban unemployment is attacked, and taxation of industrial output is easier; in addition, urban standards of living appear to improve. It will also be necessary for long run growth and diversification. This course proved most attractive in the 1950s and early 1960s. By contrast, rural development may be stressed, calling for productive incentives

---

[13] Edward Mason, *Economic Planning in Underdeveloped Areas* (New York: Fordham University Press, 1958, 87 pp.), pp. 18-20. In contrast, see R. J. Holt and J. E. Turner, *The Political Basis of Economic Development* (New York, Van Nostrand, 1966, 410 pp.), Ch. 7.

for the farmer and a multiple attack on rural backwardness. These will provide certain political assets in rural areas and will be necessary in many countries if food production is to keep pace with population growth and the agricultural sector is to generate savings. It also aids in earning sufficient foreign exchange to fund imports and finance external borrowing. In the short run, however, it may risk political unrest in the cities and generate political demands in the countryside more rapidly than they can be met.[14] In reality, agriculture and industry depend on each other. To provide necessary inputs for an expanding agriculture, certain types of industrial enterprises are vital. If the urban populace is to be fed and if a domestic market—sufficient to generate an expanding and real demand for growing industrial production—is to develop, agriculture must be improved. The real choice, then, is one of emphasis and pace, not either/or.

Rulers may lay stress on improving human resources as the first step, through generalized or highly specialized education and training programs and heavy investment in social overhead. If the type and size of training is kept commensurate with the growth of opportunity, the development of an increasingly impatient body of educated unemployed may be limited. Thailand, it appears, has geared its educational programs to job openings longer than most countries.[15] However, if education is rapidly expanded, as in India and Ceylon, numerous articulate and disgruntled young people are in the making.

In dealing with these alternatives, a government may attempt to influence the process by providing incentives and creating an environment designed to induce the desired activities. By contrast, it may seek to manage the economy by detailed physical controls, specific directives, and governmental operation of selected enterprises.

A regime's approach to development policy—and the political implications of these policies—will be affected by whether the regime is freely choosing the course of development or is responding to immediate and urgent politico-economic pressures. The conscience

---

[14] On the relation between agricultural development and industry, see Wilfred Malenbaum, "Some Political Aspects of Economic Development in India," *World Politics*, Vol. X, No. 3 (April, 1958), 378-86, 382-83.

[15] On Thailand's approach to this problem, see Wilson, *Politics in Thailand* pp. 103-04.

of the ruling group may find it intolerable that the people must, on the average, live on less than $100 per year. The leader's other private impulses may also impel him to press for development, for he may want to prove to himself, his former associates in the metropole, or foreign visitors that he is modern and determined to change the lot of his people. Resources available from abroad may in themselves be a catalyst, making conceivable economic steps hitherto out of the question.

The urge to develop may also derive, however, from a more immediate political calculus. Increasing demands may be pressed upon the leadership by spokesmen for larger and less well-favored groups in the populace who are no longer content with what they have, and who make demands in the here and now for a larger share of opportunity and consumption.[16] In this case much will depend upon who are the impatient ones, what claims they make, and how politically effective they are. In India and Pakistan, for example, mounting tensions appear unavoidable for the future unless the educated find more opportunities commensurate with their training and the organized obtain more regular employment. Rather than from immediate pressure, the motivation for development may come from projections into the future of what current trends of population, employment, and growing group expectations portend for five to ten years from now. Leaders in such countries have a wide choice of development strategies and face lesser political risks if their policies prove incorrect. In some countries where resources are plentiful and expectations remain limited, as in Thailand, projections of future political pressures growing out of economic cramp suggest little urgency.

The ideological predilections of political leaders will necessarily limit their view of whatever economic options might theoretically exist, given their country's resource endowment and institutional equipment. "Socialism" is widely accepted as a good thing in most emerging countries. To support socialism is to put one on the side of the anticapitalist angels. The capitalist targets of socialist criticism have historically been foreign enterprisers, usually associated with the European rulers. They may have been regional minorities of higher energy and sharper business acumen, like overseas Chinese

[16] Hirschman, *Journeys Toward Progress*, p. 308; Kingsley Davis, "Social Changes Affecting International Relations," in Rosenau's *International Politics and Foreign Policy* (New York, The Free Press, 1961, 511 pp.), pp. 137-39.

in Indonesia and Malaysia, or Indians in Burma. As pointed out in Chapter 3, socialism represents the search for a more just and equitable society. Commitment to socialist doctrine calls for ever increasing use of the government bureaucracy to manage economic enterprise.

Which course of development will appear plausible depends in part upon the economic effectiveness and political standing of existing institutions capable of promoting economic growth. Characteristically, for example, the private business sector in many countries is believed insufficient to the task.[17] By comparison, national hope has been fixed upon the political leaders, who brought independence, and on the bureaucratic frame, which appears to embody the nascent nation and to be the only institution working for the general interest. Although the bureaucracy itself is often held to be filled by time servers and men responsive to the already well-placed, private business is seen as working for the benefit of far narrower special interests. On the other hand, the ability of government administrations to implement the policies assigned to them is often in doubt. For these tasks require administrative talent, energy, and a nice perception of ways to economize scarce resources—qualities rare in any bureaucracy.[18]

Accordingly, different approaches to economic development will contribute to different political results. The few observations below are by way of suggestive commentary only on a subject deserving much more attention than it has yet received.

SOME POLITICAL ADVANTAGES OF ECONOMIC DEVELOPMENT

Development may provide certain short run gains in welfare which may have political returns. Dramatic changes in the standard of living may not be necessary for a regime to gain some advantage from development policy. The tastes of the bulk of the population

[17] Mason, *Economic Planning*, p. 15.
[18] On the need to economize, see Zinkin, *Development for Free Asia* Part II. For a comparative historical analysis raising doubt about the bureaucracy's ability to cope, see Holt and Turner, *Political Basis of Economic Development*, Chs. 3, 4, and 7.

in most emerging countries are starkly simple. Extra food in most seasons, more cloth at reasonable prices, inexpensive lanterns, stoves, cooking utensils, flashlights, and cheaper bicycles are the basic consumption items desired. Apart from agricultural improvement which often requires a subtle combination of incentives and technological and administrative innovation, these consumption items may be produced by small-scale plants. The latter do not require a large initial investment while yielding their output to the market relatively quickly, compared to capital goods industries. Expenditures on schools and dispensaries are also in high demand, and, judging by their rapid spread, rulers must believe them to be highly useful politically.[19]

Success in these seemingly modest objectives can be perceived by the populace. A sense that the government cares for the small man is enhanced and mass unrest minimized by such steps. Overstressing these and similar short run returns, however, will absorb too many resources and further delay economically more ambitious—and sophisticated—investment. Admittedly, too, such modest gains in themselves will not impress the middle and upper middle classes from whom most political spokesmen are drawn, since many of them want their country to become more modern—an aspiration which seems to require a move into industry. De Tocqueville was probably right when he argued that when some abuses are ameliorated, those which remain stand out in bolder relief, intensifying rather than moderating impatience.[20]

Nevertheless, to dismiss the probable political returns of such simple distributive policies is to ignore political imperatives and, perhaps, be beguiled by the fascination of oversophisticated economic calculation, as well as the chimera of catching up with the developed countries within the century. The modest first fruits of such development can be of real political importance, making the more extreme criticisms of the opposition seem unreal. It has been reported, for example, that a sharp increase in the Ivory Coast's ability to distribute welfare and other services greatly eased the government's problem for a time. The moderation of Malaysia's communal relations

[19] For their role in Nigeria, for example, see Sklar, *Nigerian Political Parties*, p. 504.

[20] Alexis de Tocqueville, *L'Ancien Regime*, translated by M. W. Patterson (Oxford, Blackwell, 1952, 233 pp.), p. 186.

until recently has been attributed in part to the government's extensive services and development activities.[21]

Development may provide an integrative goal after independence is achieved. After the temporary unity derived from the independence struggle, the objective of "economic development" is often the next promise held aloft by hard-pressed leaders. In contrast to patronage-type rewards, where advantages are distributed in a highly specific and discriminating fashion, the generalized goal of economic development holds out promise of something for everyone. As noted in Chapter 3, bureaucrats expect to have greater responsibilities; intellectuals hope to lend their wits to the planned national endeavor; business expects capital assistance and an expanding and protected domestic market; trade unions anticipate a growth in candidates for unionization; and leaders of deprived ethnic groups may expect their sons to gain access to opportunities they never dreamed of.

Indeed, without some promise of improvements in elementary standards of living or of expanding opportunity for the more numerous educated, one can expect in most countries a growing sense of ineluctable struggle among traditional groups, socioeconomic classes, and better organized interest groups of many kinds. Growing social tensions, mutual hostilities, and increasingly frequent social conflicts are perhaps ineluctable concomitants of social mobilization accompanying independence in emerging countries.[22] But it can hardly be argued that a stagnant economy will be more likely to hold such conflicts in check than one which is able to offer a somewhat better standard of living and increasing opportunity to a more numerous, better educated and organized, and more aspiring populace.[23]

Economic development decisions may help to counteract centrifugal tendencies. Tribal, regional, or other demands for independence by people along the country's frontiers may be contained

[21] Coleman and Rosberg, *Political Parties and National Integration in Tropical Africa,* p. 262. Interviews in Kuala Lumpur with officials and journalists, 1967.

[22] Karl Deutsch, "Social Mobilization and Political Development," *American Political Science Review,* Vol. LV, No. 3 (September, 1961), 493-514.

[23] In "Economic Development and Political Stability in India," Bert Hoselitz and Myron Weiner make this same point, reprinted from *Dissent* (Spring, 1961), p. 3. M. Olson, Jr., "Rapid Economic Growth as a Destabilizing Force," *The Journal of Economic History,* Vol. XXIII (March, 1963, pp. 529-59), 534.

by the selective application of development resources. Investment in roads, dams, irrigation works, major infrastructure projects, or large industrial units such as oil refineries may provide the government with ways to reward those local leaders who make only moderate demands. Such rewards may also dissuade them from pressing their parochial claims. The Government of Pakistan invested more than it might have otherwise in the tribal areas of West Pakistan in an effort to encourage the political acquiescence of tribal leaders.[24] India located oil refineries contrary to economic advice, in order to assuage the sensitivities of Assamese leaders.[25] Investment, too, may go into specific enterprises either run by scions of local families or with joint ownership, etc., giving to the locally influential an economic stake in the enterprise and the wider national market.

Too many instances of such "solidarity" investments may be unbearably costly in an economic sense. They are likely to lower the rate of economic growth below what is theoretically possible. But if a substantial measure of political stability and internal peace can be purchased in such a way, it may prove to be a first-class economic bargain, as well as represent a political success for the regime in power.

Certain tendencies toward political fragmentation are too deep to be dealt with simply by providing improved incomes, economic opportunities, or credible expectations. And it is difficult a priori to distinguish what a local notable may feel is a dishonorable bribe from what appears as an honorable reward recognizing the status deserved by local leaders and the unique cultural and other values they believe they represent. The way economic development policies are determined may contribute to a sense that the status of local leaders will be improved if they collaborate with a national regime. For example, local leaders may be drawn into consultations on a footing of equality with the representative of the central government in such devices as development councils, regional committees, etc., to help decide how development resources should be spent locally. Thus to consult local interests may delay investment decisions. It is also likely, however, that when local leaders are consulted and come to see a common interest in the endeavor, the work will proceed

---

[24] Interviews.

[25] Weiner, The Politics of Scarcity, pp. 205-07.

more smoothly and contribute more to the desired political objective of greater unity.

A prudent administration will seek ways to draw young people from the outer margins of the realm into satisfying activities relating them to the wider nation. Investment in education may raise the general level of skills, thus satisfying a widespread demand for more opportunity. It may also contribute to reducing centrifugal tendencies. Parents may be induced to accept a regime if they see their children receiving sufficiently promising educational opportunities. Heavy educational investment may be necessary if younger people in incipiently dissident communities are to have competitive access to the wider national life in roles other than the most menial. Socialization in national values thus may be facilitated. Of course, raising educational levels may also promote local self-consciousness and produce more skillful and sophisticated leaders of regional opposition movements. This has occurred in the Mizo and Naga hill areas of India, and among Kachins and Karens in Burma. National leaders have little choice in most areas, however, but to expand educational facilities, ensuring as best they can that curricula meet the desire for respected status and cultural autonomy while promoting skills and attitudes useful to the wider national community.

Economic development programs usually improve a government's instruments of control. Infrastructure investments in road, rail, and air transport are usually important to bring new areas into the market economy, to permit greater specialization and division of labor, and to ensure that areas hard hit can be succored in times of national disaster such as floods, drought, or disease. Telephone and radio communications also promote economic growth by linking different levels of economic activity across distances. But these road and communications facilities also improve the mobility of government forces, providing the government with new means of asserting its authority beyond the precincts of the capital, even into more distant areas where the regime's writ may never have run before. Not only will the government's surveillance capacity be improved, but it will also be able to activate the rural population to political participation, as Menderes did in Turkey.

Improving communications and mobility is double-edged, however. With improved communications comes new awareness and increased demands, as the successors to Menderes have discovered in Turkey. Troubles which hitherto were isolated may cumulate and interact with one another. Dissidence started in one place may become more widespread with improved movement of men and ideas. With new communications, a government can no longer properly disregard disasters or civil commotion it could afford to ignore before. Accordingly, if infrastructure investment in roads, public transport, and so forth is to enhance governmental controls, governments must function at a higher level of effectiveness than before.

As a specific objective, or as a by-product of development activity, new institutions, such as cooperatives, village councils, small-scale credit institutions, and the like, can grow. These may serve many economic functions. Indeed, their main rationale may be to induce initiative for constructive activity by utilizing abundant spare time or to provide through local channels those resources individuals may need to promote greater productivity, such as the distribution of credit, seeds, tools, and certain consumption requisites as well as the collection and sale of crops. Few of these can evolve without the application of new resources of cash and management. In addition, however, almost all of them may lend themselves to improving a government's ability to influence the behavior of the populace, to penetrate further into the social hinterland, and to provide more adequate information on local grievances or individual opposition.

On the other hand, these institutions can also provide means for hitherto quiescent groups to draw together, discover, and amalgamate their separate grievances and channel their demands upward. They can be the apprenticeship institutions for democratic self-organization. Through them, the more numerous lower layer in the rural areas may eventually displace a more privileged, less numerous group which may have dominated local rural affairs for generations. Indian Brahmins discovered this to their sorrow.[26]

Whether or not such new institutions represent improved means of government control or become instruments for altering local power relationships depends on how the regime manipulates the resources channeled through these institutions, and on how effectively opponents of the regime or of the locally influential use these institutions as means for building opposition to those in power. It could probably be shown, for instance, that Pakistan's use of union councils in East Pakistan temporarily strengthened the government's

---

[26] Susanne Rudolf, "Consensus and Conflict in Indian Politics," *World Politics*, Vol. XIII, No. 3 (April, 1961), 385-99.

hand at the expense of the urban-based politicians who had earlier been East Pakistan's political spokesmen. In Madras State, on the contrary, it is more likely that the structure of local governing bodies provided the lowest level framework for the organizational activities of the Dravida Munnetra Kazhagam (DMK) which routed Congress in 1967.

Economic development policies may permit the government to provide additional resources to large groups in the society which it fears otherwise may become disaffected. Although major decisions of developmental policy are often argued on technical economic grounds alone, the political implications for a leadership group may be critical. Indeed, choosing among alternative developmental policies is essentially a political act, for the choice will affect the distribution of economic benefits and costs and may even contribute fundamentally to the survival or demise of identifiable politico-social groups or of the regime itself.

For example, in some countries, both economic rationality and political judgment may argue the virtue of channeling more resources into the urban centers. Here are large numbers of people who are more politically aware than the rest of the population. Whether key sectors of the work force are organized in trade unions or easily coalesce into urban mobs, inattention to urban unrest can spell the downfall of city-centered regimes. Only by expanding opportunity or subsistence aid in urban areas can such unrest be held in check. Large public works to beautify the city and bring to it a grandeur characteristic of Paris and London may satisfy the urge for symbolic equality on the part of the educated who know the metropole. They may also provide jobs to the jobless and lucrative opportunity to friends of the regime.[27]

Economic theories may urge the necessity for simultaneous investment in many industrial enterprises, to the end that they reinforce each other and finally move the economy forward. Industrial investment may also be undertaken with an eye to the urban unemployed, to the frustrated half-educated white collar clerks who desire more important jobs, to the young men who aspire to supervisory jobs in

---

[27] David Hapgood, *Africa: From Independence to Tomorrow*, put it this way: "Government spending goes to satisfy a profound need for status, as well as privilege. Since these are the educated Africans who worked for the colonial administration, status consists in having what the Europeans had." p. 67.

industry or the bureaucracy, and to all those who disdain rural life and look on the peasantry as little better than animals.

Fiscal and pricing policies may also favor the city man. An important proportion of resources needed to promote such a big push must come from foreign exchange earnings or from foreign assistance. The peasantry must continue to produce and improve its output so that more foreign exchange can be acquired through primary product exports. But domestic prices for agricultural products must not be allowed to rise, since that will adversely affect the urban cost of living and will promote unrest among the urban proletariat. Yet no increase in the price of agricultural commodities is likely to result in stagnant rates of growth in the agricultural sector. The dilemma is real enough and, until the acute food crisis of the mid-1960s, most countries opted in favor of holding rural incomes low by restraining food prices; at the same time, they attempted to concentrate development in the urban and industrial sector.

Alternatively, where the leaders are less interested in promoting industrial investment in the short run they may lay greater stress on the rural sector. It may be believed that since they must first feed their populace and promote exports as a means of gaining foreign exchange to pay for industrial imports, as did Japan, the rural sector should have greater priority for economic reasons. They may see in the rural masses a strategic political reserve which, if it can be gained, will lend the strength of numbers against their city-based political opponents. D. S. Senanayake was said to have done this with extensive land development schemes in Ceylon. They may believe that the landowning peasantry are more conservative and less likely to promote radical solutions than the more easily organized urban workers who are often led by Marxist-inclined union leaders with left party affiliations. Improving rural conditions may be the only way to slow the explosive rush to the cities.

Whether justified on economic or political grounds, many policies favor elements in the rural population. Land development, irrigation investments, the promotion of new credit institutions, organizations to distribute farm production requisites and to improve storage and marketing facilities, price supports, and other inducements to greater productivity—all may be used to strengthen a regime's following in the countryside, at least in the short run. Since resources are scarce, investments and effort applied in these directions are often at the expense of developments in other sectors, and they may begin to activate a hitherto inert rural population, creating new political problems for the future.

Certain tribes or regional or even ethnic groups may benefit from the policies adopted or from the way they are administered in detail. Particularly where identifiable groups preponderate in the administration of development policies or in specific lines of business, it is likely that their coreligionists, fellow tribesmen, or members of their own ethnic group will be quietly favored where discriminating decisions are to be made.

Economic development policies may also be used to undermine particular groups considered likely political opponents or whose destruction will win popularity among the politically relevant. Investment decisions may be made at the expense of chiefs, dissident regions, or specific groups a regime wants to punish or of which it wants to make an example, demonstrating the costs of not cooperating. Nearly all societies contain groups whose economic activities have been resented for generations. They are usually politically vulnerable, and a government program designed to take from them what can be distributed to others is usually popular. The Chinese in Southeast Asia have been victims of such policies. Land reform is as much political as economic. It is usually designed more to eliminate wealth of possible political rivals and to lay the political base of a conservative peasantry than it is expected to expand economic output, which it usually does not do. As Vatikiotis notes, Nasser's land reforms directly attacked the position of Egypt's landed and were a "means for striking a sensational note with the Egyptian masses."[28]

No doubt additional political functions can be served by successful economic development. It should be of little surprise, therefore, that most regimes have by now adopted economic development as one of their goals. Yet economic development policies in themselves may pose serious political difficulties.

POLITICAL LIABILITIES OF ECONOMIC DEVELOPMENT POLICIES

Advantages can always be gained by a government in a position to spend money on programs of its own choosing. But there are

[28] Vatikiotis, *The Egyptian Army in Politics*, p. 75. Micaud reports this motivation behind Tunisia's land reform, *Tunisia: The Politics of Modernization*, p. 161.

political costs in making economic development decisions, as there are in implementing them.

A major difficulty derives from the need to accumulate resources, for *finding the resources is usually politically painful.* Most regimes seeking to develop must raise the levels of taxation. A regime is fortunate if its colonial predecessor imposed heavy and regressive taxes. It is politically easier to retain colonial tax rates than to raise them, if they will provide sufficient returns for investment programs. More typically, however, most new regimes have faced the difficult task of having to impose new and heavier taxes at a time when its own political position was not yet secure nor its claim to rule unquestioned. Import, land, income, or sales taxes must be initiated or sharply raised. Tax collection must be improved to permit the government to extract resources from individuals who otherwise would have been immune.

The returns on improved export earnings may not go to the producers of commodities but be retained by government for development purposes. Inflation may prove a tempting indirect device for channeling resources to the government without heavy direct taxation. However, as an ever greater proportion of the population enters the cash economy, consequent rises in the cost of living can be politically inflammable. Nearly all groups will feel the new pinch if substantial resources are to be directed into heavy early stage infrastructural, industrial, or extensive agricultural capital improvements requisite for broad-gauged economic development. These are costly and take time for the fruits to become available. The problem of sharing the burden of accumulating necessary resources will be central to all governmental discussions of development policy.

It may be possible to ease domestic pressure by seeking resources from abroad. Few economies in emerging countries, apart from the oil-rich areas of the Near East, are likely to be able to promote sufficient investment on the basis of their own resources alone. Indeed, the need for more resources from abroad is becoming increasingly apparent to leaders of most new countries. Yet seeking assistance may appear to threaten independence; aid donors do not always share a government's understanding of its own political vulnerability and requirements. Donors may define conditions on purely economic grounds which may only accentuate political vulnerabilities. If assistance is in the form of loans, the pain may be postponed until the economy can bear the burden more easily but, in the end, the costs may be higher because heavy interest payments may more than offset the gains from the loans. There may be implicit if not explicit political conditions, which can easily be met if there is no opposition. However, a lively and articulate opposition can use such conditions to dramatize the regime's alleged lack of concern for national independence and sovereignty.

Moreover, spending on investment instead of welfare may prove politically costly as increasingly articulate political groups seek more immediate returns than can be expected from capital investments.

Development benefits are often only long run, but costs are immediate. The political returns from patronage-type activities are likely to be prompt—and probably short-lived. Expanding educational opportunities, confiscating the property of those who are widely disliked, undertaking land reform, instituting consumption or production subsidies, and certain other distributive policies associated with economic development may show quick political results.

But the substantial returns expected from genuine economic development come only over time. Standards of living will rise almost imperceptibly at the outset. Only gradually will new and better opportunities evolve for large numbers of people. Changes in the nature and style of life will take years. The underlying—and costly— infrastructure and more directly productive investments will not produce for a long time returns commensurate with their immediate costs. Yet the aggregation of political power is a short and middle run activity. A long run political tomorrow is reached only by political success in a series of short runs, often in a succession of political challenges barely overcome. Political futures cannot be thought about in the same terms as can long run returns on an industrial investment.

Hence, the shrewd political leader will weigh with care the real and present political risks he may run on behalf of some economic advance which will not present its political return until a number of years have passed. He will therefore search out the politically tolerable relationship between present sacrifice on behalf of some future economic benefit and his assessment of the immediate benefit necessary to assure political continuity until that happy and hypothetical tomorrow.

Economic development goals have an apparent measurability about them, but they are usually unrealizable in the short run. Development goals are usually stated in quantitative terms that refer most often to the rate of growth, the proportion of GNP plowed back into investment, or changes in per capita income. There is a double difficulty here.

Development goals are often beyond what can be achieved. To enlist necessary effort requires an overstatement of intent. To paint a vision of that future toward which a leader seeks to move is to highlight the virtues and returns and underplay the magnitude of the task. Goals as stated may be intended only as suggestive guidelines in the general direction the leader wants to go. Even an economic development "plan" may do little more than provide indications of the targets toward which one should aim, rather than state with assurance and commitment realizable objectives to be achieved.

Unavoidably, when development goals are stated in quantitative terms, they have an apparent firmness about them which easily becomes a yardstick to measure a regime's performance. When that occurs, economic failures are all too obvious. When the promised 8, 10, or 15 per cent growth rate is not achieved, the government can be accused of failure on the basis of evidence it provides against itself. If prices rise sharply when price stability was promised, obviously the government has not kept its promise. Factory building or new major public works may be necessary for the maturing of the long run economic plan. They are also tempting ways of demonstrating economic activity. However, premature emphasis on such conspicuous investment to prove one's attachment to change may consume an undue proportion of available capital, a waste of scarce resources an economy can ill afford. Such enterprises are almost inevitably behind schedule, their costs are likely to be higher than originally promised, and launching them into economical production takes more time and requires more capital—and managerial skill—than estimated. The critical can find in these matters grounds for arguing incompetence or corruption. The promises, spelled out in plans or public statements, when unfulfilled, can give critics demonstrable and manifest grounds for opposition.

If economic development could be promoted without detailed and defined statements of vaulting purpose or if specific steps could be implemented without definite targets or publicity, efforts to promote economic development would be less ambiguous political assets. Yet the apparent concreteness of goals defined in numbers has, in itself, political advantages. And a serious shortfall can be blamed on a scapegoat—the United States congress or administration, the International Monetary Fund, the International Bank for Reconstruction and Development, or even the weather, thus relieving the government of a responsibility it may, in fact, justifiably share.

Economic development requires change, and change is psychologically disturbing. More regular and precise work habits by a people may be necessary and will call for effort under the eye of some unknown supervisor instead of the local notable or family head. Workers may have to labor in cooperation with those from a different tribe, caste, or ethnic group, when such differentiations and social distance are an important source of one's self-esteem. Instead of performing the total productive process, they may now have only a specialized segment of the task to perform, monotonously, day after day. The lowborn may rise beyond their station, one tribe may adjust more rapidly to change than another.

As David Apter put it: "In most new countries there are mixed feelings about the consequences of economic development, and, while few would disagree with the material benefits of a rising standard of living, many have bitter feelings about the organizational consequences and demands made upon individuals which such a process exacts."[29] Political leaders who are sensitive to their populace will know of this ambivalence, and their enthusiasm for development will be moderated by this knowledge, since they, too, are beset by such contradictory feelings.[30]

When development policies are implemented, they do not in fact spread advantages equally. Economic development as a goal has the virtue of promising something for everyone. But as soon as specific decisions have to be implemented regarding raising the resources or defining priorities, more people are likely to be disappointed than satisfied.

If development policies give scope for individual initiative, certain groups may take the lion's share of resources or make the most rapid social and political advances. In India, the great Marwari and Parsi families stand out among those who have done well under planned development (as they did before). In Pakistan, industrial expansion has been notable, but the fortunes of a few families, such as the Adamjees or Isfahanis, have advanced conspicuously. In Malaysia,

[29] David Apter, "Systems, Process and the Politics of Economic Development," paper read before the North American Conference on the Social Implications of Industrialization and Technological Change, September, 1960, p. 9.

[30] Kingsley Davis makes the same point, "Social Changes Affecting International Relations," in Rosenau, *International Politics,* pp. 133-34.

despite government efforts to favor the Malay community, Chinese and Indian enterprisers are making the most of industrial development. The Burmese government of Ne Win appears to have preferred economic stagnation to permitting that type of development which will improve the fortunes of individuals or minority ethnic groups.

The articulate and well-organized have pressed their own advancement. Labor unions and ethnic associations seek out ways to make the most of development opportunities, leaving their less active and ill-organized neighbors to get along as best they can. In practice, therefore, economic development may not be equalizing but is more likely to raise some groups more rapidly than others, creating new tensions as old stratifications break down.

If economic development is successful, it is likely to under-cut at least some of the support for an existing regime, and it requires adroit political maneuvering to ensure that rising groups are won to the side of the regime in power, as the older supporting groups are weakened.

In the cities, a number of changes associated with development are also likely to weaken the group in power. Industrial development brings men together for new purposes and in ways likely to weaken established political machines. Trade-union organizations may come to replace the organization of the local boss or traditional ethnic leader, which focused on neighborhood. Public service institutions gradually make the party's service activities less relevant, as the New Deal's agencies displaced the ethnic boss in *The Last Hurrah*.[31] Younger men push forward, with new skills, higher levels of impatience, and a sharpened sense that the old compromising, adjusting city "boss" is out of step. It is not so much the direct effects of new industrial investments which undercut the city organizer. It is rather that the changes in communication and the opening of alternative organizations, indirect by-products of development activities, help to inflate aspiration, promote activism, and lead to politics against the regime, whoever is in control.

Changes in the countryside designed to promote productivity or equity may also weaken the local position of rural notables on whom a regime may depend. New village councils, cooperatives, lending institutions, and extension advisory services provide opportunities for energetic, capable younger men from lower positions to

---

[31] Edwin O'Connor, *The Last Hurrah* (Boston, Little Brown Press, 1956, 427 pp.).

demonstrate their worth and gain to positions of local responsibility. To the extent the local notables depended upon their monopoly control of farmers' requisites like credit, seeds, bullocks, and fertilizers for their political influence, to that extent will these innovations diminish their influence—unless they are able to control the new institutions from the outset, as sometimes occurred in India. But the sweeping political changes noticeable in India's 1967 elections suggest that the Congress Party's structure of support in the countryside, dependent to an important extent upon the continued influence of rural notables, has been drastically weakened, as was Ceylon's United National Party's strength in 1956. Indeed, a careful analysis of election statistics would probably show that where economic development had gained the most momentum, as in Madras and the Punjab, congress's rural foundations had been most thoroughly weakened. This is not to say that the new rural institutions directly undermined congress notables. But the new institutions gave opportunities to new men, provided the framework within which the opposition could organize, and enlivened a sense that change is possible where relatively unchanging stratification had been the norm before.[32]

A sharp rise in the industrial sector or successful agrarian reform thus promotes new power groups in the city and weakens a regime's support among the traditionally influential in the countryside. New groups will not automatically support the regime which provided the conditions for their growth, since their aspirations are likely to grow more rapidly than the regime's capacity to satisfy them.[33] Trade unionists or white collar workers may seek more rapid improvement in their working conditions than the new industries and government agencies can effect. An awakened peasantry may demand more fertilizer, better tools, and improved distribution and collection than a government can manage to provide. At the same time, the older interests will have been weakened by taxes or other measures and will no longer have either the influence or, probably, the desire to provide support to the regime which allowed their positions to be weakened.

[32] For a discussion, see Susanne and Lloyd Rudolf, "New Era for India: Politics After the 1967 Election," unpublished manuscript.

[33] For the political problems posed to Haile Selassie by the new business classes and his way of coping with them, see Levine, *Wax and Gold*, pp. 183-90.

Economic development policies require stability and order, but political survival may also require color and drama. While the economic development specialist may wax lyrical over upward curves of growing Gross National Product or a favorable turn in the balance of payments, this provides little direct satisfaction for the bulk of the populace. The very orderliness and predictability desirable for economic growth call for a minimum of demagoguery, a maximum of matter-of-factness in political expression. Excited passions may lead to disorders; verbal attacks on foreign or domestic enemies may impede the investment climate. Promises of foreign adventure or an evocation of the great religious traditions may excite passions disruptive of developmental processes. Regimes dedicated to creating the conditions necessary for speedy economic development, therefore, must take special measures to meet the subjective, passionate side of political imperatives. And this is a difficult prescription to combine.

In many countries, regimes have no other present alternative than to attempt to promote development. Rapid population growth and increased popular demands leave them no option. They talk a good development game. And most of them mean it to some degree. But the short-run political costs of raising the resources and making hard choices are likely to be serious. There is no assurance that if the pace is speeded substantially, the regime in power will gain from the new forces it will have promoted. It is no wonder, then, that men in power do not always adopt policies which economic rationality would commend.

11 Expand (or Contract) Political Participation

> In due course, political consciousness and participation extends to the lower middle class of the towns and cities, to the urban working class, and to the peasants. . . . The expansion of participation in an underdeveloped political system . . . which lacks strong and adaptable political institutions, simply increases the alienation of some groups from the system and leads to overt or covert civil strife.
>
> Samuel P. Huntington

When men out of office aspire to responsibility or incumbents feel threatened by the growing popularity of their opponents, either will be tempted to dip lower in the society to enlist new supporters who have hitherto been politically quiescent. They may be ahead of history, activating the passive in order to undercut the base of their opponents; they may be yielding to what they consider to be the inevitable, attempting to gain credit for opening the door which the more numerous lower strata are about to push open. The Reform Bills of 1832 and 1867 in Great Britain were constitutional landmarks in such a change.[1]

"Political participation" encompasses a range of possibilities.[2] At

---

[1] The Whigs in 1832 and the Conservative Disraeli in 1867 played these opposite historic roles. See, for example, Norman Gash, *Politics in the Age of Peel, a study in the technique of parliamentary representation 1830-1850* (London, Longmans Green, 1953, 496 pp.); William H. Riker, *The Theory of Political Coalitions*, pp. 200-01.

[2] For a further discussion, see Chapter 3 above.

one end of the spectrum, individuals may be activated to cheer a leader as he rides by or to register a plebiscitary yea. They are not politically quiescent, nor are they participating in the sense used here. They may, by contrast, participate by registering a choice, as in a free election, with or without prior discussion of the issues and personalities. They may also participate as part of a party cadre, with an eye to affecting the choices of others. Participating in party affairs can be a full-time, professional activity, a way of life. Participation may take the form of guerrilla insurgency. Great personal risks may be run. The range of "participation" is therefore wide, although the following discussion does not attempt to distinguish where in this range each example of political participation should fall.

AN EXAMPLE: BANDARANAIKE OF CEYLON

The success of Prime Minister S. W. R. D. Bandaranaike is an example of how expanding political participation of the hitherto quiescent can be of advantage. He used this strategy to undermine the incumbent regime and to help sustain his position once in power. By a remarkable effort, mainly in rural areas, Mr. Bandaranaike activated the Sinhalese rural middle class and through them the peasantry. In 1965, he overwhelmingly defeated the incumbent United National Party, the party of independence that had sustained general communal harmony since independence in 1948. While Ceylon had had universal suffrage since 1932, the 1956 election was the first in which the bulk of the rural population was activated to lively political participation.[3]

Most of his competitors were either city men or those so well placed in the rural society that they counted upon the local political influence normally available to men of property in the countryside. By contrast, Mr. Bandaranaike built on many years of effort in enlisting support of less prominent rural figures. For more than a decade prior to 1952, when he resigned from the United National Party cabinet, he had been Minister of Local Government, in close

[3] For a detailed discussion, see my Ceylon, particularly Chs. 6, 7, and 9; also Robert N. Kearney, Communalism and Language in the Politics of Ceylon provides more detail on the communal and social background, Chs. 4 and 6, and pp. 50-51.

touch with elected village committeemen and such local men of modest, albeit locally important, position as village school teachers, *Ayurvedic* physicians, Buddhist monks, and small businessmen. He used their grievances regarding the language of government and the role of the Buddhist religion to enlist them in his cause; and they in turn activated the peasantry on behalf of his party.

Mr. Bandaranaike demonstrated that he understood their frustrations, and in articulating these "primordial discontents" he made their sense of grievance more acute.[4] Compared to their English-language colleagues, the Sinhalese school teachers were virtually second-class professionals, their salaries were poorer, their career opportunities less spacious, and their general standing conspicuously lower. And many of their graduates, skilled only in the Sinhalese language, could not find jobs commensurate with the status they expected as high school graduates, particularly in the largely English-speaking public service.[5] The *Ayurvedic* physicians felt their traditional profession was looked down on by the English-speaking bureaucracy and medical profession, as large sums went for medical schools, hospitals, and the development of a national health service based on Western medicine, while relatively few resources were devoted to their traditional skills. The monks felt that the government and bureaucracy were disproportionately manned by Tamil Hindus or by Sinhalese or Tamil Christians and did not give due place to Sinhalese Buddhists or to traditional Buddhist institutions and values. Other political leaders worked their rural constituencies only intermittently; Mr. Bandaranaike assiduously traveled the rural areas and consolidated the network of relationships he had built up when dealing with local government affairs, and he actively encouraged organizations of Buddhist monks who were working on behalf of a change of government.[6]

Unemployed students and younger monks had time on their hands and served as volunteer electoral agents canvassing door-to-door to urge townsmen and villagers to vote Mr. Bandaranaike's ticket. The physicians and teachers lent their substantial status in the eyes of the villagers to his support. In the event, he achieved an overwhelming victory, taking 51 seats and leaving the United National

[4] On the problem of "primordial discontents," see Geertz, "The Integrative Revolution," in *Old Societies and New States*, pp. 105-57.

[5] Kearney, *Communalism and Language*, pp. 61-62.

[6] Wriggins, *Ceylon*, pp. 337-48; Kearney, Ch. 4.

Party only 9. The results astonished the winners as much as they dismayed the defeated.

In 1956, for the first time, in the secrecy of the voting booth, large numbers of the townsmen and villagers voted against what their local notables preferred. After the election, hundreds of villagers and townsmen swarmed into the parliament building for the first time, demonstrating their belief that the parliament now really represented "the people." And the business of parliament increasingly was conducted in the vernaculars. By broadening popular participation, Mr. Bandaranaike had succeeded in creating a new coalition of political forces, undermining in the process the base of support put together before independence by the United National Party. Vertical national integration had begun to bridge the cultural distance previously separating rulers from ruled in Sinhalese areas.

In the main, the new groups activated for the election sustained their participation after the victory was won. The Buddhist organizations, particularly, continued to press their case for rapid language changes and for "restoring Buddhism to its rightful place." The professional associations of teachers and *Ayurvedic* physicians did not revert to quiescence but continued their pressure.

The language issue, more than any other, disrupted Ceylon's communal harmony. Sinhalese agitation during the election frightened the Tamils, who feared for their future opportunities on the island. The defensive measures the Tamil leaders of the Federal Party took in efforts to guarantee their bargaining power vis-à-vis the majority were those steps best calculated to antagonize spokesmen for the majority. Mutual suspicions increased sharply, producing unfamiliar but no less vicious riots. A modus vivendi was worked out by the Prime Minister, in consultation with Tamil leaders. It protected the "legitimate rights" of the Tamil minority while assuring the Sinhalese of rapid progress toward establishing the official standing of the Sinhalese language. But it provoked such demonstative opposition among Sinhalese Buddhists and language enthusiasts that Mr. Bandaranaike felt forced to repudiate that agreement. This further accentuated the Tamil sense of fear and weakness.[7] Tragically, before another compromise could be negotiated, the Prime Minister was assassinated by a monk in collusion with the head monk of one of Ceylon's most important temples. In the wake of this tragic event,

[7] Kearney, pp. 83-89, 107-12.

communal impatience calmed temporarily as did the ardor of most of the activist groups pressing for rapid language and religious reforms.

As a result of these political developments, the English-educated strata of Ceylon found their position weakened as the non-English-speaking Sinhalese majority of the population experienced a closer sense of identity with their government than they had ever had before. The vertical social and political distance between rulers and the majority of the ruled had been diminished. In the process, traditional and parochial values had been reasserted, the Tamil minority had been alienated and distrust between the communities rendered more intense.

It is obvious that Mr. Bandaranaike was not the sole cause of these developments. The communications system in Ceylon was probably more intensely developed than in any other Asian area apart from Taiwan, Japan, and Singapore. Years of expanding education led to growing numbers seeking middle class employment in the few public service openings. Growing literacy in the vernaculars produced increasing self-consciousness among both the Tamil and Sinhalese as separate communities, each with a long history of past hostilities toward the other.[8] But Mr. Bandaranaike's efforts to stimulate into political activity groups which hitherto had quietly followed local leadership illustrate the political advantages and some of the liabilities of such a strategy. A more general discussion may suggest other aspects of the strategy of expanding political participation.

To some extent, of course, increased participation appears to be occurring quite without political intention. With the penetration of the money economy into the countryside comes greater ease of movement: more farm-to-market roads, the increasing use of the bicycle, truck, and bus, and more widespread schooling. Other factors include migration to the cities, growth of industry, and a rapid increase in public communications media of all kinds. Such changes are penetrating and breaking down some of the old isolations and bringing men and women into contact with one another across old barriers of isolation as never before.[9] Moreover, rapidly expanding school systems are providing education which politicizes most of its students and leads them to believe they should have a role in politi-

[8] Wriggins, Ceylon, Chs. 6 and 7.
[9] K. Deutsch, "Social Mobilization and Political Development," pp. 493-514. Lerner, The Passing of Traditional Society, particularly Chs. 1 and 2.

cal life. They are trained in skills which are not yet wanted, but, at the same time, they are instilled with values which make them unwilling to accept the jobs that are available.[10] These social and economic changes need not, in themselves, produce political results, but they are likely to weaken traditional authority structures as they strengthen parochial self-awareness. They tend to shake traditional passivity and prepare an increasing proportion of the population to be susceptible to political organization and activation.

The independence struggle itself usually broadened participation. New leadership gained prominence through the independence movement, and the position of traditional leaders who often were closely associated with the foreigners was weakened. In India the princes were undermined; in Ghana the chiefs were weakened; in Vietnam the mandarin families were generally displaced. When agitation for independence extended over a long period of time, as in South Asia, it left numbers of groups with the experience of articulating demands and pressing their interests, often in direct and disruptive ways. New, more accessible representative institutions, such as panchayats in India or village councils in Ceylon or elsewhere, provide the framework at the local or district level within which the hitherto quiescent may become politically active under the stimulation of the national leaders being considered here.

This new susceptibility can be used by leaders for a range of political purposes after independence is achieved. Once in a position of responsibility, the leader may serve his purpose by drawing into politics those who have still remained passive. In India, for example, Congress Party politicians in Madras found it electorally expedient to activate more numerous lower castes, weakening the standing of the well-educated, prominent but numerically small Brahmin groups. A leader may simply want to weaken accustomed loyalties in order to undermine the assured support possessed by the traditionally prominent men—the chiefs, the district notables, and communal or religious leaders. In so doing, he may hope to increase his bargaining power over these traditional leaders without necessarily seeking to displace them. He may, however, hope to undermine them altogether and win their former followers for himself.[11]

[10] Shils, "The Intellectuals in the Political Development of the New States," *World Politics*, Vol. XII, No. 3 (April, 1960), 329-68.

[11] Coleman and Rosberg, *Political Parties and National Integration in Tropical Africa*, p. 281.

He may seek to mobilize the wider populace on behalf of vaulting goals of social and economic transformation.[12] In this endeavor, the leader may wish to evoke energies he believes to be latent in the population. If this leads to enlarging opportunities for real political choice, he will be broadening political participation. However, he may also be attempting to encadre political energies, thus shaping party auxiliaries within which all aspects of individual lives may come under the surveillance and control of the state.[13]

In Ghana, for example, Mr. Nkrumah increased the activation of lower strata, resulting in a net reduction in that kind of participation which extends the scope of political choice. He started out with a moderate regime, based largely on the Western-educated bureaucracy, intellectuals, and businessmen in collaboration with certain of the chiefs, as the main base of his nationalist movement. Through his activities as Youth Secretary of the United Gold Coast Convention (UGCC), he developed a wider, more popular and more excitable following, including numerous "Standard VII boys" who had not been able or did not wish to go beyond, roughly, grades 8 or 9. He early showed his oratorical and organizational abilities. After independence, he came to contend more directly against the chiefs. As he sought to push toward radical goals requiring intensive mobilization and an increasingly authoritarian regime, the educated became ever more critical of his ambitions and his methods. In an effort to find more malleable followers and a broader base of support, he reached lower into Ghanaian society and activated the less educated. They proved to be more amenable to his organizational requirements and more susceptible to his Pan-African aspirations than the cooler, less excitable among the more highly educated. The Standard VII boys were better able to excite the wider masses in the city and those in the countryside who resented the archaic pretensions of certain chiefs.

Accordingly, by changing the composition of his alliance and reaching downward to activate broader strata of society, Nkrumah displaced the moderates who came into power with him and developed his own form of authoritarian regime. His new supporters were willing to intimidate with more enthusiasm than were his previous associates, and some of his former allies left the country. Insofar as

---

[12] Apter, *The Politics of Modernization*, Ch. 10.
[13] Kautsky, *Political Change in Underdeveloped Countries*, pp. 94-95.

he drew lower strata into political activity, he extended activation. But as these efforts narrowed the range of political choice, on balance they worked to reduce genuine participation.[14]

In developing the Neo-Destour, Bourguiba succeeded in attracting a wider spectrum of support than the leaders of the older party, who were interested in recruiting only the traditional intellectual elite.[15] Nasser helped sustain his position by his ability to implement long-delayed land reforms, which appealed to the peasantry, and to symbolize Egyptian and Arab self-respect, attributes which attracted the town and city lower and middle classes. In the Ivory Coast, Houphouët-Boigny encouraged group representation through corporate bodies as a way of organizing the support of those it might be more difficult to win through residential representation.[16]

If a leader is to engage the support of new strata in the society, he may well have to devise new methods for identifying himself with the masses. He must demonstratively take on characteristics which the groups he wishes to attract respect or in some ways aspire to. The untimely deaths of Jinnah and Liaquat in Pakistan removed the two most respected leaders who had enthusiastic and potentially sustainable followings of broad national scope. Successors depended too much on the skills of the lawyer, the symbols of traditional religion, or acute localism, or they retained too obviously the colonial style of vice-regal rule to evoke a substantial base of popular identification or channeled participation for the long pull.[17] Diem was unable to overcome his mandarin symbolic character and win support of the educated and rising new skill groups. In marked contrast, Bandaranaike in Ceylon, Nehru and some of his colleagues in India, Bourguiba in Tunisia, and a number of others managed to project an aura of accessibility in distance, of understanding the needs and values of the masses or of rising groups while underlining the leader's own distinctive—and admirable—difference from them. Strategies for projecting the personality and building an organization combined to activate new levels on behalf of new leadership.

---

[14] For this interpretation see Austin, *Politics in Ghana*, pp. 16-17; and Arthur Lewis, "Beyond African Dictatorship," *Encounter*, Vol. XXV, No. 2 (August, 1965), 3-18.

[15] Clement Moore in Micaud, *Tunisia*, p. 82.

[16] Zolberg, *One-Party Government in the Ivory Coast*, p. 278.

[17] On the problem of insufficiently persuasive leadership in Pakistan, see van Vorys, *Political Development in Pakistan*, p. 108.

Particularly if he came to power through a coup d'état, the ruler will be concerned with the problem of broadening participation. His first requirement will be to restrict participation so as to ensure that only the handful of loyal followers have access to powerful positions and can exert that influence on behalf of his objectives. But sooner or later he will need to respond to growing pressures for participation of some kind. Ayub's search for a middle ground in Basic Democracies only partially succeeded. Open challenges to his regime in 1968 and 1969 illustrated the more general point that it is more difficult for such regimes to institutionalize a gradual expansion of popular participation than it has been for those which established the processes and institutions of participation during the independence struggle and have been able to maintain them. Similarly, where political competition has been narrowed and replaced by the single-party state, moving toward a reopening of participation will be both dangerous to the rulers and difficult to institutionalize.

ADVANTAGES

The strategy of broadening participation has certain advantages for the man in power who wishes to prevent an opposition from gaining a popular base or to weaken the position of his well-established but not sufficiently acquiescent allies. It can also be used by the man who is not in power but who wishes to gain power by undercutting the traditionalist base of his opponent, so long as the regime permits free opposition activity.

The strategy of promoting participation has a constructive role to play in bridging some of the political gaps observed in emerging countries.[18] By and large, the political leaders at independence were mainly city men, whose eyes were fixed on developing the capital and a modern industrialized economy. They tended to disdain the countryside. Though talking democracy, it was the rare exception to find a political leader, like Gandhi, who took the peasantry seriously. More recently, there has been a change as the problem of food production presses home the need for activating the peasantry and rural middle classes on behalf of improved agricultural performance. In

[18] Shils has identified these gaps in considerable detail, *Political Development in the New States*, pp. 30-31.

the interim, the desire of men of politics, like Mr. Bandaranaike, who were seeking to broaden their base of popular support took them to the countryside, where the numbers are. They articulated the aspirations of peasants and townsmen, and attempted to deal with major peasant and townsmen grievances.

Increasing opportunities for political participation draw into political life growing numbers of educated young men and women with more populist convictions than their parents, or with a more discerning eye for grievances to be corrected or changes to be made through the available political process. Such a strategy may be a prerequisite if socioeconomic change is to come about. It makes less likely the type of disruptive direct activity outside the political process which sometimes leads to such disarray as will tempt the military to stage a coup d'état. The need to enlist the support of numbers has also led to the encouragement of trade-union organizations as instruments for activating support of numbers in the urban areas. These have come to voice the demands of urban workers, provide means for checking the excesses of primitive indigenous capitalism, and help to sensitize well-off politicians to the needs of the urban work force.[19]

Such a strategy encourages political leaders to deal with lower class grievances in timely fashion, before the political pressure cooker nears the bursting point. Leaders responding promptly to popular needs encourage a national awareness and sense of having a stake in the polity among those who otherwise might feel excluded. From the leader's point of view, promoting certain types of participation may hold out promise of enhancing his control as lower levels of society and youth are encadred in the party's activist institutions.

DISADVANTAGES

Political leaders wishing to activate groups which have hitherto been quiescent are likely to probe for grievances, sharpen awareness of inequities, and help the disadvantaged to formulate demands and press their claims on the total polity. In winning concessions that the previous leaders would not make, the aspiring leader acquires popular loyalty. But such activities may intensify contention to levels that threaten the integrity of the nation itself. Mr. Bandaranaike's

---

[19] Millen, *The Political Role of Labour,* especially Chs. 3, 4, and 5.

efforts to enlist lower levels of the Sinhalese majority exacerbated relations with the Tamil minority. Gandhi's efforts to mobilize the Indian masses to participate in the independence struggle often appealed to traditional values with Hindu religious overtones. This was the natural way for him to move the Indian multitudes. But in the end, despite Gandhi's expressed interest in all religions and his many efforts to reassure the Muslims, his mobilizational activities contributed to Muslim fears for their future and helped induce them to mobilize on the basis of Muslim values.[20]

Where food, jobs, and status are all scarce, heightened demands may only sharpen mutual hostility. The political parties, legislative bodies, and courts or other institutions for voicing and adjudicating conflicts may be insufficient to deal with intensified differences.[21] Many demands by newly emerging groups are put forward in an all or nothing mood. There is little experience with incremental improvements. A minor concession which falls far short of the total demand is often seen as a major defeat rather than a possible first step in a series of favorable adjustments. Disorder may be accentuated, and group tension may rise sharply beyond what the shaky political institutional frame can withstand. If this occurs, mobilization has outrun institutionalization. The regime may have increasing difficulties in promoting a necessary minimum of public order, or performing other necessary functions.[22]

Particularly where competing leaders have turned to the urban proletariat and have sought to activate them on behalf of one political leader or another, violence may easily erupt. In Middle Eastern countries, the urban mob has become a notable factor in political life. During the Mossadegh era in Iran, his efforts to mobilize urban unrest on behalf of acute nationalist demands brought near anarchy. The Tungku's opponents in Malaysia sought to arouse nationalist Malay sentiments against his regime which was promoting a moderate approach to the Chinese minority; this intensified Malay fears of Singapore Chinese, as did the organizational activities in Malay-

[20] Percival Spea., India, A Modern History (Ann Arbor, University of Michigan Press, 1961, 491 pp.), pp. 360, 391.

[21] Weiner, "Political Integration and Political Development," The Annals, Vol. 358 (March, 1965), 52-64, 60.

[22] For a detailed discussion, see Samuel Huntington, "Political Development and Political Decay," World Politics, Vol. XVII, No. 3 (April, 1965), 386-430.

sia itself of Singapore Prime Minister Lee Kuan Yu's party, the People's Action Party.[23]

Economic problems may become acute as a result of politically motivated gestures designed to win the backing of the hitherto quiescent. Particularly where export earnings are subject to sharp fluctuations, a generous gesture to win popular backing in one year might be quite reasonable while in another it would be more than the economy could bear; yet politically it is highly risky to withdraw what was once granted. In Ceylon, efforts to gain and hold the preponderating rural majority and to keep urban food prices down while retaining urban votes created costly agricultural subsidies. One prime minister resigned after an attempt to withdraw them, and a minister of finance was overthrown on the same issue. Mr. Nkrumah's design for rapid and conspicuous investment brought his country to the edge of bankruptcy.

Accordingly, ill-considered activation for immediate political advantages may impose on an insufficient economy burdens it cannot bear, risk the armature of statehood and even lead to disintegration or partition of the state.

TO NARROW PARTICIPATION

By contrast, some leaders have followed the opposite strategy, consciously seeking to contract the politically active, narrowing the circle of those with access to power or to the means of political organization.

Von Vorys reports, for example, that in 1959 (some ten months after President Ayub came to power in Pakistan), political figures of the former regime were, in effect, dissuaded from further political activity. But late that year Ayub opened his polity to a new electoral process. He established a complex system of indirect elections, which shifted the weight of electoral gravity to the countryside. This reduced the former influence of urban politicians and made it more likely that those who emerged from the successive indirect elections to man the regional and national assemblies would be more conservative and responsive to substantial governmental influence.[24] Though

[23] R. S. Milne, *Government and Politics in Malaysia* (Boston, Houghton Mifflin, 1967, 259 pp.), p. 214.

[24] Von Vorys, *Political Development in Pakistan*, pp. 196 ff.

decisively challenged in 1969, such procedures for indirect elections lasted a good deal longer than the more stringent measures imposed by General Abboud in the Sudan, where all political activity was stopped and any political expression prohibited. With no outlet for pent-up demands or opportunity for aspiring politicians, those of political bent became the focus of unexpressed protest movements. After a series of disorders, General Abboud stepped down and the system was again opened to political contention.[25]

A more frequent method in Africa has been to whittle down party competition by the gradual encroachment of one party until there is a virtual one-party system. Under such arrangements, there is no institutional way of challenging the leader himself, and anyone who aspires to political responsibility must play his part within the single, overarching party. There may be a high level of political activation, in the sense of public displays of loyalty and enthusiasm, and some organized effort to achieve the government's vaulting goals. But active participation to promote the fortunes of another leader in a competing political party is impossible, or made to appear so risky as to be not worth attempting except for the compulsive. Often there is more talk of mobilization than real achievement.[26] This is the reverse of expanding political participation although it is often accompanied by a regime's effort to bring the more numerous strata of society into political activity. In this way, democratic participation has been reduced in Ghana, Guinea, and Ivory Coast, and other one-party states of Africa, although political activation was increased, at least for a time.

Activating ever lower and more numerous strata of society is usually a strategy employed by outsiders wanting to get into power. However, even an incumbent may use this strategy if he can turn popular energies against the former privileged among his opponents and if he believes his personality, party organization, or ideology are such as to assure continued control of the masses he activates. So long as the institutional frame for politics is fragile and resources with which to satisfy increased demands are scarce, this strategy has substantial risks. Nevertheless, because of intensified political communication, expanded educational opportunities and improved levels

[25] T. E. Nyquist, "The Sudan: Prelude to Elections," *Middle East Journal,* Vol. XIX, No. 3 (Summer, 1965), 263-73.

[26] See Carter (ed.), *African One Party States:* Zolberg, *Creating Political Order,* Chs. 3, 4, and 5.

of social organization, leaders have to expect increasing demands for participation on the part of the more numerous elements in their societies. Repression can be only a temporary reply. In the end, institutions must be constructed which will permit the expression and channeling of these demands in ways the social and political system can absorb, or else the polity will suffer periodic revolution.

12 Use Foreign Policy

> The foreign policy of a new state cannot be understood exclusively in the light of domestic necessities; but unless the omnipresent task of state building is allowed to illumine the objectives and motives of foreign policy, it cannot be understood at all.
>
> Robert C. Good

Foreign policy decisions seldom result from only one consideration. Schelling rightly sees much of diplomacy as mixed-motive bargaining. Similarly, foreign policy making in real life typically results from the interplay in officials' minds of numerous, often competing, considerations and motives.[1] Rarely will considerations of domestic politics alone be sufficient to precipitate a foreign policy decision. Yet, it is clear that foreign policies often do affect a regime's domestic political position. Accordingly, it is plausible to expect that at times leaders will consciously design aspects of their foreign policies with an eye to fending off domestic oppositions or gaining support at home.

There is much truth in the contention that the well-established states

[1] Thomas C. Schelling, *The Strategy of Conflict* (New York, Oxford University Press-Galaxy, 1963, 309 pp.), Chs. 1 and 2. See also Roger Hilsman, *To Move a Nation, the Politics of Foreign Policy in the Administration of John F. Kennedy* (New York, Doubleday, 1967, 602 pp.), Ch. 1.

of the world have a fairly consistent view of their interests as these derive from their geographical location, their relative power vis-à-vis other states, and their traditional conceptions of threat and friendship. These underlying interests, it is held, are affected only marginally by the play of domestic politics.[2] The new states, however, have not yet developed a consistent and long-term perspective on their interests. They lack the years of responsible statehood which would help their leaders perceive the costs and advantages of alternative policies. Although some, like Iran, Ethiopia, Afghanistan, and Thailand, have been at the business a long time, the bulk of the countries under consideration have diplomatic specialists with less than two decades' experience. Their foreign offices are lightly manned, and few offer the cautionary advice of experienced practitioners. In most instances, the prime minister or president has a relatively free hand to lay down policies which correspond to his own views. Accordingly, where ideological preconceptions do not narrow options from the outset, one can expect a certain fluidity in foreign policy. In some states, foreign policy may be directed primarily to releasing leadership or mass emotions and to playing out old grievances or new dreams.[3] In others, there may be a more experimental search for policies best calculated to forward the interests of the state or, at the very least, of the leadership.

Rulers do not, of course, have a completely free choice of how they might use foreign policy for domestic political purposes. Their state's size, location, and history and the policies of near neighbors and distant powers affect their priorities and their room for maneuver. Their ability to generate foreign policy capability depends in part on the domestic political order and on their economic margins.[4] They may face genuine external dangers as large neighbors, traditional enemies, or big powers from outside their area bring pressure to bear within it to threaten their independence. And the first foreign policy responsibility of a ruler is to be able to cope effectively with

[2] Morgenthau, "Another 'Great Debate': The National Interest of the United States," *American Political Science Review*, Vol. 66, No. 4 (December, 1952), 961-68.

[3] Robert Johnson's forthcoming study tentatively entitled, *Prophets and Politicians: The Political Development Setting of the Foreign Policies of Less Developed Countries.*

[4] Almond and Powell, *Comparative Politics*, p. 205.

such external pressures, sometimes without calculating the short run domestic political consequences.

The religious habits or racial composition of the ruler's people inhibits certain affiliations while the fact of being an underdeveloped ex-colony among other former colonies and the pattern and urgency of their economic relationships define additional limits. But within the parameters set by these fundamentals of interstate relations, rulers may find scope for choosing among foreign policies those best calculated to promote their domestic political fortunes. It can also happen that policies which may have great utility in promoting a regime's position in one period may lead to involvements which can adversely affect its position later on.

AN EXAMPLE: NASSER OF EGYPT

President Gamal Abdel Nasser of Egypt is an example of a leader whose foreign policy activities have affected his domestic political situation. When he and his fellow officers took power in 1952, they had virtually no links with any civilian political forces. Overthrowing the monarchy, effecting land reform, passing social legislation, and bringing a halt to corruption at the top helped to give the new regime legitimacy among the Egyptian middle classes and the masses. But a dramatic and virtually unbroken sequence of foreign policy successes in the early years contributed further to improving his power position at home.[5]

When Nasser sought to define Egypt's role in the Middle East and North Africa, he stressed Egypt's humiliations at the hands of its own corrupt leaders and foreigners, the need to raise up Egypt, regenerate the Nile Valley, and draw Egypt into closer association with his Arab and African neighbors.[6] As the central figure in the government of the largest and most modern Arab state, Nasser assigned to himself the role of architect of closer Arab unity. As he wrote in The Philosophy of the Revolution: "Here is the role. Here

[5] See Vatikiotis, The Egyptian Army in Politics, Ch. 4, for consolidation of the regime.

[6] Gamal Abdel Nasser, The Philosophy of the Revolution, excerpts in Sigmund, The Ideologies of the Developing Nations, pp. 120-27; discussed in Charles D. Cremeans, The Arabs and the World (New York, Praeger, 1963, 338 pp.), pp. 213-19.

are the lines, and here is the stage. We alone, by virtue of our place, can perform the role."[7]

His early foreign policy successes were notable. He openly rejected the Western-sponsored Bagdad Pact in 1955 and induced even his conservative neighbors to be wary of close association with it. The British were withdrawn from the Canal Zone, where they had had virtual control for decades. He succeeded in procuring arms from Czechoslovakia in 1955, freeing his army—on whose backing he completely depended—from supply constraints developed by Paris, London, and Washington. In June 1956, when rebuffed by Secretary of State Dulles on the financing of the Aswan Dam because of the financial and other implications of the Czech arms deal, he nationalized the Suez Canal with a dispatch and efficiency astonishing to those familiar with previous Egyptian regimes.

This bold stroke precipitated a concerted military attack from Israel, France, and Britain, and his military defeat was swift. But he showed himself "the master of the new international politics, in which advantage is made of weakness and in which world opinion and the vast machinery of international organization were brought into effective play" against his attackers.[8] He emerged from these events with the victor's spoils returned to him, the UN policing his frontier with Israel, his position at home materially consolidated, and his reputation strengthened as the hero of the Arab world who dared to talk back to Western governments, who stood up against their military attacks and got away with it.[9] "To the average Egyptian, President Nasser appeared as the first modern ruler to be taken seriously by the Great Powers."[10]

His military associates welcomed the new arms he had procured from Czechoslovakia and Russia, since the arrangement overcame the limitations Britain, France, and the United States had sought to erect around his and Israel's military procurement.[11] He gained great status among them as a result.

The middle classes admired his daring and found satisfaction in

[7] Robert St. John, *The Boss, The Story of Gamal Abdel Nasser* (New York, McGraw Hill, 1960, 324 pp.), p. 10.

[8] Cremeans, *The Arabs and the World*, p. 45.

[9] Little, *Egypt*, p. 176.

[10] Vatikiotis, *The Egyptian Army in Politics*, p. 227.

[11] *Ibid.*, pp. 217-19; Leonard Binder, "Egypt, the integrative revolution," in Pye and Verba, *Political Culture and Political Development*, p. 400.

knowing that Egypt was in the front rank of Arab countries and asserting her active independence from Western influence. The masses saw in Nasser a romantic national hero, battling great odds, passing safely through great dangers, with hair's breadth escapes. They gained a sense of participation in great events and, by acclaiming him, confirmed his political strength in the face of possible domestic opponents.

Nasser used his position in Egypt to promote change in the wider Arab world and to expand Egypt's influence. Egyptian teachers continued to be sent abroad. Embassy personnel sought by many ways to spread the message of Nasser's domestic revolution, and the need to consolidate Arab unity. Radio Cairo penetrated other Arab countries, evoked the image of a hostile, anti-Arab world, and incited the masses to insurrection against regimes which opposed his policies.[12] Where "the word" was not sufficient, the conspiratorial experience of his own rise to power made clandestine activity particularly congenial. Police, armies, civil services, labor unions, and universities in neighboring countries were all penetrated by Nasser's agents, who found many ready recruits among the disgruntled, who were impatient with their archaic leaders or dreamed of a larger Arab unity.[13] He sent military and other support to Algeria in its fight against the French, supplies to Lumumbists in the Congo, and gave hospitality to countless African opposition groups.

International conferences were inexpensive ways of promoting his foreign policy objectives, with useful side effects at home. Periodic meetings with Nehru and Tito demonstrated Egypt's new independence in international affairs, and helped draw together the Afro-Asian forces he favored. After his success at Bandung, he invited numerous Afro-Asian statesmen to Cairo. Such confabulations held in Cairo dramatized at home and in the Arab world the central role Egypt—and Nasser—now played. And they underlined Egypt's new role in the third, uncommitted world. Russia's commitment to build the High Dam at Aswan and the flow of Russian arms freed him from dependence on Washington or London. They gave him an opportunity to play an independent game—unless he became, in the end, subject to preponderant Russian influence.

[12] Cremeans, *The Arabs and the World*, pp. 38-39.
[13] *Ibid.*, pp. 42-44; St. John, *The Boss*, p. 275.

Rhetorically hostile toward Israel, Nasser nevertheless sometimes moderated the more intense Syrian antagonism. But to help sustain his position at the head of the Arab world, he often backed the armed guerrillas who conducted hit-and-run raids against Israeli settlements. These provided Nasser with occasions for claiming "victories" against Israel, but they did not affect the real balance of forces in the area. On the contrary, they stiffened Israel's nerve and aroused sympathy for Israel abroad. Policy toward Israel could hardly have been called a success, although the rhetoric probably helped him at home.

In 1958 he received a further boost. Syria asked to join with Egypt in a federal association. Nasser was the reluctant suitor in this case, sought after by the anxious Baathi leaders in Damascus who feared a communist takeover from within. After some hesitations, he agreed to the proposal. When the United Arab Republic, combining Egypt and Syria in one regime, was proclaimed in February, Nasser's popularity at home and throughout the Arab world was tremendous. He had accomplished at one stoke, and without firing a shot, what no Egyptian leader had attempted since Mohammed Ali, his great predecessor, had been forced to give up that province in 1841. His position at home was virtually unquestioned.[14] The wave of the Arab Middle East future seemed to be carrying him inexorably forward, a mere six years after his accession to power from the obscurity of a colonelcy in Farouk's humiliated army. Even the Imam of Yemen, one of the area's most conservative and isolated rulers, sought and obtained loose association with the federation.

But it proved easier to accept power in Damascus than to hold it. Political and economic forces in Syria could not be easily organized along the same lines that had served Nasser so well in Egypt. Syrian officers were offended by high-handed Egyptian ways. Within three years a coup d'état replaced collaborating Syrian officials, and Nasser had to choose between withdrawing or fighting a war against the Syrians. He chose the former course, and the union was dissolved.[15] 1958 may have been the zenith of Nasser's leadership in the area. Never again would he have such unquestioning and enthu-

---

[14] Cremeans, *The Arabs and the World*, pp. 159-61; Little, *Egypt*, pp. 32-33, 190.

[15] For a post-mortem, see Cremeans, pp. 175-79. For a detailed analysis, see Amitai Etzioni, *Political Unification* (New York, Holt, Rinehart and Winston, 1965, 346 pp.), Ch. 4.

siastic mass support; his reputation never quite recovered from this failure.[16]

Great and heroic deeds abroad had helped Nasser to consolidate his position at home during the early years of his rule. An heroic role can become costly, however. Without identifying himself with the vision of Arab unity, Nasser might not have become involved in Syria. Radicalization of domestic policies in Egypt had contributed to his difficulties in Syria. Such domestic policies also led to growing hostility toward the monarchies, going so far as to induce the Hashemites and Saudis to align against him. In 1962 he responded to a request for military assistance from a tenuous republican regime which had overthrown the Imam of Yemen, and his armies became embroiled in an indecisive and costly campaign in Yemen, deepening the rift with King Faisal who supported the remnants of the Yemeni royalists. Dramatic gestures against the United States were good politics at home and in the Arab world. But he reckoned without the domestic political difficulties his actions would intensify for the President of the United States, thereby losing foreign aid and jeopardizing even the shipments of food which were increasingly necessary as Egypt's balance of payments deteriorated with these costly ventures and declining terms of trade.

In 1967 he had another narrow escape. As Syrian and Jordani-Israeli relations deteriorated, Nasser was confronted with the dilemma of either fulfilling his announced leadership role by taking an initiative or of foregoing his hard-won prominence. In a new bold gesture, he closed the Gulf of Aqaba to Israeli shipping. This initiative escalated into open hostilities in which the combined Arab forces were defeated, his air force and army destroyed, and the canal again closed.

But even from this debacle he extracted some domestic political advantage. In a dramatic gesture, he publicly tendered his resignation in chagrin at what had befallen Egypt under his leadership. The masses, however, would not have it. They insisted he continue. From foreign policy defeat he was able to demonstrate to his domestic and foreign enemies the mass support he could still command. The Russians quickly replaced his military equipment and sent training advisors to rebuild his army and air force. But by 1968 he was still dependent upon periodic subventions from the Arab oil kingdoms

---

[16] Little, *Egypt*, p. 196.

to keep his country solvent, a dependency unthinkable ten years before.

The example of Nasser suggests some of the connections to be discerned between foreign policy initiatives and a leader's domestic political situation. If this strategy is looked at systematically, some additional points emerge.

THE VALUE OF FOREIGN POLICY ACTIVITIES

Many foreign policy activities can promote the stature of the political leader at home. State visits abroad are highly publicized. They serve to demonstrate that the leader is being dealt with as an equal by the world's leading statemen. In receiving the plaudits of foreign multitudes, the leader dramatizes his own stature and underscores it for those at home who find their self-respect through identifying with him. The United Nations plays an important role in this respect. Membership in the UN provided an "accreditation" for the new states, a "symbolic collective recognition by the international political community that they are indeed sovereign and independent."[17] Because regimes lack capability and economic resources are scant, the day-to-day business of statehood dramatizes how ambiguous is the reality of sovereignty. By contrast, at the UN sovereignty and independence are symbolized more clearly than anywhere else. Speeches at the UN and participation in its deliberations, like the leader's movements among the chanceries, confirm the reality of independence and the status of equal independent statehood.[18] Such international recognition can be a partial substitute for more home-grown varieties of legitimacy. Following a leader's accession through a coup d'état, he will seek prompt international recognition for his regime and will angle for invitations to Washington, London, Moscow, or the capital of a regional power to demonstrate that he is accepted abroad, at least, for what he claims to be at home.

Convening international conferences in one's capital may cost for-

[17] Vernon McKay (ed.), *African Diplomacy* (New York, Praeger, 1966, 210 pp.), p. 168.

[18] See, for a discussion, Ann Ruth and Dorothy Willner, "The Rise and Role of Charismatic Leaders," *The Annals*, Vol. 358 (March, 1965), 77-88; also R. C. Good, "State-Building as a Determinant of Foreign Policy in New States," in L. Martin (ed.), *Neutralism and Nonalignment*, pp. 7-8.

eign exchange and absorb scarce resources in special buildings, as in the case of Indonesia's preparations for Bandung or Algeria's preparations in 1966 for an Afro-Asian meeting that was not held. But if the meetings are only moderately successful for their explicit purposes, they will have useful side effects. They accentuate the leader's importance and the extent to which he is recognized as a respected and constructive—or radical—member of the international community. He who can sire a major regional organization or become spokesman for a grouping of states is likely to enhance his weight in international affairs. His political position at home is likely to improve, as is suggested by one Syrian's reaction to Egypt's early espousal of Arab unity: "We noted with surprise and concern the struggle between Faruq and Nahas. We realized their chief concern in promoting the [Arab] League was not for the Arabs but for their own position within Egypt."[19]

Their competitive effort to promote Arab unity did not save them, but it is typical for statesmen to feel that speaking out on behalf of such regional entities will raise their stature at home. Sukarno saw the Bandung meetings in part in this light. The Colombo Conference preceding Bandung focused attention on the Ceylonese Prime Minister, Sir John Kotelawala.[20] Nkrumah, Sékou Touré, and other African leaders have shown the same interest in the side effects of calling international conferences in their capitals.

Foreign policy may also enhance the leader's position if he, like Horatio at the bridge, can be shown to have held back the advancing enemies of foreign influence or imminent interference. Heroically defending the nation from a host of enemies is well-calculated to strengthen the leader's domestic position.

Enemies may be real enough. Distant powers may be scheming to infiltrate and take control. Ancient antagonisms, repressed during the colonial period, may revive and pose acute local security problems, as India and Pakistan eye one another, or Burma and Thailand exacerbate each other's anxieties. Neighbors may be suspected of designing imminent attack. Successfully overcoming genuine foreign dangers may accomplish important foreign policy functions. The leader responsible for success will have his domestic position

[19] Patrick Seale, The Struggle for Syria, A Study of Post-War Arab Politics, 1945-1958 (London, Oxford University Press, 1965, 344 pp.), p. 21.

[20] Wriggins, Ceylon, pp. 441-42.

strengthened, as Prime Minister Shastri and Defense Minister Chavan discovered after the Indo-Pakistan war of 1965.

If there are no real and immediate enemies, they may be conjured up. As Ward and Rustow put it: "Once having gained independence, [the ex-colonial countries] are, if anything, apt to be even more harassed than others by fears that some aspect of their national security is in jeopardy."[21] Familiar imagery from the independence struggle tempts the leader to square off against old enemies, renewing, perhaps briefly, the solidarity experienced before. Nkrumah and Ben Bella declared that their countries could not be secure if "colonialism" existed anywhere in Africa, no doubt hoping thereby to induce a renewal of unity. By contrast, leaders of Madagascar, Ethiopia, and the Ivory Coast gave little evidence of such anxieties.[22]

National unity may be felt to be uncertain. Arbitrary colonial frontiers separate tribes and ethnic groups along lines that are impossible to police. Leaders feel their states are permeable.[23] Acute communal or tribal differences may be mitigated by reviving a sense of shared outside danger. Enemies perceived or conjured up or territorial ambitions awakened may assist the leader in sustaining unity and contending against fragmentation.[24] The West Irian issue strengthened Sukarno's domestic position, and his confrontation with Malaysia had the side effect of providing a joint enterprise for both the Indonesian army and the PKI. Confrontation facilitated Chinese integration within Malaysia, while the end of confrontation reawakened anxieties among the minority Chinese.[25] Persisting tension between India and Pakistan has probably strengthened the solidarity of both, while Syrian and Egyptian leaders have both used the existence of Israel to this end.

External enemies or territorial ambitions may also distract the populace from difficulties at home. Excitement over foreign dangers or irredentist dreams may divert attention from an insufficient har-

[21] Ward and Rustow, (eds.), Political Modernization in Japan and Turkey, pp. 448-49.

[22] I. William Zartman, "National Interest and Ideology," in McKay, African Diplomacy, p. 47.

[23] On the "permeability" of states, see Andrew M. Scott, The Revolution in Statecraft (New York, Random House, 1965, 194 pp.).

[24] R. C. Good, "State-Building as a Determinant of Foreign Policy in New States," in L. Martin (ed.), Neutralism and Nonalignment, pp. 5-7.

[25] On the role of the campaign for West Irian in Indonesia, see Hanna in Silvert (ed.), Expectant Peoples, p. 174.

vest, contracting economic opportunity, growing corruption, or a generally poor performance by the administration. Foreign enemies may help to justify tightening political control and reducing regional autonomy. They can warrant increased military budgets and provide the backbone of bold purpose to otherwise flaccid security units, as well as allow scope for the military to strengthen their position so as to balance or override other political forces.[26]

In efforts to simplify ethnic diversity and to demonstrate to the skeptical how devoted a ruler is to his people's welfare, he may seek to eliminate foreign communities which developed under colonial auspices. Chinese may be expelled from Indonesia, Indians from Burma, Indian Tamils from Ceylon, and Asians from East Africa; Europeans were induced to leave Egypt after the Suez crisis. Such steps are a cheap way to popularity. They demonstrate independence of the large neighbor or distant power whence the minority came. And new jobs, lands, or other resources can be made available to the deserving. But they involve certain costs. The economic functions these minorities perform may fall into desuetude for years or even a generation or two. Too harsh a policy may provoke an outside protector of the harrassed minority; hence, presumably, Burma did not touch its Chinese minority when it ejected the Indians. These apparently easy gestures may also create persisting discord between the governments concerned.

A leader may seek to enlist allies at home by adopting their foreign policy positions. Extreme nationalist sentiment and xenophobia periodically may burst through more reasonable approaches to the international world. Only a leader fully secure in his political position at home can stand against such popular emotions. More likely he will have to join the cry and castigate the distant larger power in order to retain the support of the more excitable among his intellectuals and newer nationalists. He may be friendly to the Soviet Union or China in foreign affairs or advocate revolution in other countries in order to gain the support of his own communist party without adopting at home the changes it advocates, as Sukarno is reported to have done.[27] He may undertake to improve relations with Western countries in order to strengthen his backing within his

---

[26] Almond, "A Developmental Approach to Political Systems," *World Politics*, Vol. XVII, No. 2 (January, 1965), 213.

[27] Feith, in Kahin (ed.), *Government and Politics of Southeast Asia*, p. 249.

bureaucracy, his business community, his non-communist trade-union movement, or anti-communist political parties.

At the height of the Cold War, some leaders appeared to undertake foreign policy initiatives vis-à-vis both "camps" in order to ensure that they could command the political center at home. One may understand at least one strand in the foreign policy thought of Mr. Bandaranaike in this way. Neutralism abroad became equated with the middle way in domestic politics, a posture well-calculated to minimize domestic frictions by uniting orthodox Buddhists, Sinhalese cultural nationalists, and Marxists into a foreign policy consensus, perhaps the one issue they could all agree on.[28]

Rarely will the desire to demonstrate one's orientation in domestic politics be sufficient in itself to define foreign policy choices. Such political symbolism is more usually a significant by-product of foreign policy decisions taken on other grounds. However, where a leader's tenure is uncertain and opposition or critical parties are well-organized or noisy, such considerations are likely to substantially influence his foreign policy posture.

Foreign policy orientations may be influenced by notions regarding how best to acquire assistance resources. Two markedly different approaches have been noticeable, although the differences are becoming less sharp as the intensity of the Cold War eased following the Cuban missile crisis.

Those leaders who joined alliances for security reasons generally believed that the best way to maximize foreign assistance was to work closely with their allies. Thus, most allies of the United States and Britain received nearly all their assistance from Western sources. In West Africa, Senegal and Ivory Coast have profited greatly from their close relations with France and their unwillingness to develop relations with the East. From the mid-fifties until the United States began to provide some arms aid to India, Pakistan depended entirely on Washington and London for its military supplies. The philosophy appears to have been that with loyalty and unambiguous alignment, rewards would be sufficient to meet critical resource needs and to overcome possible domestic criticism.

Other leaders have taken an opposite position, holding that the best way to maximize resources and to assure continued independence is to seek assistance from both the West and the East. Some

[28] Wriggins, *Ceylon*, p. 397.

argue that seeking help from both sources reduces the threat to independence thought to be implicit in accepting aid from only one of the major powers. Critics often held that it is a device for playing off Cold War competitors against each other in an effort to get more. For whatever reasons, India, the UAR, Nkrumah's Ghana and Afghanistan, among others, took this course.

Regardless of the motivation behind either approach, economic or military resources received from abroad serve a number of important political purposes.

Foreign assistance may provide the panoply of military might and independent statehood, represented by streaking jets, tanks, staff cars, and modern communications gear. Symbolizing national independence may be its first purpose. But military assistance can also provide the sinews of coercive power. It may thus serve its explicit purpose, to improve a country's ability to deal with its external enemy. But as the army and police are strengthened, their ability to deal with domestic enemies in more discriminating, humane, or decisive ways can be improved through technical training, better organization, and more sophisticated and mobile equipment. They may also become simply more efficient in their ability to repress popular unrest and political criticism.

The political advantages of economic development activities have been discussed already. A margin of resources received from abroad will make it easier to reap the political benefits of development expenditures without having to face the costs of extracting the necessary resources from the people at home.

If the country providing assistance is generally respected in the recipient country, the man who initiates a new aid relationship will better his political position. General Ayub's position within Pakistan probably improved prior to his taking power when he appeared to be instrumental in obtaining quantities of military equipment. Particularly in the early years of an aid relationship, the political futures of different ministers may be affected by their ability to obtain assistance from major donors, as Hatta's was strengthened in the early days in Indonesia.[29] However, this becomes less apparent as assistance moves increasingly toward programs which have a certain momentum and continuity of their own and are thereby less dependent upon the skills and relationships of any one minister.

[29] Feith in The Decline of Constitutional Democracy in Indonesia, p. 52.

But there are liabilities. If opposition is permitted, it will be easy for the regime to be criticized for risking its independence in order to receive foreign exchange, a frequent charge suffered by the governments of Ceylon, India, and Pakistan. If a recipient government becomes obviously dependent upon one donor which does not wholeheartedly support his client when in major difficulties, the regime will face acute criticism for having allowed itself to become overly dependent upon an "unreliable friend." President Ayub experienced such difficulties when U.S. military aid began to flow toward India in 1962 and when U.S. military supplies to both India and Pakistan were cut off during the war of 1965. If aid flows are stopped abruptly, the recipient government will have to curtail certain programs. If the military became too closely linked to outside sources of supply, the civilian leader's ability to retain control of the military may be diminished.

Aid programs have other possible political implications. Any aid program is likely to promote the impatience of younger men, provide new skills for which there are not yet sufficient openings, and set examples of higher living standards than the local economy can afford. Economic assistance may be essential to provide resources to meet the challenges of impatience. But where economic development is taken seriously in countries not yet experiencing a high level of restlessness, the foreign assistance relationship may become a disturber of a hitherto placid polity.

Foreign assistance tends to be channeled from government to government, meaning, in practice, from officials in the donor country to officials in the receiving country. It is the bureaucrats, the economic development technicians or the military, whose positions are directly strengthened by foreign assistance. This may—or may not —serve the interest of either the political leadership or long-run growth of a balanced polity.[30]

Nevertheless, despite the political difficulties inherent in programs of assistance, for most recipient countries in today's world there are simply not sufficient resources available to meet their politico-economic requirements. Leaders must therefore find ways of obtaining additional resources while limiting whatever political risks they believe may be inherent in acquiring them from abroad.

[30] Riggs, "Bureaucrats and Political Development: A Paradoxical View," in La Palombara, *Bureaucracy and Political Development* (pp. 120-68), p. 149.

Scapegoats are necessary to most leaders in order to shift the blame to others where their own performance is insufficient. This was familiar in interwar Middle Eastern affairs, as the British government was regularly assigned responsibility for every ill wind that blew. It bids fair to be common practice today, when the United States or the Central Intelligence Agency, the Soviet Union, or the Chinese are blamed when things go wrong. Particularly where there has been a close relationship of assistance and obvious dependency, if the donor does not do all that is expected of it as a protector and supporter, heavy blame is likely to be heaped upon the donor country or its representatives.[31]

A foreign scapegoat can become a target outside the nation, attracting free-floating hostility which might otherwise be directed against the leadership. The presumed hostile intent of the scapegoat may be used to rally disparate elements at home which might otherwise be locked in internecine struggle. Economic difficulties can be explained away by identifying this or that state as responsible for the economy's poor performance.[32] The source of economic or military assistance to a neighbor is often a convenient explanation for why relations with that neighbor are not better. The Government of India often argued this way in reference to American assistance to Pakistan as later did the government of Pakistan in regard to Washington's aid to New Delhi; Sihanouk has made the same argument about U.S. aid to Thailand. At the same time, none of the parties to these local disputes took serious steps to improve relations.

The leader wishing to use foreign scapegoats for his domestic political purposes may himself identify scapegoats in his own speeches or symbolize his views in the way he deals directly with foreign diplomats. In the more rigorously organized polity, however, it may serve his purposes better if the press or radio uses the invective, or the crowds demonstrate before the selected embassy or burn the cultural center or library, while he himself expresses regret at the incident and retains a more benign posture, as Nasser and Sukarno did in the early 1960s. This focuses local hostilities without engaging the leader so directly.

[31] For an interesting study of the psychological reactions to the withdrawal of Western power both in colonial territory and among the colonial rulers themselves, see Dominique O. Mannoni, *Prospero and Caliban, The Psychology of Colonization*, trans. by Pamela Powesland (New York, Praeger, 1956, 218 pp.).

[32] Kautsky (ed.), *Political Change*, p. 96.

If foreigners can be made to appear responsible for domestic evils, it will become especially expedient to identify one's domestic opponents as friends and dependents of the foreign enemy. Business interests can be identified with the United States; communists with Moscow or Peking; disliked ethnic minorities, such as Chinese in Indonesia or Tamils in Ceylon, may be alleged to be more loyal to their ancestral regime than to their present homeland. National sentiment can thus be enlisted to devalue if not to destroy one's domestic rivals.

THE LIABILITIES OF USING FOREIGN POLICY FOR DOMESTIC POWER PURPOSES

Dramatizing regional enemies may promote domestic solidarity. But it may also provoke neighbors into fear, an arms race, and perhaps even direct retaliatory action. This will consume resources which might otherwise be more efficiently directed toward internal development. Such a policy could precipitate a diplomatic or military conflict which may risk the future of the regime, as Nasser discovered in 1967.

To make scapegoats out of those who provide substantial assistance runs the risk of cutting off that assistance on which the state has come to depend. The U.S. assistance programs are declining in part because of reiterated criticism of these programs often voiced by major recipients. The euphoria of cutting ties with the former donor may carry a regime for some months, but sooner or later the pinch of resources will make itself felt, and the regime's domestic political pressures are likely to increase, as occurred in Guinea in 1958.

Agitating foreign policy issues may divert attention from domestic difficulties. This may help the regime temporarily. But it will also distract effort from domestic development. The energetic and the skilled may be caught up in military preparations or in promoting agitation elsewhere; scarce material and organizational resources may go toward the instruments of regional military power which are likely to become rapidly obsolescent, as occurred in Indonesia under Sukarno, instead of toward laying the productive base for a more prosperous, long run future.

Moreover, leadership time and energy is finite. The more its efforts are focused on foreign activities, the less time, imagination and art will be left to deal with intractable domestic relationships and complicated policies which require subtle judgment and insistent persuasion if they are to be successfully implemented at home.

There is some political utility in promoting excitement over foreign policy issues. But the net effect is often to accentuate unpredictability and a sense of uncertainty in relations with other countries or within one's region. This has its costs. Apart from the exceptional Kaiser investment in Ghana, few investors were likely to run long-term economic risks under Nkrumah. Sukarno's penchant for promoting foreign policy drama in his area probably would have discouraged foreign investment, even if his policies toward investment had been more encouraging. It appears increasingly unlikely that a network of economic relationships will evolve to permit one's own country as well as the foreign economic associate to gain returns so long as unpredictability is deliberately encouraged.

In sum, there are a number of ways in which the leadership's concern for strengthening his domestic position may find its reflection in alternative foreign policy moves. Real foreign or economic policy interests may sometimes be sacrificed in the name of sustaining and improving the leader's power position at home.

Where countries are far from the major confrontations between great powers, some foreign policy risks can be run safely in order to support the domestic position of the leader. But if a country is near to an area of contention between the major powers, it is chancy business to put domestic power interests above foreign policy calculations. Where local disputes risk armed conflict or when economic imperatives require sustained assistance, prudence would seem to recommend that short run domestic political necessities be dealt with in other ways than by using foreign policy.

As time goes on, leaders of new countries are likely to make a more accurate assessment of the foreign policy risks worth running on behalf of domestic political gains. With sustained independence, the edge of anxiety about whether or not one is really independent will be dulled, and state relations among the newly independent may become more like those among the more established states. Where feasible, regional arrangements may well emerge to deal more effectively with mutual antagonisms and those other problems which may be dealt with locally and in a quiet, orderly way. However, where regimes are unstable and new groups come rapidly forward

through coups d'état, foreign-sponsored insurgency, or genuine domestic revolution, the zealous or inexperienced are likely to ensure
a substantial measure of continued unpredictable state relations.

Statesmen are not always prudent; foreign policy rationality cannot be assumed. Except in times of foreign policy crisis, domestic
political considerations are likely to preponderate. Accordingly, leaders can be expected to continue to use foreign policy as part of the
strategy of aggregating power at home.

IV

**Coalition Building:
Strategic Mixes
and the
Purposes
of Power**

13 Strategic Mixes, the Longer Run, and the Purposes of Power

Each statesman fashions from a number of political strategies his own grand strategy for remaining in power and pursuing additional purposes. The strategy combinations he seeks to use result from the way he perceives his political resources in relation to his goals; how he came to power; his own personal qualities; assets of support, organization, and political resources available to him; locally accepted rules of the game; and who his opponents are and how they seek to displace him. A fully developed theory of strategy choice would have to take all these and more into account.

For purposes of this essay, however, it will be enough to note how four questions regarding political strategies may lead to suggestive propositions deserving closer examination. (1) Which strategies are likely to be useful in drawing different political groups into the ruler's coalition? (2) Which strategies give promise of helping a ruler to pursue his immediate goals beyond mere political survival? (3) Which strategies depend upon other strategies? and (4) which can

be substituted for other strategies? These questions will be discussed
in turn, and a number of brief examples of strategic mixes will
illustrate them further.

STRATEGIES AND THE SEARCH FOR ALLIES

Each of the political strategies discussed can contribute to
aggregating power by helping to attract different political groups
to the ruler's camp or to coordinate their activities with the ruler's
purposes. In no instance will the following generalizations reflect
exactly the untidy real world, but certain general propositions nevertheless can now be made.

No strategy has been more widely used by civilian governments
than that of *projecting the personality*. In Southeast Asia, South
Asia, the Middle East, and Africa new leaders have mustered whatever assets of personality and organization they could and directed
them toward enlarging the public vision of themselves until they
appear to be all-knowing.

No other single approach seems more likely to attract a broad
coalition from among the variegated components of the traditional
society in transition. Personal relationships are at the heart of loyalty
and motivation; formal political institutions which are not yet well-
established count for relatively little. Groups may be historic rivals,
but they may experience a sense of unity in following the uncommon
leader where little else unites them. By his personal appeal, the
inspiring leader may be able to penetrate directly beneath traditional
or other intermediate leaders who oppose him. He will weaken their
position and reduce their bargaining capacity while enlisting their
former supporters directly into his own following.

Civilian bureaucrats and the military rarely are caught up in
uncritical enthusiasm for the personality. They are more likely to
perceive that there is somewhat less in the leader than meets the
public eye, and in the main they are sustained as supporters more
by the results he can achieve and the rewards he can provide than by
his public style or the emotions he stimulates. Students will be drawn
if he is young and personifies promise of change. Men of the press
and other mass media will be a major means of forwarding his
enlargement, but they may also become disenchanted and contribute
to his deflation unless he persuades them to support him by other

means. Rank and file trade-union members may be impressed, although their leaders are likely to be moved only if results are substantial. The appeal of personality will normally have little effect on large landowners, although a Gandhi can touch the hearts of the landed as well as of big and small businessmen. If the personality wishes to attract religious leaders, he will have to personify traditional religious virtue and pay at least public deference to the local priesthood and those in the wider populace endowed with sacred qualities.

For successful personal leadership, the ruler must sustain his image of possessing near magic qualities. This is increasingly difficult over time. The inspiring rhetoric loses its capacity to move; the promise to resolve all problems becomes less plausible as the same difficulties persist or worse ones cumulate. The posture of daring fighter against all enemies becomes less persuasive. Indeed, the personality may be driven to undertake ever bolder enterprises in efforts to hold his followers spellbound, which may lead to overly ambitious domestic efforts or too risky ventures abroad.

To organize is to develop a more stable base for any power aggregation. A communal, ethnic, or tribal party is not hard to organize, if a leader has blood or obvious cultural ties within that group. It will easily win a loyal if narrow following. With it, he may at least be able to improve the relative position of his followers. But if he has wider national ambitions, the leader of such a party will have to find a broader base for his activities.

Patron parties will generally appeal to the senior levels of the army and bureaucracy and can usually negotiate a following with the leaders of traditional groups. Students and trade unionists are not likely to be enthusiastic about a patron party; larger businessmen and landowners will find it convenient.

The patron party represents a loose coalition or federation. The model authoritarian mass party, by contrast, seeks a monopoly of integrated power and usually sets forth bold purposes. Upper levels of the army and bureaucracy are likely to be replaced by more enthusiastic younger men, who will enjoy expanded responsibility unless the party apparatus itself begins to encroach on the bureaucracy's and army's responsibilities. Traditional local leaders will be undercut as the party gains direct access to their erstwhile followers and seeks to involve these in party auxiliaries. Action programs attract students and the rank and file of labor; businessmen find substantial opportunities within the expanding development programs the mass party seeks to mount, unless the mass party aims to eliminate their activities altogether. Landowners are often ignored or may be swept aside by radical land reform.

The authoritarian mass party sets up such high goals that it is impelled to be increasingly active or repressive. To hold the indispensable cadres, at least in the early years, it must be ever more zealous with higher promise and intensified enthusiasm; otherwise the cadres will become disenchanted. After a time, however, even they become fatigued and tempted by the perquisites of power, thereby losing both zeal and persuasiveness. Increased repression may be necessary to intimidate those inside or outside the party who come to oppose specific party programs or who become frustrated by the leader's or party's unavoidable insufficiencies. Repression has its own requirements of surveillance, secrecy, and intimidation.

A consensual democratic mass party will set less ambitious goals and will press change less rapidly. It will attempt to build a broader base of support while allowing other parties to exist on the political margins. It will press for compromises which do not eliminate political opponents but keep their followers divided. The party will demand less of the bureaucracy and army than an authoritarian mass party, and is likely to permit more diversity. It will ask less of students but a reaction of boredom and political withdrawal will not be as likely. Businessmen, trade unionists, and landowners may all find some place within it. Such parties in India and Ceylon have provided orderly civilian transfers of power to new men when death took prominent leaders or elections displaced them.

Approaching the political task of coalition building through the *use of ideology* has advantages, since nearly all components of social power can be attracted by some aspects of ideological politics. But there is a major difficulty. The ideological appeals acceptable to all are often mutually contradictory or so bland as to be useless in inspiring any one.

The bureaucracy and army are likely to be attracted if the ideology lays stress upon efficiency and order, thus emphasizing their special roles in public life. Traditional groups will be influenced if the ideology plays up the distinction between the disruptive modern forces emanating from abroad and from the cities and the pure qualities of the untouched society—often identifiable with the traditional religion. Those who are restless with the cramping restraints of the old society may be appealed to by ideas of social transformation, but these risk alienating those who presently are influential in traditional groups. Landowners are not likely to be moved.

Arts students and faculties are likely to be attracted by complex and emotion-charged ideologies. Engineering, medical, and business students and faculties, by contrast, remain relatively uninterested in ideological politics. Those who stop school before completing high school or the holders of school diplomas who cannot get jobs are the most susceptible to ideological appeals. They are literate, they derive status from manipulating concepts and ideas, and they are acutely frustrated.

The businessmen, on the whole, are unlikely to be impressed with ideologies, being more committed to pragmatically solving specific management or production problems. They may praise laissez faire as a theory. However, their ability to reach working arrangements with the bureaucracy, and the gains they make from the quasi-monopolistic position these permit suggest their ideological commitments do not decisively affect their actions. Trade unions generally find Marxist ideological themes congenial, stressing as they do class struggle and radical change presumed to promote worker interests.

Rewarding the faithful or intimidating the opponent or the wavering may help to aggregate power. Rewarding the faithful by office is usually limited to those who are either close to the leader through past associations or are known to be influential already. When they are induced to associate with the government, they bring to it a substantial increment of power. Prominent men of influence may be intimidated by the tacit (or explicit) threat of economic deprivation through administrative decision or, what is more serious, by deprivations of personal liberty and in many other ways.

Critical sectors of the bureaucracy can be won by job rewards or policies which meet the bureaucracy's conception of what needs to be done. If a blind eye is turned to modest corruption, officials at a number of levels can arrange their own direct rewards to make up for admittedly insufficient pay. The threat of being sidetracked, demoted, or removed will deter officials from outright insubordination, but such intimidation is unlikely to win energetic application to the job at hand.

The military can be rewarded with equipment if the foreign exchange or military assistance is available, as well as by personal rewards of promotions, decorations, foreign training, or opportunities for personal enrichment. Too many individual rewards for the senior personnel may provoke splits in the army as junior ranks not so favored will increasingly object. Equipment will enhance the pride and scope of activity of all grades, but carries with it the additional hazard of improving the army's ability to impose its own will in the event it should turn against the civilian leader. Intimidation is difficult to apply against the military, although assignments, promotions, and perquisites can be manipulated to induce support on the part of potentially powerful officers, so long as key positions are held by those assuredly loyal to the ruler.

Traditional groups may be rewarded in a hundred ways, through providing offices and honors to their leaders, allowing preferential scope for political organizations favorable to traditional values, assigning development resources to their bailiwicks, and so forth. Intimidation can be effected by withholding resources, stationing troops in their neighborhood, reducing the freedom of the leaders, and threatening to deprive them of resources and activities they hold important.

Students and unemployed intellectuals are difficult to deal with through reward unless the economy is expanding generally or new job opportunities are consciously created for them. An expansion of the regular bureaucracy to accommodate many of them is a tempting step, for its serious long run costs are not likely to be as apparent at the outset as its immediate political advantages.

Individual businessmen may be rewarded by policies favorable to their businesses, by honors, social access, or whatever else they may want. Their political cooperation may be useful if it increases the economic resources available to political leaders or results in political guidance to the businessman's work force. The entrepreneurs' economic energies may be indispensable if the economy is to expand. They are susceptible to intimidation of various degrees of intensity by withholding licenses, foreign exchange allocations, and so forth, but their productive business activities are likely to contract as intimidation against them increases. Too obvious association with them can be a political liability for a ruler, since generally they are disliked.

Trade unionists can be won by wages and hours legislation and by freer scope for organizational activities. But where unemployment is prevalent, the strike weapon is usually of limited value. Unions are often riven by traditional-type rivalries or by political competition among their leaders. These circumstances weaken the leverage trade unions can bring to bear against a regime or the support they can organize from within it.

Specific *developmental policies* will affect the aggregation of power in different ways, depending upon the type of economy, its level of growth, the general thrust of economic policy, and the particularities of the leader's political situation.

Nevertheless, to oversimplify, the bureaucracy will generally support a regime devoted to economic development, for its responsibilities will be enhanced, and a sense of constructive purpose will be evoked. The military will cooperate if they believe the country's logistical infrastructure or arms production capability will improve, or if they have a role to play in development activities. Development policy will draw neither the bureaucracy nor the military, however, if expenditures on productive investment or social overheads are so high as to materially cut into their supporting budgets.

Traditional groups and the more conservative and absentee landowners are likely to be dubious about development. Some generalized innovations may have substantial political costs for certain traditional groups. On the other hand, specific capital investments or the introduction of new institutions like cooperatives, marketing organizations, and so forth may even strengthen the position of those with local wealth and influence, at least in the short run. Even the most conservative will not object to changes which promise to increase their incomes without adversely affecting their influence in the countryside.

Students will see hope in development plans and rightly assume that as an economy develops, there will be more opportunities for them. Businessmen are likely to expect expanding opportunities for their activities if a government pursues development, but the way development policies are administered may have a good deal to do with whether the business community is politically won or alienated. Trade unionists are also usually in favor of development in general, unless the resources are to be obtained by stringent labor discipline which will impede the unionists' organizing activities and will hurt labor's chances of improving its position vis-à-vis other groups in the society.

Increasing participation of the hitherto quiescent will affect the aggregation of power, depending upon whose participation is being encouraged and how this is channeled. If the rural population is being

activated by cultural or religious appeals, by reference to their economic grievances, or by direct organizational activities, winning
them can substantially increase a regime's support in the countryside.
As the peasantry is won, however, landlords usually will be alienated, though the largest landholders can usually be attacked without
provoking the enmity of the more numerous smaller landowners.
If urban workers are similarly activated to participate in politics,
businessmen and those government servants who are part owners
or who manage government enterprises may be lost to a regime. If
religious figures or more parochial, region- or district-oriented rural
populace or townspeople are drawn into politics, the more modern
secular and Marxist inclined will feel their interests challenged.
Despite these and other differences which may be precipitated by
expanding popular participation, activating the hitherto quiescent
may so broaden a leader's coalition as to decisively help him to
acquire power or consolidate his position.

While a regime's *foreign policy* can affect a leader's political position, its influence on a leader's supporting coalition is often subtle.
The bureaucracy is likely to approve of a foreign policy which brings
pride to the country or foreign assistance in ways that enhance its
responsibilities and the resources at its disposal. It will resist such
policies if donors seek to intrude too directly on the responsibilities
the bureaucracy is accustomed to.

The army will be likely to rally around a regime which can ensure
that if the country's independence is threatened, substantial support
will be forthcoming from reliable allies or from those who can
provide the army with improved equipment, training facilities, and
prerogatives. Some may favor a policy of foreign policy adventure
to enhance national solidarity, increase the scope of their own
activities, and perhaps lead to social or other changes they favor.
In the event they consider the policy to be militarily or politically
hazardous, however, they will be a force for foreign policy restraint.

Traditional groups are rarely moved by foreign policy considerations, unless the policy appears to oppose those modernizing
outside powers which the traditionalists fear are undermining their
status and influence. Anti-Western and anti-communist policies may
find considerable resonance on these grounds among traditional leaders. Students and intellectuals are likely to gain satisfaction from
foreign policy actions which dramatize independence or which gen-

erate a sense of common national enthusiasm in opposition to a neighboring traditional enemy.

Businessmen generally will favor foreign policies which are consistent with setting limits to foreign business competitors while they remain able to sustain profitable economic links with outside enterprise. They are likely to recognize the desirability of acquiring resources from abroad rather than sharply raising taxes, but they are not necessarily pleased to see the bulk of the new resources allocated and dispersed by governmental decision. Trade unionists tend to follow the government's lead rather than have an independent view on foreign affairs, unless they have organized links with communist countries and thus may be subject to Moscow's or Peking's guidance.

This summary discussion suggests that preliminary generalizations can be made about the way in which different strategies affect the ability of a regime to develop coalitions of support.

INTERDEPENDENCE OF STRATEGIES

Political strategies can be looked at in another way, i.e., the extent to which they are dependent upon and consistent with one another.

It has already been pointed out that for a leader to project his personality, he needs some organization to assist him. An organization, to have focus and to be able to evoke a sense of loyalty, requires a leading figure. The stature of the leader will be enhanced if it is demonstrated that he contributes to and shapes an ideology; the ideology itself may stress the role of the indispensable leader. Rewarding the faithful requires an organization to allocate rewards in a politically discriminating way and sufficient governmental performance and economic growth to ensure there are rewards to distribute. Intimidation requires prior control of key elements of the bureaucracy for surveillance and for the means of intimidating only those the leader intends. Extending participation implies an inspiring leader able to evoke new activity and sufficient political organization to channel the energies of the newly awakened and to hold popular excitement within bounds. To use foreign policy for domestic political purposes requires the pre-existence of a state apparatus of some kind capable of first having a foreign policy. It depends heavily upon leadership, organizational capabilities, and economic margins to sustain interest, to select and implement policies, and to provide resources for foreign policy activities.

STRATEGIES CAN BE INTERCHANGED

Certain strategies can substitute for others; there may be trade-off possibilities among them. A leader may discover that a vivid projection of his own personality or certain ideas can be a partial substitute for developing a political organization, as Mr. Bandaranaike demonstrated in Ceylon and Sukarno did in Indonesia. Ideology, to some extent, may also substitute for organization, at least in the short run, if the enthusiastic support of influential men or large numbers can be won by an ideology. Some organization, of course, is necessary, even to promote a personality or an ideology. But this organization is far less demanding than that necessary if a mass political party, such as the Congress Party in India or the Convention Peoples Party in Ghana, is to be created.

Organization of some kind is particularly necessary if the leader seeks to use his time in office to realize major goals beyond mere survival. Organization will be necessary if he hopes to leave behind him some armature around which political power can be aggregated to legitimize and sustain his successor. If a regime lacks a developed political organization capable of aggregating and responding to urgent demands and possessing suffcient power to get things done, it remains vulnerable to coups d'état. When a leader lacks a party with political links to the main components of social power in his society, he must accept the limits set by a more authoritative type of organization based on his own personal following placed in key positions in the military or civilian bureaucracies, as in the case of President Nasser.

Rewarding the faithful will contribute to aggregating power so long as the rewards can be continued and gradually increased. The policy of specific reward tends to be most efficient when applied to a society in the early stages of the transition to modernity, since only the relatively few leaders of traditional groups need to be rewarded. As participation expands and larger and larger groups of people begin to act politically, the rewards must be more widely distributed. Their cost will rise accordingly, and they nearly always have to be less discriminating. Nevertheless, if economic development gains way, increasing resources may be available to provide substantial rewards to the faithful. An inspirational personality may require less in the way of tangible rewards, for the direct subjective returns he provides to the faithful may prove to be an economically inexpensive substitute, though its long run political costs may be high, as Indonesians have discovered. A capable party organization may reduce the need for widespread reward, though keeping party lieutenants up to scratch may call for highly specialized rewards in the form of ideological satisfactions, perquisites, or office.

On the other hand, where it is possible to broaden participation in order to bring enthusiastic popular support to a particular leader, as Mr. Sukarno was able to do for so long, he may not need to supplement his personal position by promoting rigorous organization, demonstrating performance in the fields of economic development or more direct welfare, or defending his position by increasingly heavy intimidation.

Where the personality is bland, where organization is weak or merely defends the position of the privileged, and where foreign policy provides few domestic political assets, the level of intimidation may have to increase. When all these elements of political strategy are in low account, intimidation may still be kept to a minimum if there are sufficient desirable resources to provide ample and widely distributed rewards. Where intimidation does increase, it can be a substantial substitute for other strategies for a long time in certain countries, as in the extreme case of Haiti. But in most countries which have experienced more open forms of rule without intolerable disorder, a high level of intimidation will usually generate its own resistance.

Economic development, if it can proceed without imposing undue deprivation through taxes or without providing outrageously large rewards to only the few, may sustain a regime which lacks a vivid personality, plays down ideology, uses intimidation to a minimum, and follows an unexciting foreign policy. If so, however, its bureaucratic organization must be efficient, and the civil servants must understand the art of economizing resources and releasing or generating productive energies in the population. The regime's political organization also must be accessible to the newer groups being formed by successful economic development while not provoking intolerable antagonism from those who have held positions of wealth or influence before and who now see these customary advantages going to others.

Foreign policy in itself can never be a sufficient strategy, but adventure abroad or sharpening a sense of acute outside threat can be a partial, and probably only a temporary, substitute for other political strategies.

STRATEGIES AND SHORT RUN POLITICAL GOALS

Different strategies will commend themselves, depending upon which goals beyond political survival a ruler seeks to achieve or which issues are most salient. In real political life, rarely can a ruler pursue one goal at a time. Usually he cannot avoid dealing with several objectives simultaneously. Yet some hypotheses can be suggested by looking at goals as if they could be pursued in isolation.

If the goal of *national independence* is prominent, foreign policy will preoccupy him most. The ruler will devote substantial energy and resources to demonstrating that he and his regime are unambiguously independent. Underlining international recognition, arranging state visits and promoting regional discussions are symbolic steps in this strategy, dramatizing his personality or his country as sovereign independent actors on the world stage. If a genuine security threat besets his country, he will give high priority to acquiring arms, training defense forces and finding allies. He will seek to tighten national, political, or economic organizations in order to better ensure that his polity can respond in a unified fashion to international threats. He will have to promote a nationalist ideology. Economic development programs will be designed to reduce dependence on outsiders or to broaden trading options in order to free the economy from overdependence on one or two markets or suppliers.

National unity may be the most urgent need. Projecting the personality will often be the easiest way to tackle this problem, unless he himself comes from an area, a minority, or a personal background looked down upon by substantial numbers of influential individuals or groups. Developing a political organization is indispensable if faltering national unity is to be corrected. Improving the effectiveness and responsiveness of the bureaucracy may be a first important step. Where differences are notable and he hopes to avoid authoritarian rule, the leader will seek to assemble loose political structures, such as the Congress Party in India or the Alliance in Malaysia, and combine these with personal leadership and economic development policies. Alternatively, he might try an authoritarian mass party as in Ghana or other single-party states in Africa, perhaps providing more opportunity for participating in nationwide enterprises which overcome traditional differences while requiring—as it facilitates—substantially more intimidation. As another possibility, the bureaucracy may be the principal instrument for restraining the expression of differences and for providing conditions conducive to economic growth. Special representative devices may be established to permit a gradual renewal of political discussion and participation, as was tried in Pakistan. Personality and organizational strategies will be supplemented by energetic efforts to popularize a unifying ideology and by the policy of reward to buy off potential dissidents or individuals with local influence who cannot be won by more usual political party or bureaucratic influences. Unity will be favored if minorities are brought into more active political participation, as long as the developing economy is providing increased opportunities desired by growing numbers of the more highly educated and those who hitherto felt excluded. A foreign policy crisis, real, provoked, or imaginary, may help consolidate national unity.

If *social transformation* is of high priority and calls for dynamic change, greater equality, or more participation, the strategies of personality, organization, ideology, and expanding participation will be called into play. The personality will have to be able to evoke a readiness to accept sacrifice on behalf of change. The ideology will have to demonstrate the necessity for change, the direction to move in, and the steps to take. Substantial change through the bureaucracy alone is unlikely, unless the bureaucracy is itself unusually capable of implementing the ruler's will. Normally, a more explicitly political party-type organization will be necessary. This will have to be activist and disciplined, encadring large numbers and giving drive and direction to their activities. Together with the police and bureaucracy, it will have to be able to intimidate those who cannot voluntarily support or acquiesce in the changes to be brought about. Reward for the risk-taking militants will be necessary to sustain their dedication, as will a measure of intimidation to discourage corruption and privilege-seeking. Increasing political participation will draw new groups forward and broaden the base of the regime responsible for their activities, at least for a time.

But if the pace of transformation is not to be so rapid, a mobilizationist political organization will not be necessary. A less disciplined, more open political organization may induce greater genuine participation. Economic development, if effectively pursued with sufficient resources, will produce fundamental changes in the longer run although increased equity may not result in the short run.

Economic development may be of central importance. Unless the economy is unusually favored by specific natural resources, as are the oil-rich kingdoms of the Middle East, finding the resources will be of major moment. At the same time, serious development will require changes in attitude, organization, and ambition, and these may be unwelcome to important elements in the bureaucracy and populace. The personality can help to induce the necessary sacrifice of current consumption. Organizational changes in the bureaucracy may be necessary to shape and implement effective development plans or to induce investment and production. Various types of political organization will prove more effective in different economies, depending on the type of development desired. In general, however, investment resources must be available to those who are economically dynamic, whether they be in the bureaucracy or private sector. Mass demands must be held within some relation to increasing productive capability, and a reasonably high degree of predictability and public order must be maintained if economic development is to gain way.

STRATEGIES AND THE LONGER RUN PURPOSES OF POWER

There is a certain interchangeability among strategies so long as the political objective is simply to stay in power. But if the leader has wider ends in view beyond mere survival at the apex, his choice of strategies for aggregating power will have to be more discriminating, since some strategies may contribute to his power position in the short run, but may actually work against his longer run purposes.

As already pointed out, the strategy of *personality* is likely to promote a broad coalition. If, however, the leader looks beyond his immediate problem of political survival, he will perceive that convenient as it may be for that short run and narrow purpose, the strategy of personality will not provide the means for implementing in the here and now intricate policies requiring sustained and orchestrated action. Nor will it equip the polity to deal with the crisis of succession which is bound to follow his demise, for after his passing, the aggregation of power must begin again around a new personality, usually after intense and highly disruptive rivalries.

Different kinds of *political organizations* will have generally foreseeable longer run consequences, as suggested in previous chapters. The parochial minority party will solidify small traditional groups, but it will exacerbate divisions and factions in the country, impeding national unity. The patron party will combine some degree of national unity while disturbing traditional ways as little as possible, but not much change will be likely. An authoritarian mass party will promote maximum direct mobilization of effort looking toward change and may induce a rapid although often superficial improvement in national unity. But it risks generating antagonism which may require increasing intimidation to contain. It is also likely to postpone the growth of the practice of compromise and mutual adjustment among semi-autonomous power groups on which successful democratic growth appears to depend. If leadership is adequate and political conditions are in other ways propitious, a democratic consensual mass party will be most likely to combine the need for overarching unity with conscious efforts toward change and the arts of compromise and adjustment necessary for reasonably democratic rule. Since a democratic consensual mass party is more flexible, it is less brittle than an authoritarian party; and as it is less claimant, it will provoke less opposition. It combines sustained aggregation of sufficient power with a checking of that power by orderly representative devices more satisfactorily than is characteristic of any other type of polity outside the Atlantic democracies. But it is not easy to develop, since it requires unusual leadership qualities and many years of effort. It is prone to stalemate as the demands of its multiple components cancel each other out, and it becomes increasingly dependent on patronage reward as early idealism fades.

Ideology is necessary to give a sense of common purpose and mutual identity and to popularize ideas of political cause and effect. It will also help to enlist enthusiasm for national effort. Depending upon its substance, it can either promote authoritarian tendencies or it can define rules of the game of a more open political system. Experience would suggest that ideologies of democratic practice conceived prior to independence have often given way before the more immediate imperatives of leaders seeking first of all to remain in power. Most have felt impelled to deviate from their democratic ideology and have whittled down the area of open political contention in the name of minimum order and personal political survival. Ideological politics, as pointed out above, may turn attention from real problems to unreal issues and divert action from useful tasks. Ideological categories may inaccurately type-cast labor, management, other political groups, or specific foreign countries as friends or foes, while the realities of specific local interests might lead to very different and more fruitful combinations.

Rewarding the faithful or intimidating the opponent has short run advantages, as noted above. However, too blatant *rewards* to only the faithful will sharpen jealousies, misallocate scarce resources, and postpone the development of a civic sense. When the law designed for all is too obviously flouted by the privileged, the law will fall into general disregard. The task of governance will become ever more difficult as each seeks to ensure his own uninhibited advantage at others' expense. If *intimidation* is too prevalent, men will walk in fear; they will take no initiative because of the apparent risks in making errors. The leadership will have to invest increasing resources in informing itself of the true state of its affairs. The intimidatory services themselves will become increasingly costly and influential; economic development will be deterred. Desirable rules of the game cannot develop where there is unregulated and pervasive intimidation. Too much corruption and intimidation may make a regime so repugnant as to provoke sincere and patriotic men to attempt a coup d'état.

Expanding political participation serves the short run political purpose of enlisting the hitherto quiescent behind the leader who awakens them. It is likely to induce political leaders to be more responsive to the less well-placed in society. This may challenge haughty bureaucracies to serve the populace more directly and is likely to increase the pressures favoring policies designed to raise levels of consumption. It may reduce the need for intimidation if pent-up resentments thus find opportunity for politically fruitful expression. For the longer run, if political institutions are resilient enough, increased participation is a step toward more popular, democratic government. On the other hand, expanded participation may rapidly increase demands and risk the institutional integrity of the political system, as contenders generate new grievances more rapidly than fragile political processes can contain or satisfy. Too rapid a mobilization may awaken intense communal jealousies or lead to such unrestrained group competition as to threaten chaos and political disintegration. The temptation is great, therefore, to discourage participation except as a means of gaining power or where a regime is certain it can contain the pressures a wider participation is likely to generate.

Economic development has long run implications. If successful, it should promote more diversified and accessible opportunities and ease a government's task of providing necessities for a growing and more demanding population. As increasing numbers are brought together across traditional communal, tribal, and class lines through more sophisticated economic relationships and as economic opportunity generally expands, traditional rivalries are likely to decline more rapidly than new types of contention will increase. Yet economic development also poses long run political problems. The groups most adept at economic activities may make gains in their economic position and show pretensions to a new social status which arouse the jealousy of those who are less economically ingenious but traditionally better placed. As new groups come forward through successful economic growth, they must be brought into the ruling coalition; this requires adroit political maneuvering on the part of the leadership. In this process, the traditionally influential will have to yield some of their privileges and prerogatives, a change in relative status which may come hard to those who lose position.

Resources from abroad will ease domestic tax pressures, but may subject the regime to accusations of failing to protect national integrity and independence. Conspicuous investment may tempt leaders who seek to impress the populace or to make an international splash and may divert resources from more immediately productive ventures; it may create unproductive indebtedness that future generations will have to find ways of repaying.

A *foreign policy* adopted primarily to improve the short run domestic political position of a regime is not likely to have beneficial side effects for the longer run unless the threat it dramatizes or generates will add to real solidarity without provoking hitherto nonexistent foreign policy dangers. Alternatively, a regime may gain if the resources it obtains from foreign policy are wisely used to promote the longer run domestic goals a regime asserts it is pursuing. An overactive foreign policy may mean involvement in costly difficulties for the longer run, or facing, in solitude, dangers that were foreseen but left unheeded.

Politics is not simply the art of the possible. It also requires a refined—yet unavoidably uncertain—assessment of short run as opposed to long run gains and risks. Many strategies useful in the short run have long run costs. Yet to be so concerned with the logic of the long run gain may risk losing in the short run and thus forfeiting the opportunity to affect affairs of state in the long run altogether. Accordingly, political leaders who are successful in the long run are either just plain lucky or they have acquired that particular political knack of double time vision. By calculation or art, they succeed in identifying those strategies which appropriately combine and balance short run imperatives and the logic of the longer run.

EXAMPLES OF STRATEGIC MIXES

The men who have survived in politics for some time have shown themselves versatile in the way they orchestrate different elements of these strategies, laying major stress on a few, yet not forgetting that most may have some utility.

For example, Sukarno developed his coalition of support by combining a number of strategies. His unusual personal qualities made his search for charismatic leadership as natural as his role in the independence struggle made it easy. He had little success in developing his own political organization. Instead, the Indonesian Communist Party (PKI) and the army developed relatively independent of his immediate control. As they balanced each other off, he hoped to retain the critical weight at any one moment. His flexible and capacious ideology allowed room for the more rigorous PKI doctrine and the emotional nationalist enthusiasm which contributed to national solidarity in the face of enormous problems of geographical and cultural diversity. Developing the economy was for him politically unimportant. At critical times, he provided substantial rewards to those whose support he needed. Relatively little drastic intimida-

tion was permitted while he retained dominance, although some
opponents were jailed and others went abroad. A foreign policy of
confrontation against the Dutch in West Irian and against Malaysia
across the Straits of Malacca induced elements of the army and the
PKI to collaborate and elicited popular enthusiasm for a time. But
these were costly in resources and helped consolidate his threatened
neighbors. His combined strategy drew support from many sources
of power. His coalition did not embrace the Muslims and important
regional interests, however, and he remained anxious about his army.
His strategy helped to hold to him those who could be won by stressing national solidarity. But a political organization did not develop
to provide an armature for the sustained aggregation of political
power, apart from either the army or the PKI. Many governmental
functions considered desirable in most countries were not performed,
and by the time he was pushed aside, his economy was in disarray.

In sharp contrast, several statesmen in French West Africa, perhaps epitomized by Houphouët-Boigny of the Ivory Coast, have
looked on their task in a fundamentally different way. Their states
have been much smaller, but they, too, have been faced by problems
of internal diversity. They have put little stress on ideology and
have undertaken no foreign policy enterprises comparable to Indonesia's. Each has placed major stress on three other strategies. They
all projected the personality, pushing the leader into the center of
the political process and seeking for him a position not unlike that
of the traditional tribal chief. Each invested heavy effort in building
a political party. The structures have differed, but nearly all sought
at the beginning to build a sophisticated party apparatus, led by one
or a small group of top personnel, who sought to penetrate and
influence numerous components of social power below. All have put
major efforts into acquiring the resources necessary to continue
economic development. Instead of assuming that perpetual revolution
or drama on the international stage would serve to overcome faction
and ethnic diversity, they appeared to believe that economic growth
would give scope for the ambitious in competing tribes and ethnic
groups. Development would permit personal leadership and an organized party to sustain national integrity, promote well-being, and
keep the leadership at the helm; only moderate intimidation and
some measure of reward was used. To this end, some have been
willing to retain close links with France and restrain the pace of

social transformation in order to acquire economic resources and promote productivity. This strategy has been rejected by others out of ideological conviction and fear that such policies would diminish their independence, as in Guinea, or be used against them by their domestic political opponents.

In India, the Nehru regime drew upon the personal qualities of the well-born, leading personality. But it also depended on the versatile and resilient Congress Party organization to aggregate power throughout India and on the bureaucracy to promote economic development. The party's very survival, in turn, appears to have depended upon a combination of Mr. Nehru's charismatic presence and its early reputation as the party of independence, as well as tough party organizers in key states, the use of rewards for the more important among the faithful, and very moderate types of economic or, in certain cities, machine-type intimidation. Preventive detention has been used in communal emergencies or in dealing with leading personalities likely to arouse frontier minorities, such as Sheik Abdullah of Kashmir. There has been some stress on ideology in political matters and particularly in economic policy. The latter may have slowed economic development, but it at least provided a rationale for a substantial development effort which might not have been forthcoming without it. The ideology also served, at least in the early years, to hold the urban intellectuals and important segments of labor. A foreign policy of originality dramatizing India's independence and its special role in international affairs strengthened the ruler's position, until the Chinese–Indian conflict of 1962 challenged its assumptions and dramatized how little real help India would receive from the nonaligned. Substantial foreign economic assistance eased the burden of a complex economic development program. As a by-product, development activities provided additional opportunities for the use of a strategy of reward. As Nehru's own energies slackened and newer segments of Indian society became politically more active, the liabilities of the Congress Party—acute factionalism, a tendency toward immobilism and unduly obvious rewards to the faithful— came increasingly to the fore. These trends were accentuated under his successors and contributed to the party's substantial setback in the elections of 1967.

In all these regimes popular activation and, in some, genuine political participation have increased over time. The passivity of the traditional populations has been done away with, probably for good.

Certain military regimes, by contrast, have tried to reduce participation. The Abboud regime in the Sudan, for instance, was widely welcomed to power in 1958, for it held out hope of overcoming the stalemate among civilian politicians, coping with relations with Egypt, and correcting the economic policies of the fumbling civilian regime it replaced. While promising a return to civilian rule when conditions permitted, General Abboud nevertheless ended all open political participation by attempting to suppress political parties altogether. Beginning in 1963, he instituted a system of partially elected councils at the local, provincial, and national level, but these were not influential enough to attract the best talent, and unrest continued to grow. He himself lacked color, and his regime became increasingly criticized for corruption. In the end, in October 1964, he was not willing to use the coercion necessary to retain power when popular unrest, pressing forward through old parties and certain new professional groups, was directed against his regime.

Menderes in Turkey built his coalition by consciously promoting the political participation of rural interests—landowners and the peasantry. He also drew on businessmen and labor leaders who had not been welcomed by the previous paternalistic and *étatist* ruling party. He developed religious and economic policies attractive to the peasantry and to these urban interests, and he obtained substantial foreign assistance resources to support these policies. His personality gained a devoted following in the countryside, and his economic development policies for a time were widely welcomed. However, his expansive economic development policies and resulting inflation lost him popular backing in the cities. As popular unrest grew, he increasingly resorted to intimidation in an effort to silence his opponents. Important segments of the army became restless as their own relative position declined vis-à-vis the new business and technical groups who were prospering. When he attempted to use the army to intimidate his political opponents who were themselves highly respected by the army, the military removed him and then returned power to a caretaker civilian government.

These examples illustrate how each leader has sought out his own combination of these distinguishable strategies. For some, the strategic mix they chose was adequate to their situation. Other leaders were less successful. If more systematic attention were turned to the comparative study of political strategies useful for the aggregation of power, more precise propositions could be developed.

Abraham Lincoln at one time declared that "it is a grave question whether any government not too strong for the liberties of its people, can be strong enough to maintain its existence in great emergencies."

This essay has been concerned more with the question of how governments in Asia and Africa make themselves sufficiently strong to implement policies they consider essential than with the problem of containing the possibly overly ambitious pretensions of the prime minister or president. To concern oneself with the aggregation of power is not to suggest that the ends and qualities of limited governance are not important. It is to underline, however, a nagging question besetting all men at the apex of governmental power in the former colonial countries now come to independence or in the awakening archaic kingdoms. Where peoples are divided— often speaking a multitude of languages—where the effective reach of government is uncertain, where economic cramp is growing, and where political contention is likely to be intemperate, much depends upon a government's ability to stay in power and to become more effective in its rule. To look at the political leader's world through the strategies he uses or might adopt in his efforts to gain and maintain the capacity to govern, is to look at what probably preoccupies him most.

For when the history of our time is written, the struggles of newly independent countries or of the archaic kingdoms to find their modern statehood will be among the more exciting—and perhaps tragic— dramas to be reconstructed. Some peoples by then will have succeeded in forging sound polities based on a viable balance between governmental power and individual liberty that we would find congenial to our ideal. And this is what one wishes for them all.

Some countries may survive as states only within a framework close to tyranny. Some of the people will have become habituated to their unhappy circumstances, tyranny being the best they can imagine. Others will find their circumstances intolerable, and the more desperate or optimistic among them will seek to overthrow the tyrant and establish something better. Those who seek to replace the tyrants, in their turn, will have to gather to themselves sufficient power to retain control, using more acceptable means in the pursuit of those better ends which the tyrants neglected. Other peoples may not erect states at all, but may succumb before the exigencies of international life. They may be overcome by external force or taken from within by subversion supported from outside. Still others may be torn asunder by faction and internecine strife; only anarchy and chaos will be left behind.

However the drama is to be understood, success in the search for viable statehood will have required something akin to what has been called here the aggregation of power. Without that minimum necessity, governance is impossible. Without at least having some success in aggregating power in the hands of reasonably capable leaders over a substantial period of time, institutions for defining public purposes and for channeling public energies cannot be erected and the inescapable crises of succession overcome.

The challenge facing leaders in Asia and Africa is how to combine sufficient power to sustain continuity for a period permitting governmental effectiveness, while seeking means to permit those necessary elements of representation, openness to innovation and access to rising groups, without which sound and humane government in an era of rapid change cannot be established or sustained.

This essay has sought to illuminate aspects of this process and has suggested a conception of how leaders have actually tackled their predicaments thus far. If it has raised questions readers believe deserve further attention, it will have served its purpose.

Index

265